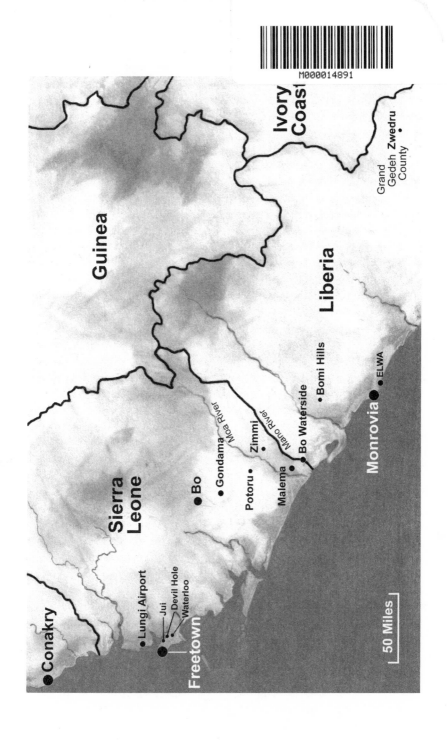

SO FAR TO RUN

The Memoir of Liberian Refugee

SO FAR TO RUN

Louise Géesedeh Barton

Louise G. Barton

BASCOM HILL PUBLISHING GROUP

BASCOM HILL
PUBLISHING GROUP

Bascom Hill Publishing Group
212 3rd Avenue North, Suite 290
Minneapolis, MN 55401
612.455.2293
www.bascomhillbooks.com

ISBN-13: 978-1-935098-92-8
LCCN: 2011939176

Distributed by Itasca Books

So Far to Run Website: sofartorun.com

Cover Design by Alan Pranke
Typeset by Madge Duffy

Printed in the United States of America

DEDICATION

This book is dedicated to my dear late mother, Boahn Gouria Josephiné Barton (commonly known as Boahn Sophené)—your spirit lives within my heart; to my late father, Charles Barton (also known as Kohoun Charley), who instilled in me a love for education and provided a means for me to gain one; to my late Uncle Siah Willie Nyoun, who saved my life and is immortalized in this story; to my brother Solo, who loves me so much he named a daughter after me; to my cousin Jacob Roger Gouria, who my heart goes out to because he lost his sight while he was only a teenager; and to Jesse Lee, my wheelchair-bound, special-needs son who has cerebral palsy—my love goes out to you forever.

ACKNOWLEDGEMENTS

This memoir would not have been possible were it not for the dedicated efforts and support of many people—not the least of whom were my two outstanding editors Allen Stalvey and Diana Neff.

I would also like to thank Jerome Quaye and Emmanuel Clark, fellow refugees who aided me in recalling and substantiating key events documented in this memoir; Abel Quoi, without whose love and support this story could not have been written; Mother Dora Dumuya, for her prayerful encouragement and advise; The Old Soldier, who, as described in this memoir, pleaded my case to his commander while I was on the run for my life, resulting in my being able to continue my journey to freedom; Janet Massaquoi, one of my closest friends and strongest supporters; Elizabeth Deah, for providing a helping hand, including cooking meals for my family, as I worked on my memoir; Zoawan Kayea, my childhood friend who migrated to America two years before Liberia erupted into civil war; and Christopher D. Bernard, for his wise counsel.

In addition, I would like to thank Bonnie Kearns, Mark Rohde, Debbi Mygatt, George Weaver, Tracey Gonzalez, Esperanza and Joseph Duarte, Edgar and Carmen Pierre, and John Hammer for aiding me in getting settled in America soon after my arrival.

CONTENTS

INTRODUCTION

I was born in Monrovia, Liberia, but raised in a humble village over two hundred miles east of my birthplace as a member of the Naio clan of the indigenous Krahn tribe. In order to secure a quality education for me and to afford me the opportunity of an upbringing in modern society, just over two years after enduring the trauma of separation from my mother, my father sent me to live in Monrovia as a domestic servant at the age of seven.

My life as a domestic servant was extremely difficult. I subsisted on three to four hours of sleep each night and emotional and physical exhaustion were my constant companions. Yet during this time, I learned of God's unfathomable love and received a divine gift as evidence of His hand on my life. Moreover, I learned that I was related to the family of Liberia's President Samuel K. Doe, who was also a member of the Krahn tribe and the first member of an indigenous tribe to serve as the president of Liberia since its founding in 1847 by freed American slaves.

Samuel Doe had assumed power via a military coup in 1980 that toppled the Americo-Liberian government, which had ruled the country for 133 years. The Americo-Liberians, who could trace their ancestry to freeborn and formerly enslaved African-Americans, immigrated in the 1800s to found Liberia, as well as other colonies along the coast. These Liberians call themselves "Americo" or "Congo," while they call those who are indigenous to the land, "Country." Although they comprised about five percent of the population of Liberia, they dominated the intellectual class, controlling more wealth than the indigenous Liberians.

On December 24, 1989, a few months after I completed my high school education and started college in Monrovia, a band of Libyan-trained, Liberian rebels, who called themselves the National Patriotic Front of Liberia (NPFL) and were led by Charles G. Taylor (a former government official), invaded Liberia from the Ivory Coast. Their goal was to overthrow what Taylor called, "The corrupt and dictatorial regime," of President Samuel K. Doe.

Some politicians and Liberian citizens hailed the rebels' actions, because they did not support Doe's regime. What resulted, however, was a horrible reign of terror that led to the death of tens of thousands of innocent people.

With the outbreak of the civil war, my being a member of the native ethnic Krahn tribe and related to the first family made me an instant target, and forced me to run for my life. Rebels consisting of men, women, and children pursued me. Children as young as six or seven, drugged and trained in killing techniques, went into the battlefield. They were fearless, totally ruthless, and inhumane. They often killed fleeing civilians simply because they did not like their faces. They made people dance, laugh, and clap while watching their relatives or friends being butchered. These children were, without a doubt, capable of the worst acts human beings could perform on each other.

Making matters worse, Charles Taylor additionally trained and supplied a Sierra Leone-focused rebel group known as the Revolutionary United Front (RUF), with the intention of destabilizing the country. After barely escaping with my life into Sierra Leone, I found myself chased across the entire country by RUF rebels, who, like the NPFL rebels, were killing almost everyone in sight. The RUF also used children soldiers, and included at one point up to 23,000 of them—many of them murdered their own parents.

This story is the firsthand account of my life as a struggling young girl who desperately wanted acceptance and love, and as a refugee who spent more than ten years as a hunted animal. To survive, I traveled over three hundred miles through two countries, and journeyed in a small boat over seventy miles through high seas to escape to Guinea, where I was falsely accused and thrown into jail. I was hunted, hounded, brutalized, starved, and flogged; yet, throughout my struggles, whenever there appeared to be no way out and no hope of survival, God provided miraculous sustenance and means of escape.

My life has been a series of vast contrasts, where I have experienced the deepest valleys and the highest peaks, and have suffered unspeakable horror buttressed by unbelievable kindness. In the midst of it all, I learned to forgive, not blame; to love, not hate; to live in peace, not turmoil. God strengthened me, and my tears of misery transformed into those of joy.

Many times, I thought I had breathed my last breath, and were it not for God's grace I could not have survived to tell this story. My God-given gift saved me, as well as many others, from certain death during those many years of running as a refugee in the midst of the Liberian and Sierra Leonean civil wars.

It is my hope that my story will inspire and encourage you to prevail against any obstacles that may come your way.

PREFACE

This story is a true account of the more than ten years I spent on the run and hunted down as a Liberian refugee, as well as my early childhood that provided me the foundation I needed to survive the ordeal. As the author of this memoir, I take full responsibility for any errors or omissions, as well as any details I purposely left out to shield readers from the blunt trauma more graphic details of unspeakable horror might cause.

Due to the sensitive situations and times described in this book, and to protect the innocent, I have changed some names.

CHAPTER 1

Destiny

Ruthless young rebels with AK-47 rifles and sharp knives tormented the terrified crowd of refugees. Shoving their hands in our faces to show us their wooden voodoo rings they said, "These rings have special voodoo powers, and when they're near a member of the Krahn or Mandingo tribe they get hot and burn our skin!"

One rebel boy thrust his closed fist at unsuspecting people, screaming, "It's getting warmer!" Reaching me, he shouted, "Oh, oh, it's burning me!" as he opened his fist and frantically shook his hand in the air. He announced to the others, "Hey, I've got a firecracker over here!" He looked me straight in the eyes and said slowly and pointedly, "Today could be your lucky day." I begged for mercy as he laughed hysterically.

Another rebel boy boasted loudly, "Our voodoo magic and our voodoo spells protect us from bullets. We cannot be shot and killed because bullets bounce off us as if they were made of rubber, and bayonets break like twigs." He continued, "One time a soldier aimed his AK-47 at me and all the bullets that struck my body bounced off me and fell to the ground and did me no harm. That soldier wished he hadn't met up with me. Do you know what I did to him? I sliced him into a million pieces!" He picked up and twirled the good luck charm he had hanging on his necklace and said, "This is his trigger finger."

At one point, the rebel boy with the trigger finger necklace playfully skipped over to where twin, teenaged girls were holding each other. The boy danced around the two girls as they trembled in fear and tried to turn away from him and his taunting.

"My finger is burning hot and you two are going to die." He was sure they were Mandingo girls because of their ebony skin. The twins were dragged behind the hut. Their screams for mercy pierced our hearts for we knew there was no one to rescue them. When the rebels had run out of strength, they forced the girls to stand naked along the side of the road, and shot them down. Two delicate and beautiful, ebony girls were dead.

Another rebel danced his way through the crowd and stopped abruptly in front of the four young brothers I had been following down the trail earlier. As he shoved his voodoo ring in their faces he said, "My ring is getting hot again." He quickly pulled his hand away, shook it violently in the air, and said, "Ouch! I got a hot one over here."

Two other rebels came running over to check it out. They shoved their voodoo rings toward the boys and they all danced and joyfully proclaimed, "Oh yeah, they're hot for sure!"

I had become faint and thought I would vomit. One of the rebel boys who came over tilted his head from side to side as if noticing something about the brothers. His eyes narrowed and he looked straight into the oldest boy's eyes and growled, "Don't I know you?"

The boy froze with fear and could not respond. The rebel reached out his hand with the ring and joyfully chanted, "Yes, yes, yes. You are a Krahn. A dirty rotten Krahn dog. My ring never lies. I recognize you from school." He turned and looked at the other three boys and said with a wicked smile, "What do we have here? Did we hit the jackpot? Are these your brothers?" The youngest of the four cried; he had soiled his pants. I had followed this family through the forest and we had shared our joys, hopes, and fears with each other. I shook violently as they were forcibly ushered out of the group.

The oldest boy, shot in the head, collapsed to the ground. The youngest ran to his side and was blasted with bullets. The other two fell under waves of gunfire. That wretched scene was committed to my memory as if branded there by a hot iron.

A rebel yelled, "Give me six feet," as he motioned for the crowd to move back. He felt six feet would give him ample clearance and, before I could blink my eyes, I saw bullets rip through the entire family he had ousted from the throng.

One of the rebel executioners took out a sharp machete and with one sweeping blow beheaded the father. Grabbing the head by the hair, he brought it over to me and told me to hold it and dance with it in celebration. When I refused, he hammered me with his fists until I passed out.

While I lay on the ground in a heap I dreamed of my mother—when she had blessed me with rice and water, saying, "May your life be full. May success follow you. May you live very long to see every strand of hair on your head be as white as these grains of rice, and may many years lie before you. Blessings will flow from above, and you will be strong and great."

A rifle fired near my head, and the resulting loud ringing in my ears jolted me back to consciousness. I gasped, realizing I was again in hell.

Destiny is somewhat like a musical orchestration. A skilled conductor chooses the piece, yet allows each musician to express his or her own individuality and creativity. One thing is for sure, God's orchestrating hand was on my life even before I was born.

My mother learned it was her turn to play her instrument when an old woman she did not know politely, but boldly, approached her on the street and said, "Beautiful lady, you're going to get pregnant and give birth to a little girl."

The woman's words surprised her because she was not pregnant at the time and was focusing on her music career. In a hurried manner, the woman finished her message, saying, "You will give birth to a little girl and she will go through many terrible struggles in her life. Don't be afraid, she will experience victory over them all. Your daughter will grow up to love God and serve him all the days of her life."

My mother, Josephiné, was a very attractive woman and a talented musician and singer. My father, Charles Barton, also known as Kohoun Charley, met her at a wedding ceremony in the Ivory Coast, where she was a guest performer. During her performance, she dazzled the guests with her singing and dancing. My father, not taken only by her beauty but also by the aura that exuded from her, said to himself, *This is the kind of woman that I would like as one of my wives.*

After several months, my father secured the hand of my mother, making her his fourth wife, and she joined him and his other three wives in Monrovia. In the African tradition, polygamy is a common way of life; having many wives and children is a sign of wealth and prestige.

A few years later, my mother became pregnant with me. Basking in the joy of her new pregnancy, she walked to the local market. It was a scorching hot summer day in October. She could not hide her joy at carrying a child; she smiled and hummed as she walked down a dusty road. She squinted at the bright sunlight and her flip-flops kicked up small clouds of dust. At one point, she stopped to rest with one hand on her belly and the other supporting her lower back.

A few children passed by, running and giggling down the road, and she smiled at their free spirits. My mother knew all too well that not every child in Liberia has the privilege of such freedom. Many children, especially those of impoverished families, became servants at a very young age, exchanging their freedom for the opportunity to secure an education.

My mother often wondered if she was going to have a little girl, as the old woman had said. She thought, *If I am to have a daughter, I will teach her to sing and to play musical instruments, and I won't grow old alone because I will always have her beside me.*

A month later, I was born and the family held a naming ceremony in my honor. The celebration brought many well-wishers bearing gifts of food, wine, and other handmade gifts for mother and baby. In Africa, it is the father's responsibility, and joy, to name the child.

Traditionally, baby girls receive the names of their paternal grandmothers. I was given the name Diehi Louise Barton, but was called by the nickname Géesedeh.

Although my mother was uneducated and illiterate, she had grown up in large cities and, as a sought-after musical entertainer, was accustomed to plush surroundings. When I began crawling, she would place a *lappa* on the ground for me. *Lappas* are beautifully colored, sheet-like cloths that African women use for everything from carrying babies to wrapping loose items into huge, hobo-like bundles that they balance on their heads. They also wear them wrapped and tucked securely around their waist as a full-length skirt.

When I had crawled to the end of the *lappa*, she would lay down another one. I became so accustomed to the routine that when I came to the end of the *lappa* I would stop crawling and wait for my mother to place the next one down. Other women marveled at my mother's special attention, and her way of treating me as if I were royalty.

My father was a Liberian soldier posted as a guard at the old government hospital on Ashmun Street. His income, however, was not sufficient to keep his many wives and more than a dozen children from destitution. We lived in the army barracks at the Barclay Training Center, where families shared common bathroom facilities and showers, and washed clothes in large outdoor washing tubs with washboards. Families cooked outside on "coal pots," metal pots heated by charcoal fires. We subsisted on bags of rice provided by the army and the few fruits, vegetables, and meats we could purchase in the open market.

It was not uncommon for children of the indigent to complete no more than the seventh or eighth grade and then leave school to learn a trade. In the hope of providing one of his children a better future, my father approached a well-to-do and well-educated man, who worked at the hospital, and asked if he would be willing to assist my older brother Solo. After much consideration, Mr. Smith agreed to allow Solo to work for his family as a domestic servant; in exchange, he would be housed, fed, educated, and given the opportunity to grow up in modern society.

Not too long thereafter, when I was just a toddler, the Liberian Army transferred my father to a post in the city of Zwedru, in Grand Gedeh County, over two hundred miles east of Monrovia. There I was first introduced to village life—a life I soon grew to love. My older brother Solo, however, stayed behind with the Smith family.

As the years sped by, I grew more and more in love with my new surroundings. One of the highlights of my life in the village was the annual celebration held in honor of the men who would soon leave on a dangerous but essential elephant hunt. At that time, elephant hunting was legal, and every portion of the elephant was utilized to sustain the village's way of life.

Laughing children weaved in and out of the day's preparations. Enticing aromas escaped from large pots simmering on open flames, women swept the ground with their woven brooms, and older men conversed with one another under the shade of the knobby old tree. All of this activity added to the joyful anticipation of the upcoming evening festival. Women prepared the celebration meal while hunters skillfully and painstakingly painted their faces with white chalk. These specially designed markings represented the individual characteristics each hunter either possessed or aspired to have—bravery, fierceness, strength, or fortitude.

We viewed our beloved hunters much like superheroes; Superman, Spiderman, Batman, and the like. Each had his own mask-like markings to identify him as brave, fierce, or strong. Women, old and young alike, took their very best *lappas* and laid them on the newly swept ground. This kind and loving gesture was done out of deepest respect, in honor of the hunters. The master drummer's hands began to fly rapidly in succession on the tightly stretched head of his handmade African drum—and with a single nod of his head the men broke into a traditional hunters' dance.

The barefooted hunters stepped onto the multicolored *lappas* as a band of drummers skillfully led the men in a hauntingly captivating, traditional tribal dance. Bodies bent down and rose up; arms reached to the heavens while they swayed left and right; again and again feet pounded the ground to the beat of the drums while strong and well-defined muscles glistened in the campfire's light. It was a beautiful display of pure, masculine strength; affirming the hunters' confidence, power, and unity. The dancers danced for each other, and with each other, drawing the onlookers into the shared energy as their hearts filled with the anticipation of the good hunt to follow.

Beautiful, young women with sun-kissed, mahogany skin—robed in bright canary yellow, lemon-lime green, mango reds and oranges, and other brilliant rainforest colors—joined the dance. Before long, the rhythm enveloped the entire village, which danced and swayed to the beat, anointing the hunters with the courage and energy they needed for a successful hunt. Hundreds of miles by foot and many weeks of hardship would follow the evening's party, but it would only take one sure arrow, shot with precision, to bring home enough meat to sustain the village for several months.

Whenever our hunters killed an elephant, they presented the tail to the village chief as a trophy of victory. An elephant is a magnificent creature known for its keen intelligence, loyalty, sensitivity, and physical strength; although small, the tail represented the entire elephant in all of its grandeur.

After one successful hunt, the chief decided to award the elephant's tail to someone in the village whom he felt exemplified the elephant's character and stature. He called everyone together and said, "Tonight we are gathered to recognize and honor a woman who lives among us. She has great wisdom and loving compassion for her neighbors. Her strength of character, mind, and body is well recognized, not only here in this village, but also in distant villages." Much to her surprise, he called my mother out of the crowd and awarded her the coveted elephant's tail, with its black tuft of hair cascading down from the tip.

Before the next hunt, my devoted and loving mother felt compelled to divorce my father and return to the Ivory Coast. It must have been a heart-wrenching decision because she knew she would have to leave me behind at the tender age of five. In my culture, it was customary for the children of divorced parents to stay with their fathers.

My father was a quiet and easygoing man. I believe he was good to all his wives and children. Even though my mother was very kind, she did have an explosive temper at times. She often struggled with the other wives, which by that time had grown to six, and felt tormented by some of them.

I did not know my mother had decided to leave until the day before her departure, so I hardly had time to digest the meaning of what was happening until she had already gone. I learned she was leaving when she took me by the hand and said, "Come with me, I have something to tell you." She led me to a cocoa tree that we often sat under as she told me interesting stories of the goodness of God.

Cocoa trees grow best in the shade of other, larger trees because they need to be shaded from the strong tropical sun and sheltered from the wind. I suppose my father was not able to shelter her from the hardships of village life, neither could he protect her from the strong winds of personality conflicts involving his other wives.

My mother knelt down beside me and hugged me close to her bosom. Her voice was weak and quivering and her tall, thin frame bent over slightly under the weight of what she was about to share. She cried softly, saying, "Oh, my beautiful little Géesedeh Dekontee," lovingly using the name that was mine alone. She raised her head and shoulders, breathed in deeply, smoothed her skirt and looked at her closed right hand. I leaned in to see what she was holding.

She slowly opened her fingers to reveal kernels of white rice. My mother lifted her hand and showered my head with the kernels while gently chanting traditional words of blessing, "May your life be full.

May success follow you. May you live very long to see every strand of hair on your head be as white as these grains of rice, and may many years lie before you."

She took her right hand, lifted up a cup of water toward the heavens, and said, "I raise this cup with my right hand. I do this with my right hand for it stands for leadership and nobility." She raised the cup toward God, from whom all blessings flow, and said, "Blessings will flow from above, and you will be strong and great."

She asked me to stand up and look toward the heavens while she knelt down, brought the cup of water to her lips, and took a mouthful. She folded her hands in prayer, gazed toward heaven, and sprayed the water like a mist onto my feet. Four times she showered my feet while turning me in the four directions of the compass, signifying that in any direction I would go I would find favor with people.

She said, "Géesedeh, walk forward." Lifting the cup one more time she sprinkled my path with the rest of the water and solemnly said, "May you find favor with all people everywhere. You will shake hands with great people, and you will be a blessing to many."

My mother pulled me close to her and cried. I felt her bony frame heaving against my body. Placing a hand on each of my shoulders, she gently drew me from her chest. With the hem of her *lappa*, she wiped away the tears from her eyes, but could not remove them from her voice when she cried, "Your Ma is going away and will not be returning. You will stay here with your father, and grow up with your brothers and sisters."

I was too young to understand why she had to go. I clung to her hand and tightly held her *lappa*, but she pulled away from my grasp and said firmly, "You have to be strong." I cried uncontrollably, saying, "You're leaving me? Don't go, Ma, please don't go!"

I refused to leave my mother's side, and asked, "Don't you love me?" I was wondering if I had done something wrong. She tried to hush my crying, but there was no quieting my shattered soul. I hated the cocoa tree I had once loved. My heart was breaking and I thought I would never be happy again.

I ran to my father and pleaded with him, "Papa, Ma is leaving us; don't let her go!" He turned away from me, not knowing what to say. I persisted and ran in front of him. The sadness on his face revealed his inner torment. "Papa," I said, "Please, make Ma stay." He bent down, picked me up, and said, "I wish I could make her stay Géesedeh, but your Ma has made up her mind."

I had thought he could make her stay, yet, out of his goodness, he felt he had to let her go. I changed my plea and cried, "Papa, I want to go with Ma. Please let me go with Ma." I could not say any more for the tears choked my words. He could not explain adult things to me because I was not yet mature enough to understand the complexities of marriage. It did not matter to me why my mother was leaving; I just wanted to be with her.

The sky was darkening; a storm was coming and the wind shook the trees, much as I shook to my very core. I could smell rain in the air. The heavens seemed to know the ache in my heart and would soon join in my tears. My mother would be leaving in the morning and everyone in the village wanted to spend these last moments with her.

The other women in the village prepared a farewell dinner. At the dinner, as was customary in our village, all of the women and children, along with my mother, sat in one circle, while the men sat in another. An elderly woman named Soueh, who often sang with my mother, said, "Your songs and the echoes from your voice will remain in our ears and be forever in our hearts." Her words made my mother cry. Turning her gaze to her friend she said, "Don't only remember the echoes of my voice, but also remember my daughter when she cries for me. Let her know I am always here with her in spirit and I will always love her." She paused and closed her eyes tightly in the hope of holding back the tears. Upon opening her eyes, she glanced around the circle of women and said, "When you sing my songs, love my daughter like

I have loved her."

I leaned against my mother's breast and softly pleaded, "Please stay, Ma; please don't leave me." I will never forget the love that poured forth from her eyes. My mother tenderly said to me, "I'm going away, but my heart will be left behind. My empty shell is leaving, but my heart will be with you forever. I love you so much." Huge tears dropped from her face onto my shoulder. She cried so hard that she could no longer eat.

To lift our spirits, old man Leahe, who was the most skillful drummer in the village and could make his "talking drum" speak volumes, picked up his hourglass-shaped instrument and tucked it under his left arm. With his right hand, he rhythmically tapped on the drum with a bent stick and made beautiful tonal music that sounded like our language. The tones he played were unmistakable, and cried out, "Josephiné, Josephiné, your songs have blessed us. Grace us with your voice again. Josephiné, Josephiné, before you leave, please sing for us." Everyone agreed with the words from the drum, and chimed in, "Sing, Josephiné, sing."

My mother got up, walked over to her hut, and picked up her *sasa*, a musical instrument (also known as a *shekere*) made from a whole gourd covered in a netting of beads or shells that makes rhythmic sounds when shaken and tapped. She slowly walked to the center of the circle that had formed in front of her hut.

Ma closed her eyes and sang, "Kohoun Charley, see your daughter, care for her like a leopard cares for her cubs, like an eagle cares for her young, like you care for your own eyes." Her voice drifted off. She hummed the melody until she regained her voice.

I listened to her and tried with all my heart to let the sound of her voice flow in me, through me, and around me, to be etched in my memory forever. I absorbed her voice, allowing it to soak into me and made a mental image of her face, her teeth, the way she smiled, her eyes, the way she moved, and the way she loved and blessed with her songs.

Soon, a renewed spirit came over my mother and light-hearted songs poured from her heart. Other women joined in, singing songs of unity, harvest, blessing, and love. We sang and danced all through the night, until the sun peeked over the horizon. It had been a night filled with joy and sadness.

With rains approaching and everyone exhausted from the long night of dancing and singing, we all went to our separate huts to get a few hours of rest. I followed my mother into her hut, curled up next to her, and listened to her breathing. She whispered to me, "I am so proud to be your mother. Sleep now, everything is going to be okay." I did not want to sleep. I only wanted to look at my mother; yet, I was so tired I could not keep my eyes open another minute and fell fast asleep.

As I awoke, I saw my beautiful mother standing before me. Her countenance and stature were otherworldly. She truly looked like an angel, or an African princess. She had packed a few belongings, including her elephant's tail and her *sasa*, in two small trunks. The one thing she had to leave behind, though, was her heart; it beat in my chest.

In the hope of comforting me, my mother said, "Géesedeh, I will walk about three hours and then cross the big Cavalla River, which separates Liberia and the Ivory Coast, but I want you to know that no river will ever be able to separate me from my love for you."

All of her friends and relatives came to accompany her out of the village and walk with her to the Cavalla River. She left me standing with my father, my six stepmothers, and most of my brothers and sisters. My mother stood at a distance from me with tears in her eyes. I watched her as she turned, walked away, and disappeared down the dirt path. I was a brokenhearted little girl; limp and worn; reaching out my arms in despair; pleading, begging, and crying as my mother faded from view.

CHAPTER 2

Servant Girl

They called me my father's handbag, a child a parent takes along everywhere they go. I loved traveling at my father's side, or on his shoulder; however, these trips were out of necessity, not merely pleasure, because I had ended up in the care of his remaining six wives. Two of my mothers lived in Gienwen, two in Bawaydee, and yet two more in Zwedru. While I enjoyed being with my siblings, and now had over twenty, none of these extended families could care for me for long; and every two weeks or so, just as I began to feel at home, I was unceremoniously juggled from one to the next. When I turned six, my father asked Diehi Lucy, one of my older sisters who lived in Zwedru, to take me in so I could begin first grade.

Attending school was new and exciting, and I looked forward to going. I did well, and at the end of the year I was promoted. Unfortunately, Lucy could not afford to continue caring for me; so as summer began, I resumed being juggled from family to family. My father, who was illiterate, often told me he believed a quality education was a steppingstone to a better life, and was something that could never be taken away. Knowing my being shuffled from home to home every few weeks would prevent me from ever getting an education, he contacted the family in Monrovia with whom he had left my older brother Solo, asking if they would take me in as well. Mr. and Mrs. Smith responded, saying that they would allow me to join Solo as a domestic servant in their home. I would attend school in Monrovia.

The day he decided to break the news of my upcoming departure, my father gave me a live fawn. While I admired the delicate creature, he told me of his plans. A quiet resolve creased his face as he said, "I've found a way for one of my daughters to be educated and live in the modern world. She must be at least eleven, though. I know you're only seven, but I think you can do everything expected of an eleven-year-old girl, and I want you to have this opportunity. You have to be a big girl now, and you must not tell anyone your true age, ever."

I questioned him, "I can be grown up enough to be like an eleven-year-old?" My father's nodding with certainty made it so; I only knew to trust him. And yet, I did not want to leave him, so I grabbed him around the neck with all my might. His decision was made, so he gently but firmly removed my arms, looking deeply into my eyes as if he were willing me to be eleven.

"You will be living with the Smith family in Monrovia. Your brother Solo lives there. You haven't seen him since you were a baby. You'll have a wonderful time. It'll be an exciting adventure, and you can attend school there." Before I could respond, he quickly emphasized, "And you'll become civilized!" I did not know what the word, "civilized" meant, but I did know it was something my father highly prized.

While he explained the benefits of higher education and living in the civilized, modern world of conveniences, I stooped down and considered the fawn. It was young, innocent, and without its parents. I realized that I was about to be in the same position. I knew I had no choice but to comply with my father's wishes. I picked up my little fawn and nuzzled its neck for comfort. It looked at me with its big, deep brown eyes. I squeezed it more tightly and kissed its neck. "Little friend, I'm going to be without my family just like you; but don't worry, we'll have each other. I will never leave you."

On a cool and dry morning in early January, the day of my departure had finally arrived. My father arranged for me to travel to Monrovia by mini-bus with my cousin Amos as chaperone. I was miserable because I was about to leave my family and all that I called home.

I had never been away from my family and I was still just a child. I clung to my father, much as a drowning person clings to their rescuer, and pleaded with him not to send me away. My father took me into his arms, tousled my hair with his hand, and said, "Don't cry, everything will be okay. I will visit you often, and you will be joining your brother Solo who will help you get used to your new surroundings." With some excitement in his voice he added, "Remember, this will be your new family. You're going to be babysitting Mrs. Smith's youngest daughter, and her other children will all be there to play with you."

He felt he was giving me the greatest gift he could give to any of his children, and he truly believed this move would be the best thing for me. Even though it did sound exciting, I was not convinced. My father was an amazing man. He was a good soldier, farmer, husband, father, and friend; and I loved him so much that I simply could not imagine life without him.

My cousin Amos showed up just before the bus arrived and quickly loaded a sack of rice, five caged chickens, and a crate of dried meats, which my father had prepared as gifts for the Smith family. My cousin climbed aboard the bus and found a seat near the back. I followed him by climbing over other passengers and their animals until I could reach him; because there was no other room available, I sat in his lap with my little fawn on mine. It was so tight that there was not even room to readjust ourselves.

My father poked his head inside an open window to look at me one last time; the bus was so crowded with people and their animals that he could barely see me. He stretched out his arm toward me and I reached across the lap of another passenger so I could grab his hand and hold it tightly. I knew at that moment that I would deeply miss the warm touch of his hand. He was crying and praying aloud, asking God to give me long life. I cried, too, and my fawn licked the salty tears off my cheek. The last words I heard from my father were, "God bless you, my little Kwe Jeeyah," which, loosely interpreted, meant, "God bless you, my little civilized daughter. No matter what happens, everything will be okay."

As the driver started the engine, my father pulled his hand away from mine. I shouted, "Papa, I love you," as I watched him standing on the side of the road while we drove out of sight. It was a long while before I could stop crying, and when I did I let out a sigh and wiped away my tears with the back of my hand.

The cacophony of sounds coming from within the mini-bus was maddening. Goats, chickens, and sheep were all bleating and crying. Feathers and puffs of wool floated around the passengers. My nose began to tickle, and several times I gave way to the overwhelming need to sneeze. I looked up into Amos' eyes, and he smiled kindly at me. I chuckled as I noticed that some of the floating debris had landed in his hair. Before long, the driver, who could not take the noise anymore, screamed out loudly, "Shuuuuuut Uuuuuup!" The sound of his voice rang in all of our ears. The bus quickly went silent, as if someone had pressed the mute button on an invisible remote control. For the first time since the trip began, everything seemed quiet—almost peaceful.

We sat so long in the cramped condition that our legs grew numb. We traveled all night before the driver stopped for us to get out and use the bathroom; by then, we all smelled of goats and animal urine.

Since there was no law against it, there were even passengers riding on the roof of the bus. I have no idea how they managed not to fall off during the journey. It is no exaggeration to say that people, along with their belongings and their animals, filled and covered every inch of the vehicle.

Two long and arduous days passed before we arrived at our destination. Chicken feathers, and the smells of the animals we had ridden with, covered us. Fellow passengers, hoping to procure the favor of government officials, had brought most of the animals as gifts.

My cousin Amos noticed before I did that my sleeping fawn was no longer sleeping, but had died in my arms from the stress of the trip.

I saw that it was limp when Amos gently and tenderly took the fawn from my arms. He said, "Géesedeh, your fawn isn't sleeping anymore. It has died." I was stunned. I had already lost my mother and had left my father. I could not believe my sweet fawn was dead. Amos looked at me consolingly and said, "Stay right here—I'll be right back," and headed off before I could stop him.

When Amos came back, he no longer had the fawn. I looked at him and cried, "Where's my fawn?" Amos knelt beside me and said, "Everything's fine; don't worry."

Before I could protest, Amos stood up, flagged down a taxicab, and asked me to get in. If the driver had not needed the money badly, he would probably have passed us by. Amos hurriedly picked a few feathers from my long hair, and brushed me off with the palm of his hand. We climbed in with all of our belongings, including the caged chickens. The taxi driver grunted something unintelligible and grudgingly headed toward our destination.

As Amos placed his arm around me to comfort me, I leaned on his chest and cried. Since I had been raised in a remote village, all the sights and sounds of Monrovia were foreign to me. My mouth dropped open and stayed that way for quite some time as we drove past what I felt must be mansions. My amazement was interrupted when I heard my cousin Amos say, "We're here now; come on, get out of the car."

Amos unloaded my belongings and the gifts for the Smith family, and piled them on the sidewalk. After paying the driver, Amos handed me my things, balanced the caged chickens in his arms, and asked me to follow him down an alleyway between the houses. My steps were slow and uncertain. After a short walk we reached the Smith's home. I stopped abruptly as I gazed up at the front of the Smith's grand home.

Amos looked down at me and smiled as he said, "This is going to be *your* new home." As I looked up at the massive house in wonder, a pretty woman, carrying her beautifully adorned baby, hurried out the front door. Amos looked up, cleared his throat, smiled timidly, and said, "Hello, Mrs. Smith, I'm Amos; and this is Louise Barton." I was stunned at the beauty of the woman. Her curly hair bounced around her face as she walked toward us. The first thing I noticed was her lovely smile. She had a perfectly curved body and shiny, dark ebony skin. She sported a fashionable and lovely pantsuit that neatly hugged her figure.

Before anyone else said anything, I chirped in and said, "Hello, Ma," which is the traditional greeting used when addressing an adult female. She took one quick look at me, turned to look at Amos, and said rather roughly, "Take her to the house. I'll be back later. I'm taking my daughter to a birthday party."

The baby stared at me with her big brown eyes and giggled. I smiled back at her and thought, *I sure am going to have fun taking care of that cutie.* Just then, a shiny new taxicab drove up, and Mrs. Smith slipped into the back seat with her child.

Amos' nudge brought me back to reality, and he gently guided me to the back door of the house. When Amos opened the door, the pleasant aromas that came from the kitchen nearly knocked us over. An exotic flower arrangement sat on the counter next to the window and the smell of freshly baked cornbread and other delectable foods filled the house. I swallowed hard because I was very hungry—hungry for food, love, and the hope of a better future. I thought, *My father was right; this will be an exciting adventure that I'll greatly enjoy.*

As I stood dazed in the kitchen doorway, I saw a boy who appeared tired; he was walking our way very slowly from one of the back rooms. As he approached, Amos reached out to him, gave him a hug, and said, "Solo, I brought your little sister Louise." When I looked up at him, I could see that he looked just like our father, except for the dark circles under his eyes.

Solo smiled, patted me on the shoulder, and greeted me in English. Although I knew a few words in English and French, I only spoke the Naio dialect of the Krahn language, so Amos had to interpret. Amos said, "Your brother is happy to see you." Unfortunately, Solo had been with the Smith family so long that he had forgotten his mother tongue, and he could only speak English. I suddenly realized that I would not be able to speak with my brother, or anyone else at the Smith's home, until I learned the language.

When Solo bent down to give me a hug, I noticed he had a bald spot on the top of his head. Amos rubbed the spot and said, "What's this?" Solo replied, "Oh, that's from carrying a heavy cooler every day to sell items at the beach for Mrs. Smith."

Before I could even begin to get my wealth of questions out, Solo said to Amos, "Please tell Louise I can't stay and talk because I have too many chores to finish;" and then he wearily walked away. Not knowing what else to do, we stepped onto the back porch to wait for Mrs. Smith to return home.

Cousin Amos stayed with me until Mrs. Smith returned later that night. Finding us on the porch, Mrs. Smith looked down at me and then quickly turned her gaze to Amos. He pointed to the gifts sitting on the ground and said they were from my father, who was grateful for her taking me in and providing me the opportunity to get an education.

Mrs. Smith yelled, "Solo, come get your sister and take her into the house." After she headed inside, my cousin Amos leaned over and said, "Louise, I need to go now. I will come and visit you often. I promise." I looked up at Amos and, with tears in my eyes, fell onto his neck.

I was filled with fear—fear of the unknown, fear at seeing Solo looking so haggard, fear of not knowing the language. I did not want Amos to leave me. I pleaded, "Please don't go!" In his loving way, he wrapped his arms around me and said, "Louise, I have to go. Don't cry. You'll be all right. You're going to have a lot of fun living in this beautiful house." Amos wiggled out of my grasp as my brother came out to the porch and took me by the hand, leading me into the house.

Since Solo didn't speak Krahn and I didn't speak English, he silently guided me into the kitchen, where I saw three children washing their hands in the sink. *Where was that water coming from?*, I thought. I was amazed to see water coming from a pipe, pouring into a large bowl, and then disappearing down the hole at the bottom. The children turned to look at me, wrinkled their noses, and seemed equally surprised. I became aware of how ragged I looked, and how disagreeable I smelled after the long bus ride. They giggled and whispered to each other. I attempted to be friendly, saying something to them in Krahn, and they giggled even more.

Mrs. Smith's younger sister, Hope, who lived in the Smith home while attending college, came into the kitchen and told Solo to get back to his chores. He responded with a low, "Okay," and then was gone. I found I was to be in this woman's charge for the evening.

After walking briskly to the counter, and scooping some food from the stove into a bowl, Hope rummaged in a drawer and pulled out a spoon. She handed both to me and pointed toward the porch door. Once on the porch, she waved for me to sit down on the steps. It didn't take me long to eat what was in the small bowl; and when I had finished, Hope took me back inside where she pointed to the large metal bowl I had noticed earlier, and motioned that I was to wash my bowl and spoon.

Mrs. Smith's oldest daughter, who looked like she was about my age, entered the kitchen with a towel, and waved for me to follow her outside. About thirty feet out into the yard she picked up a small plastic utility bucket, handed it to me, and pointed at a hand pump. Realizing I had no idea what to do, she pushed my hands and the bucket under the spout and dragged the pump's handle up and down until water began to flow. She turned the process over to me, and I finished filling the bucket. I realized I was to wash myself when she motioned for me to remove my clothes. I slipped them off and began splashing myself. I shivered from the cold water and the cool night air, and thought about this strange place so far from my family and the village I loved. Satisfied that I had washed off enough of the dirt and odors from my trip, Mrs. Smith's daughter handed me a towel and guided me back into the house, leaving my soiled clothing on the ground.

I followed her to a room where Hope stood in the doorway. I was amazed when Hope flipped a switch that instantly flooded the room with light. She motioned to a mattress on the floor and to a nightie neatly folded on top. She handed me the nightie, and as I dressed, I looked around the room with my eyes wide; I saw so many things I had never seen before. Against one wall was a fancy dressing table covered with luxurious-looking bottles. I also saw a necklace, matching earrings, and a watch. A box mounted in the wall rumbled and made a humming sound as cool air flowed from it. Against the opposite wall was a bed, where Hope sat while watching me.

After I had dressed, she pointed again to the mattress and gestured with her hands against her cheek, letting me know that was where I was to lie down and sleep. Kneeling down, I ran my hands over the smooth, floral-printed sheet; I patted the pillow that was lying there, soft and inviting. Back in the village, I had slept on a small mattress stuffed with newly cut grass. This bed did not smell the same, but I was sure I would like it. Worn out from the long trip, I was very much ready for sleep. I slid between the sheets, smiled at the woman, and was happy to see her smile faintly back at me.

After Hope had finished readying herself for bed, she walked back over to the doorway and again flipped the switch, plunging us into darkness. At first, I found it difficult to relax. I was in a strange new world, surrounded by things my mind could not comprehend; but, before long, my desperate need for rest won over my curiosity, and I fell asleep.

At 4:00 AM, I was startled awake by a loud voice shouting words I could not comprehend. "Get up, get up!" I was still tired, and weakly responded in Krahn that I couldn't understand and I wanted to sleep. I closed my eyes and the next thing I knew the sheet was pulled off me and I heard, much louder now, "Get up, get up, get up!" This jolted me out of my comfort and I quickly hopped off the mattress, trembling in fear, wondering what I was supposed to do next.

The disconcerting figure of a woman dressed in a nightgown and robe, and with curlers in her hair, motioned for me to follow her. When we reached the kitchen, I saw Solo and another young servant boy busily working. I realized it was Mrs. Smith who had gotten me up, and was focused on getting me to work. When I saw Solo's tired demeanor and the other boy's downcast eyes, I knew this was going to be difficult; it would certainly not be the fun and exciting adventure I was told it would be. I thought, *If this is what things will be like, I'd rather go home to the village and be seven years old again, and not have to pretend to be all grown up.*

The language here baffled me and all the modern appliances totally surprised me, though I quickly learned to turn the electric lights on and off, to use the oven, dishwasher, and washing machine. I made mistakes and received harsh corrections.

If I served coffee in a cup without a saucer, I received a smack, causing the cup's contents to splash on the floor and me. If I brought butter to the table and forgot the butter knife, I received a quick and sharp smack on the back. Mr. and Mrs. Smith often corrected me; I quivered whenever they called my name—and as the days dragged on, I wondered, *Will I ever be happy again?*

I was even afraid of Ripsy, the family dog. He was as big as a lion and had a long coat of hair and big white teeth. When I first laid eyes on him, I thought I was going to be his next meal. Ripsy would playfully follow me as I tried to run and "defend" myself by pushing him away. He was insisting that he wanted to be friends and I insisted that I did not. He was determined to win my heart and get a friendly pat on the head. I do not know how long it was before I actually trusted him, but Ripsy's patience won out in the end. Ripsy and I eventually became close friends, and I learned to count on his kind nature to comfort my wounded spirit.

The daily routine I had to endure was grueling and I could see why my brother Solo looked so haggard. Every morning I dragged my tired, worn-out body from the bed at 4:00 AM, stumbled my way to the bathroom and splashed cold water on my face to wake up. I hated looking in the mirror because I would always see bloodshot eyes staring back at me. I got up hours before the rest of the family so I could prepare breakfast, iron the children's school uniforms, polish their shoes, sweep the floors, dust the furniture, and pick up scattered items that had been left strewn about.

I had no time to relax and hardly enough time to go to school and study. My father's promise that I would have new brothers and sisters to play with rang hollow in my ears, for the family did not view me as a member. I longed for my own family; although several months had passed, I had not seen my cousin Amos, even though when he left me on Mrs. Smith's back porch he had assured me he would visit me often. I wondered what had happened to him, and why he was unable to keep his promise.

I was not the only child servant working during these early hours. There were three of us moving about quietly while the Smith family lay sleeping in their beds. Solo and I were strangers living and working in the same house. We lived in constant fear of receiving sharp and sometimes brutal correction; so much so that we kept our heads down and our focus on our chores. The only interruption to the daily drudgery was when Mrs. Smith would summon me by name.

One morning, upon hearing my name, I quickly scurried to her room and knocked on the door. Mrs. Smith's tired voice announced, "Louise, I'd like to take my tea in bed."

"Yes, Ma," I said, and ran quickly to the kitchen. "Yes, Ma," and "no, Ma," was how I primarily responded to Mrs. Smith.

When I reached the kitchen, I opened the cabinet door searching for her favorite cup. I found it and placed it on its matching saucer. Scolded so often for making mistakes, my hands trembled as I poured the tea. As I hurried back to her room, a few drops bounced out of the cup and onto the saucer. I wiped it off quickly because a simple spill would bring disciplinary action.

I was hoping Mrs. Smith was not feeling poorly; if she decided to stay home from work I might miss another day of school doing additional chores for her. Since I had to give up my freedom for an education, I wanted to make sure I got one. Much to my relief, she came down for breakfast and was dressed and ready for work.

The house also seemed to breathe a sigh of relief once everyone had left for the day and I ran as fast as I could to complete the rest of my chores. I washed the dishes, put away the food, and scrubbed the floors as I watched the clock and pushed harder and harder to finish on time. I took one more glance at the clock and fought back the tears, because I was late again. I grabbed a piece of cornbread and my books and ran out the door.

Even though I arose at 4:00 AM, it was still impossible to get all my chores done before school started. I cried as I alternately ran and walked down the road to school. Who could or would understand; who would even care about a servant girl and her education?

My life as a servant was hard, yet I was thrilled to go to school and be among other children. As long as I was in school, I felt no different from anyone else. However, once I returned home, the story was much different; I was once again a servant girl and I felt isolated and insulated from love and acceptance.

I attended Daniel E. Howard Elementary, which was about a mile from the place I was born. Whenever I was late, I was usually sent home in disappointment. On this day, however, I was surprised, and was allowed to attend the rest of my classes.

The school principal and my teachers must have discovered that I was a child servant and not just a lazy student who was not interested in showing up on time. I had tried to keep this fact hidden from my friends and made feeble excuses for why I could not stay and play after school. They did not realize that I had to rush home to make the Smith's evening meal and serve the family their dinner.

Each evening, after serving dinner to the family, I would walk out the back door and wait for my meal. Mrs. Smith would lean out the door with a small enamel bowl in her hand and say, "Here Louise, hurry up and eat, there are chores to be done." I would look down with submissive eyes and say, "Yes, Ma." The other servant children usually ate in the kitchen; however, I chose to eat my meals while perched on a bench on the back porch, with nature as my companion.

Most of the time I ate alone because the other servants' schedules and mine conflicted, preventing us from enjoying each other's company. The only company I had was Ripsy, who often joined me, along with a few uninvited guests such as ants and flies. One day, when I dropped some rice from my bowl, a tiny black ant tried to pick up a grain, only to struggle and drop it. To my surprise, another hurried over to help lift the load and the ants carried it off together. That is how it worked in my village—everyone helped each other so that no one's burden was ever too great. I deeply missed village life because, not only did we eat together, but we also fished, hunted, and shared many good times. Here, in this city, and in this mansion, I was truly alone and did not even have time to eat or speak with my brother.

As soon as I had finished my food, I got up from the bench and carried my enamel bowl back into the kitchen so I could begin my evening chores.

I was lucky if I was able to get three or four hours of sleep each night. Emotional and physical exhaustion were my constant companions. Although I managed to find a few moments to do homework and study, often by staying in the bathroom a little longer than usual, the few minutes I was able to scrounge were not enough for me to excel academically.

Unlike most workers, I worked a seven-day workweek, with no days off. My life consisted of nonstop cleaning and unending chores, except on weekends when the children begged their mother to let me play with them. I looked forward to these times because, for a moment, I could join in the fun; yet, even then, I still had to complete all my daily chores.

On sunny days, we played tag, kickball, and hide-and-seek. We blew up balloons and flew kites. We pretended to be Superman or Superwoman by draping cloths over our shoulders. We giggled and ran around the yard like raving maniacs.

If we were lucky enough to have rain on weekends or holidays, we would dance, stomp, splash, and run through the puddles. It was during these brief moments of playtime that I actually enjoyed being alive.

Friends and relatives of the Smith family often came to visit on weekends. Mrs. Smith's visitors frequently complimented the way I looked. I will never forget one occasion when one of Mrs. Smith's friends said, "Oh, look how long and beautiful that little girl's hair is. I wish I had hair like hers; and look at her beautiful big eyes—they are gorgeous!" I shyly smiled in response.

Mrs. Smith's nose wrinkled as she disgustedly said, "What? That girl is ugly. She looks like a monkey!" Mrs. Smith's eyes filled with contempt as she looked at me. She quickly ordered me to go and clean the bathrooms, despite my having already cleaned them as a part of my daily routine. I obediently went away and wiped down the bathrooms once more. It deeply hurt my feelings to hear that I was ugly and that I looked like a monkey. I was just a young child and I believed all of her hateful words.

I so much wanted Mrs. Smith's approval; however, she often called me names such as jungle monkey, beady eyes, and scrawny girl. She would smirk at me as she passed by and tell me my skin was ugly and dry. When she noticed I was doing well in school, she said I was nothing but a stupid country girl. These verbal insults caused me to become more determined to excel in my studies.

A few months after I had settled in, and after further compliments about my hair, Mrs. Smith declared that I had head lice. After treating my hair with camphor oil for a period of time, while no one else in the home was being treated, she called for me, saying, "Louise Barton, come here!" I trembled, fearing I had done something wrong. "Yes, Ma," I replied, as I ran to her bedroom door. Mrs. Smith declared, "Louise, I've been treating your hair for some time now, and without success; therefore, the only remedy left is to remove your hair. Go to the back porch." Submissively I said, "Okay, Ma," and slumped down on the bench, waiting for what would come next.

Mrs. Smith walked up behind me, grabbed a wad of my hair, and clipped it off with a pair of scissors. She made her way around my head and my hair fell at my feet until only stubble remained. I was mortified, but knew better than to protest. She picked up a razor and shaved my scalp clean. After wiping my head with alcohol, she reached for a jar of Vaseline, took out a handful, and rubbed it on until my skin shone. She wiped her hands brusquely and said, "There, that took care of that."

The next morning, Mrs. Smith's children were astonished and laughed aloud at my glistening bald head. A few tears leaked from my eyes; however, I quickly wiped them away so no one would have the satisfaction of knowing how devastated I felt.

Their reaction was mild compared with what I experienced at school, where my baldness attracted laughter, jeers, and teasing. Many of the kids bullied me, encircled me, and slapped me on the back of my head while chanting, "Who killed Goliath, *Sabu*-head killed Goliath. *Sabu*-head, *Sabu*-head." *Sabu* means "bald." Their laughing, jeering, and chanting continued throughout the day and crushed my spirit.

In sharp contrast to her standard treatment of me, Mrs. Smith, who was a faithful Catholic, took me to Mass and made sure I went through confirmation. She even brought home a beautiful, white dress for me to wear for the occasion. I was truly excited and felt almost as if I were having a birthday party. The day did not seem very different at first; I still rose at 4:00 AM and performed my chores. To my surprise, however, Mrs. Smith and her sisters cooked a special dinner in my honor and made everyone's favorite African dishes. Even then, the rest of the servants ate their meals in the kitchen and, as always, I sat outside on the back porch eating by myself from my enamel bowl.

CHAPTER 3

Eternal Love

My hair was beginning to grow back and Christmas was just around the corner. This would be my first Christmas away from home and I wondered what the holiday would be like in the big city. As a young girl brought up in a village without modern conveniences, I was still amazed at the wealth of magical things that surrounded me—electricity, indoor toilets, showers, television, an oven, and air conditioning.

Christmas at the Smith's home only added to my amazement as I, for the first time, saw things such as blown glass; rare, angel-hair ornaments; a miniature nativity scene on a white lace tablecloth; and an artificial, white Christmas tree covered with tiny lights that twinkled like fireflies on a warm summer night.

In addition to all of this, I saw a wealth of beautifully wrapped gifts with colorful bows and ribbons generously placed under the tree. I read the tags on the gifts and learned that there were many gifts for everyone in the Smith family, but not one was for me.

Christmas Eve day was extremely grueling for me. Everything was to be spotless. A large meal was to be prepared and served to the family, then cleaned up afterward. I ate my Christmas Eve dinner in solitude. After I washed and dressed Rebecca, one of Mrs. Smith's daughters, I braided her hair. She looked like a precious little angel. With all the chores I had to do there was no time left for me to look my best. I barely had time to throw on my dress, brush my teeth, and rush out the door with the family as we attended evening Mass.

Going to church was one of the few occasions that I actually sat and rested, and I loved it. I would let the music fill me; the voices in the choir comforted my lonely heart. I would smile at the statue of Jesus hanging on the cross, wondering if he might be aware of my suffering.

Since this was my first Christmas Eve service, I was not sure what to do. Should I kneel or stand, and when was I to do it? I kept a close eye on everyone else, watching so I could follow along and avoid making mistakes.

It was an evening that passed all too quickly; as soon as we returned home, I was back to my servitude. I made dessert, serving it to the family as Christmas carols filled the room. The Smith girls were looking at and touching the tantalizingly wrapped gifts, wondering what might be inside each one and which might contain something from the Christmas wish lists they had filled out weeks before.

Earlier in the day, friends of the family had dropped by with gifts for the girls; at their mother's behest, they opened them right away. They did not seem to be very excited about the new baby dolls and other toys that tumbled from the packages. Mrs. Smith's promptings brought on quick and polite thank yous from each of the girls. The girls threw one of their gifts, a beautiful baby doll, to the side. I looked at that unloved baby doll and wished it were mine; I would surely love it and care for it.

On Christmas morning, the girls arose earlier than usual. As always, I had been up since well before daybreak, doing my chores and preparing breakfast. When the family came into the living room, I could hear the girls' delighted giggles as they ripped each package open. Colorful paper drifted and settled around their feet and my task was to gather the wrappings and place them in a paper sack. I loved the paper and thought about how wonderful it would be if I could have but a small piece or two for making paper doll clothes. I would have been happy to keep but one of the ribbons.

After all the gifts had been opened, I was surprised to see that everyone sat there, disappointed that there were not more packages to open. It looked to me like Heaven had fallen from the sky and blessed everyone with everything they could possibly have wanted.

When Mr. and Mrs. Smith left the room for a few minutes, the children ran over to show me their new toys. Rebecca, Hawa, and Martha were especially happy with their new dollhouse and the accompanying Barbie and Ken dolls. Hawa shoved one of her dolls into my hands and said, "Do you want to go shopping?" Hurriedly, I sat down with her and the new dolls, replying, "Sure, let's go shopping." We happily bounced the dolls around the floor. Mrs. Smith's daughters were very sweet, and were not yet old enough to realize there was a big distinction between them and me, a servant child.

When Mrs. Smith came back into the room and noticed how immersed we were in play, she raised her voice in disapproval, stating firmly, but not so sternly as to upset her children, "Louise, hurry and finish cleaning up the Christmas wrap." The children begged their mother to allow me to continue playing with them. They delighted in my creativity.

Mrs. Smith told her children, "Louise doesn't have time to play like you do." Reluctantly, I got up from the floor, picked up all the ribbons and scraps of Christmas wrapping, and finished cleaning the living room. After I had finished straightening the sofa pillows and stacking the gifts back under the tree, the girls interrupted me and asked, "Louise, please come and play with us." I smiled at them, but had to continue my cleaning.

At that moment, a tinge of kindness touched Mrs. Smith's heart as she realized I was just a child, that it was Christmas, and that I had not received any gifts. She got up from her favorite chair and walked over to the discarded and unwanted baby doll. She looked over at me as she bent to pick it up, and then carried it in my direction. I was utterly shocked when Mrs. Smith placed it in my arms. I looked up at her and she said, "It's for you." My heart leapt for joy. I cradled and cuddled that baby all through the night.

During the next two weeks, as I did my chores as usual, I would sneak a hug or two from my new baby doll. I was so grateful and so very happy with my gift. She was the most beautiful doll I had ever seen, having a hand-painted, porcelain face and soft, pink pajamas. There was a matching blanket, in which I carefully wrapped her. I whispered into my baby doll's ears, "Don't worry, I will be right back." I checked on her as I could; not nearly as often as I would have liked to. The last time I stole away to check on my beloved baby, Mrs. Smith caught me. She snatched the baby from my arms and said, "You are not doing your work as you should." She quickly walked away with my lovely little baby; I knew I would never see my doll again.

Crushed, I felt my heart torn in two; I thought I would die.

Although Solo and I lived together in the same household, our being domestic servants and attending different schools prevented us from developing a sibling relationship. As I developed a command of the English language, I would often attempt speaking to him as we passed each other in the hallway. If we were not in earshot of Mrs. Smith, Solo would whisper, with panic in his voice, "We'll both be in real trouble." On occasion, but only for brief moments, Solo and I might assist each other with chores. Even then, we could only discuss the work at hand. If Mrs. Smith caught me attempting to have a casual conversation with anyone, Solo included, she would sharply retort, "Louise, have you finished cleaning the kitchen?" or "Louise, have you finished the dusting?" or "Louise, go straighten that room!" Mrs. Smith never allowed her domestic servants to be idle.

Around midnight each night, I would collapse onto my mattress on the floor. I was too fatigued to do any homework. I worked so hard each day that I was often too wound up to sleep and was plagued with insomnia. I was so terribly lonely and utterly unhappy that tears came quite easily.

One evening, when I was only nine, and felt I could no longer take all the abuse, I dropped my washrag and, without even trying to be quiet, pushed the back door open and let it slam shut behind me. I had no idea where to go, and I did not care; I ran hard, without looking back. I just wanted to be free.

Although it felt good to run without any restraint, suddenly a foreboding fear overtook me. My imagination transformed the shadows of the evening and the rustling wind in the nearby trees into wild animals and monsters. I ran between the houses and headed toward the beach at Coconut Plantation. As I ran in wild abandon, not even looking, cars and taxicabs sped back and forth; horns honked and drivers hurled profanities in my direction.

When I reached the coconut palm-lined beach, I ran in the sand until I was out of breath. I finally stopped running and became aware of my surroundings; couples walked hand in hand along the shore while the waves lapped at their feet. Children made their last dash into the waves as their parents gathered up belongings to head home for the evening. Down the beach, I could see the last round of a volleyball game playing out with shouts of triumph and high fives exchanged afterward between teammates. All these happy sights and sounds faded away with the last rays of the sun. I was alone.

I walked over to one of the coconut palms and leaned my back against its hard trunk, letting the weight of my body slide down the tree until I was sitting on the ground. I leaned over, hugging my knees with one arm while listlessly scooping up a handful of sand and letting it pour through my fingers. I did this over and over again, watching the grains sift to the ground in a growing mound.

I then pinched one grain between my finger and thumb and noticed its sharp edges. I rolled the grain of sand between my fingers until I accidentally dropped it and it disappeared into the infinite numbers below. I thought, *All these grains washed ashore, losing their individuality; they're good for nothing but to be trampled underfoot. My life is no different from the sand. My life is worthless.* I pulled my knees closer to my chest, lowered my head, and cried.

Darkness swept the sky, cloaking the beach in its mantle. I shivered from the cold ocean breeze as well as from the vivid thoughts of what might happen to me if I remained there any longer. My brother Solo and others had warned me many times that drug addicts, hardcore criminals, and all sorts of shady characters inhabit the beaches at night. Gruff voices and screams sounded out in drunken hilarity; horns blew and tires squealed as drivers slammed on brakes to avoid intoxicated pedestrians. The orchestra of eerie evening sounds filled me with dread and fear and I was chased back home by my imaginings, where I hid in the broken-down vehicle parked in our yard. I soon fell asleep from exhaustion.

Later that night, just before sunrise, I heard the reverberant sounds of marching footsteps, so I raised my head up slightly to peek out of the car window and see what was going on. To my surprise, I saw a group of "Society Men," as the locals called them, dressed in black and marching around the yard. These "Society Men" were widely believed to prey on human flesh for ritual purposes, and I was terribly frightened.

One of the men spotted me. Realizing no one else had seen me; he put his finger to his lips and gestured with his hand for me to duck down. I quickly dropped down below the window, and was careful not to make a sound. It was obvious he wanted to keep the other members of the group from spotting me. I quickly recognized him as one of Mr. Smith's friends.

Stories circulated of how these men would capture their victims and perform ritualistic activities, such as the extraction of human body parts. Their Voodoo doctors required these organs to perform ceremonies that would aid the "Society Men" in securing promotions in the government and power within society.

Once the sun came up, I decided not to continue with my plan of running away, but to head back into the house and face my punishment. Mrs. Smith grabbed her switch and beat me repeatedly over all my body until she was too tired to continue.

Even though every day was the same and my chores became a matter of routine, I never grew accustomed to abusive ways. I often thought, *Why must some people prey on the weak? What prevents them from showing a little kindness, or a little love, toward the less fortunate? With people treating each other like this, no wonder there is so much suffering in the world.*

One day during afternoon recess, at the end of my fourth grade year, I walked down the hallway of Daniel E. Howard Elementary School toward the doors leading outside. Across the hall I heard Ms. Comfort Smallwood, one of my former teachers, calling my name. "Louise, Louise, come here please, I have something exciting to tell you!" I hesitated for a moment, yet upon seeing her wide grin and welcoming, doe-like, ebony eyes, I ran in her direction. Ms. Smallwood told me she had just left a teacher's conference with the principal, Ms. Weeks. During that meeting, it had been decided I would be one of the students in my class to be awarded a double promotion, meaning I would be skipping fifth grade and would be promoted directly to sixth grade at the year-end graduation ceremony. "You've been selected for this most exceptional honor because you have one of the highest grade point averages in your class. We're all confident you'll do very well in sixth grade next year. I'm so, so proud of you! Your teacher will tell you formally later, but I wanted to be the first to share the news!"

I thought of my fourth-grade teacher, Mr. Isaac Woizy, who had inspired me to do my best on every assignment. Whenever I turned in work he felt was not up to my best, he would encourage me to do better, saying, "I believe in you, Louise. I know you can do it!" It was great to have someone believe in me, and I smiled as I thought, *Mr. Woizy, you were right, I can do it.*

The summer after I completed sixth grade, the Smith family decided to move a few miles away to a new home in a suburb of Monrovia called the ELWA Community; a community that had inherited its name from Radio ELWA (Eternal Love Winning Africa), the first Christian radio station in Africa, which began broadcasting in 1954.

It was quite fitting that I moved to a town with a name such as this, for I truly was looking for love—eternal love. I yearned for love as a deer yearns for water on an arid, summer day. Far more parched than the lifeless sands of a wind-blown desert is life without love.

Early one afternoon, shortly after our arrival in ELWA, I noticed Solo packing some things in a backpack as I passed his room. A bit later, I saw him heading out the back door wearing the backpack. Although I was curious as to where he was heading, I couldn't ask him and assumed Mrs. Smith had sent him on an errand of some sort. The next morning I attended to chores in the kitchen and noticed Solo was not at his usual tasks. "Where is Solo?" I asked the other servant. The boy replied, "He took off yesterday to go live with some buddies in Monrovia. Didn't he tell you?" I was shocked, and stepped out onto the back porch to be alone for a moment. I stared at the vacant road Solo had headed down the day before as various emotions flooded over me. I was surprised and saddened; and disappointed he had left without saying goodbye. Just then an overwhelming panic came over me. My last connection to my family was now gone. I felt hollow and alone, and I covered my mouth to muffle the mournful wail welling up from my throat.

Five years had passed since I last saw my cousin Amos, and I had come to believe I would never see him again. One morning, not long after we had moved and about the time Solo left for good, a soldier in army uniform approached the back door. I knew instantly it was Amos, still young and strong. I stepped out quickly and quietly to avoid drawing attention and threw my arms around his neck, whimpering with relief into his stiff collar.

After a moment, I looked up into his eyes. They were so tender and expressed his deep caring for me. "Oh Louise, you're so grown up now." When I asked, "What happened to you, Amos?" he responded,

"I'm so sorry not to have sent word. I signed up with the Armed Forces of Liberia and my assignment kept me from being able to visit. Only recently, they transferred me to Monrovia. I've been assigned as a guard at the presidential palace. I tried to visit you and found out from the neighbors you and the family had moved to the ELWA area. I came searching for you right away. I'm glad it didn't take long to find you! I can't stay long this time, but I will be back to see you often. You can believe me this time!"

Seeing Amos again, and knowing he would be visiting regularly gave me a renewed sense of hope. Although our initial visit was a short one, Amos did return frequently. Mrs. Smith must have noticed how much this lifted my spirits, because she seemed to welcome his visits, and would allow me to take a brief break from my daily chores.

During this time, I began attending the Carver Mission Academy, a nearby school, where I made some lifelong friendships with fellow students and teachers. One person who was pivotal in my life and took an interest in me was Ms. Julia King, my teacher and mentor; she was also an administrator at the school.

Mrs. Smith's philosophy concerning me was servant first, student second—and I had not been to school for several days because I was sick and had too many chores to do. Having missed me in class, five of my classmates, Musu, James, Ramona, Ludi, and Ruth, came looking for me. I do not know how they found out where I lived; I had kept that a secret so they would not try to visit me at home and discover I was a servant. Being unaware that, as a servant, I could only receive guests at the back door, they boldly walked up to the front door of Mrs. Smith's house and rang the doorbell. When the doorbell rang, I ran to answer it. I was shocked to see my five friends standing there. Mrs. Smith came out from her bedroom and said, "Who is it?"

Not wanting my friends to find out I was a servant and Mrs. Smith was not my mother, I hastily blurted out, "*Teeta*, my friends have come to see me." *Teeta* was an endearing name that her children called her, a name she had never allowed me to use.

Mrs. Smith's nostrils flared with rage. She swiftly flew into the kitchen and grabbed the largest metal spoon she could find. In a flash, she was back at my side, forcibly grabbing my wrist. She twisted and yanked it upward while screaming, "Look at your fingers, are they all equal?" She angrily pointed to each finger in turn, and continued, "Is this one equal to that one?" With a shaky voice, I said, "No Ma."

Her rage continued as she shoved my trembling hand in my face saying, "Take a good look, each finger is a different size, and none are equal!" She raised her voice so even the neighbors could hear her as she yelled with emphasis, "You will NEVER be equal to my children. Only they have the right to call me *Teeta*."

She then began to beat the tips of my fingers with the metal spoon, and continued until I thought I was going to faint from the pain. With this act, she made it very clear to me, as well as to my friends, that I was not her child. I was simply her servant and I was not, in any way, to consider myself a member of her family or her social strata.

The beating was so severe that I totally forgot my friends were at the door. I do not know how long they stood there watching the punishment she dealt out to me, but by the time the beating was over they were gone. They never returned to Mrs. Smith's house out of fear for themselves and for me. I felt totally humiliated and ashamed.

On New Year's Eve, Mrs. Smith's sister Beth and her two friends, Tracy and Janet, all home from college, came over for a visit. They spoke incessantly about something they called the "New Year's Eve Revival," which they were to attend that evening. I wanted so badly to be able to go, too; it sounded so exciting. While Mrs. Smith was out of the room for a moment, I quietly asked, "May I come along, too?" Beth glanced at me, smiled, and turned to her friends, saying, "Maybe we can take Louise. Everyone should be able to go to the revival." They all agreed and I hoped they would ask Mrs. Smith to let me go with them. I yearned to experience the same happiness that filled Beth and her friends.

I continued with my chores that evening, hoping beyond hope there was some way I would be allowed to attend the revival; I breathed a silent prayer in my heart. As much as possible, I found reasons to be within earshot of what the girls were saying. At one point, I heard Beth say, "There'll be two great preachers speaking this evening. They're known all over Liberia."

"Oh yeah," said Tracy, "I heard they speak God's Word with love and real power. I can't wait to go."

I was so lost in what they were saying that, at one point, I ended up standing spellbound, holding a dusting cloth in one hand and a broom in the other. Mrs. Smith quickly brought me back to reality. "Louise Barton!" I quickly responded, "Yes, Ma!?" swallowing so hard it felt as if everyone could hear the sound in my throat. Mrs. Smith snapped back with, "Get back to work!" I hurriedly finished polishing all the tables and chairs as I thought, *I must stay focused or I'll get in real trouble.* Once I had finished the polishing, I turned away from Beth and her friends and busied myself with the rest of my chores.

If Mrs. Smith had any idea how much I wanted to go to the revival she would have found plenty of reasons why she needed me at home that evening. I kept my mouth shut, yet took a very large emotional risk in keeping my heart open to the remote possibility that I might be able to go to the revival.

I happened to be in the living room when it was time for Beth and her friends to leave for the revival. When they got up from the sofa, Beth took my hand and walked with me toward the front door. As she opened the door, she smiled at me, turned to Mrs. Smith, and said with firmness, "I'm taking Louise with me." It was quite shocking when Mrs. Smith said, "Sure, have a good time." I could tell by Beth's determined look that she and her sister would have launched into a spirited debate if the answer had been no. As uncharacteristic as it was, Mrs. Smith had agreed to allow me to go out for the evening.

With that, we stepped out. Beth said, "Goodbye," and closed the door. Once we were outside Beth said, "Hurry up and get in the car."

I was elated to be out with Beth and her friends because Beth was different. She knew the love of God and was compassionate toward me. She said, "Tonight we will see the old year pass away, and the New Year come in. Everything will become new for each of us." As we drove away, I realized that in the five years I had spent with the Smith family, this was the first time Mrs. Smith had allowed me to travel any distance away from home.

I wondered how the family was going to manage without me that evening. I thought, *Oh, if only this night could last forever.* I felt free as a bird and light as a feather. For the first time in a long time, I was happy and smiling.

We drove past beautiful homes with well-groomed yards and flowerbeds, protected by cement walls and front gates. Hibiscus, orchids, lilies, and other tropical flowers grew up happily together in this neighborhood. Although each flower was different from the next, they all were beautiful and lived in harmony with each other. I so longed to live where people received appreciation and respect for their unique beauty and lived peacefully side-by-side.

As we drove along, I thought, *I'm going to a revival!* The funny thing is, I did not know what the word "revival" meant. All I knew was that I was going to something very special, with someone who honestly cared about me and wanted the best for me. As I thought about the word, I separated it into its prefix and root, and realized that *re-* meant "to do again," and *vive* meant "to live." I thought to myself, *I'd love to be able to be free and live again. Could I be revived? Could I regain my hope?* One thing I did know was that I did not want to live another day without hope in my life. If this revival could offer me any hope at all, I surely wanted it!

We soon arrived at the Bethel World Outreach Center, where the revival was already underway. Music flowed from the building and filled the air—voices singing and hands clapping. I had never heard anything like this before. We had arrived early enough to get a seat near the front, where we settled ourselves in and raised our eyes to the stage on which sat a large choir with heavenly voices and musicians playing the most beautiful music I had ever heard. The choir director looked out into the audience, raised his hands, and said, "Please, join the choir as we sing, 'Amazing Grace.'"

After we finished singing this beautiful song, a young and handsome preacher named Darlingston Johnson walked out on the stage with purpose and power. He stood straight as a rod and held tightly to his Bible. He smiled as he raised his hand to the audience and said, "Happy New Year! Tonight you are going to learn about God's amazing grace. Expect great things from God. He rewards those who diligently seek Him."

The preacher's welcoming smile and charismatic manner was electrifying. He preached about a young man named Joseph, the son of Jacob, one of the best-known figures in the Bible who is famous for his coat of many colors and his God-given ability to interpret dreams. Joseph was his father's favorite son and this favoritism caused his brothers to sell him into slavery, out of jealousy, for twenty pieces of silver.

As I listened to the story, I learned that Joseph became the servant of an Egyptian official named Potiphar and that he was so honest, so strong, and so handsome that Potiphar's wife became interested in him. When he refused her advances, she accused him of pursuing her, which led to Potiphar's throwing Joseph into prison, where he had little hope of escape. There also seemed to be little hope of escape for me.

I received every word personally and thought of how lost and alone Joseph must have felt, being far away from his father and mother and far from his home, with no real hope of ever seeing them again. I knew just how Joseph must have felt. Then the preacher said, "Just like Joseph, who was thrown into the dungeon of despair, found favor with God and with man, you too can find favor with God today. I want you to know that God didn't leave Joseph without hope, nor will He leave you without hope."

The preacher shared how two years after being thrown into prison,

Joseph regained his freedom because of his ability to interpret dreams and because he had gained the respect of the prison guards and his fellow prisoners. He eventually became the chief adviser to the Egyptian Pharaoh. As the preacher spoke, I clung to every word. He looked at me and said, "Young Joseph was thrown into prison for something he didn't do. If, today, you have found yourself in a position like Joseph's, do not fear. God was with Joseph, and He will be with you, too." I listened intently, because I knew he was talking to me.

Words of encouragement kept pouring forth from the preacher, "Joseph lived faithfully in that dark dungeon, day after day, and he chose to serve God where he was. Even though he was in prison, he remained faithful." All of these ideas were new to me. Could I possibly serve God right where I was? The preacher raised his voice and said, "God wants to save you today and that's why He sent his son Jesus. Let me tell you about Jesus, the Son of the living God. He was sent to give you an abundant life." I thought, *An abundant life, what's that?*

His words flowed quickly as he read from the Bible, quoting, "For God so loved the world, that He gave His only born Son, that whoever believes in Him shall not perish, but shall have everlasting life." Then he said, "All you need to be saved, healed, and protected, is the blood of Jesus. Repeat after me, it's only the blood."

The congregation joyfully chanted, "It's only the blood."

He continued, "Of Jesus," and the congregation repeated, "Of Jesus."

He finished with, "That saves us," and everyone responded, "That saves us!" His lively preaching was sinking into the depths of my soul.

The preacher cried out, "The blood of Jesus is sufficient by itself. You can't add anything to it. It's not the blood of Jesus *plus* your good works that saves you. It's the blood of Jesus *alone*." He continued, "Somebody say, 'Thank you, God, for Your remedy.'" I looked around, everyone was riveted and connected to each of his words, and the audience responded loudly, "Thank you, God, for Your remedy!" The joy of his preaching raised the roof as he yelled, "Hallelujah! Hallelujah!"

Everyone joined him like a choir chanting, "Hallelujah!"

The pastor continued by saying, "My brothers and sisters, Jesus wants to take you from the dung site to the palace. God says in His word that He raises the poor out of the dust, and lifts the needy out of the dunghill; that He may set him with princes, even with the princes of His people." He ended with, "If you hear His voice today, don't hide your heart; come now, because you don't know what tomorrow will bring!"

I felt a sense of urgency growing in me as his words rang out loudly and clearly. "Your father may fail you, your mother may fail you, your friends may fail you, the whole world may fail you, but Jesus will never fail you. Last year has passed and this is a new year for you. If you don't have a mother or a father, God will be your mother and father. If you want to know Jesus," with his arms wide open he declared, "now is the time, the doors are wide open… come!"

As he said this, he motioned with his hand for people to come down to the front to meet with him. I was so hungry for love and acceptance; I bolted from my seat and down the aisle so I could be the first one to reach the pastor.

In truth, I was afraid if I did not get down there first the pastor would not have time for me. I dropped to my knees and fell on my face, crying hysterically, "Jesus, I want you! Please help me. I want to know you."

At that moment, nothing else mattered to me. Nothing else existed but my agonizing situation. My pitiful cries echoed within the recesses of my heart and reached into the far corners of the church. I felt a loving and compassionate touch on the top of my head that actually frightened me at first because I had not received a kind touch for years. When I looked up, I saw it was the pastor and he did not take his comforting hand off my head until my crying had subsided.

The pastor then motioned for a counselor to come and assist me. A tall and very pretty, young woman, who was wearing a black skirt with a white blouse, came over and knelt beside me on the hard concrete floor. She held me in her arms, gently wiped away the tears from my cheeks, and whispered in a comforting tone, "My name is Ruth. What's your name?" I sobbed out my name, "Louise." She lovingly said, "Louise, what a beautiful name for a beautiful young woman." Ruth's soft, melodic voice continued, "Do you know that God loves you and that you are precious in His sight?" I shook my head, *No*. She said, "Well He does and he has great things in store for you. Do you know that the Lord says, "I know the plans I have for you, plans to prosper you and not to harm you, and plans to give you hope and a future," in His Word?

I had never heard anything like this before; I was amazed at the possibility that I might be precious in God's eyes, and that He might actually love me, even have plans to see me prosper. I opened my eyes, looked up into hers, and saw her smiling at me kindly. She said, "Yes, Louise, tonight Jesus wants you to accept Him as your Savior." She explained the good news of God's love for me and that Jesus had come and died for me to set me free, save me, and give me the gift of eternal life and a home in heaven someday. I so much wanted to experience God's love and acceptance that without hesitation I asked Jesus to come into my life.

That instant, God's eternal love, holy and undeniable, came into me and filled my lonely, love-starved heart. A new sense of hope welled up inside me, a hope I had never felt before, one that would stay with me forever in spite of my circumstances. I knew I would never again feel completely helpless and alone. God's peace and love swirled around me and through me; my heart danced for joy.

I found myself caught up in a vision of being with my mother in the shade of the cocoa tree she had taken me to years before, when she said she was leaving me. The loving words of blessing she had given to me that day once again washed over me and I could hear her say, "Blessings will flow from above and you will be strong and great."

I felt that my mother's blessing on my life had seen me through the darkest nights and had helped steer me to this place, on this night, so I could know the unfathomable love of God.

I would never more be dry and empty inside, because peace, like a river, had forever flooded the desert places in my soul. It was absolutely a dream come true and, oddly enough, from that day forward, as an added blessing from God, I began to dream dreams that did come true.

CHAPTER 4

God's Little Dreamer

After the evening at the revival meeting, my daily routine stayed the same, but oh, the joy that flooded my soul! I learned that I could give all my troubles and struggles to Jesus, and I did. Not by any means, however, had my life become a bed of roses; with no apparent change in my circumstances, my life suddenly took on a new reality.

Even though I still worked for her, I was no longer a servant for Mrs. Smith; instead, I was a servant of Jesus Christ. In obedience to God's Word, where it says, "Whatever you do, work heartily, as for the Lord and not for men," I did everything that was required of me, for my Savior. This new outlook on life gave me a new sense of purpose; a new sense of self-worth; and a new, inner strength. I belonged to no one but Jesus. My body was still in bondage, but my heart was free. With peace in my heart, I could inwardly bless those who cursed and ridiculed me.

Like Joseph, I began to have dreams and visions that accurately foretold of things to come. One morning I woke up after a startling dream that was vivid and quite detailed. In it, an entire ocean was running through the city of Monrovia; people were screaming and running in all directions.

I woke up from the dream, wondering and asking God, "What does this mean?" I heard the response, "War is coming and will be like the ocean rushing through the streets of Monrovia and its surrounding areas." A deep-seated foreboding came over me; I could not shake the thought that something terrible would soon happen to the city and its people.

Another time, I had dreamt of being on top of a mountain covered with something looking like snow or soft cotton. The substance gently blew down the mountainside, wafting into the valley and covering its people. During the night, I awoke from the dream asking, "God what are you trying to tell me?" The answer came, "Louise, you are becoming a leader of people. You will be as a shepherd; you will lead the flock."

There were also specific dreams about others—dreams that all came to fruition. One morning I told Tanya, one of the Smith girls, that I had dreamt about her and her sisters. As I shared the dream, her sisters ran over to hear. Later that day, everything occurred as I had said. The girls were excited and began telling their friends about me. They also told their mother, who had already noticed there was something different about me; something she could not explain. She chalked it up to my growing older and more mature.

As time went on, the dreams became more frequent; every day the children would ask me if I had had another one. They began telling me their own dreams and, to my surprise, I instantly knew what they meant. All I can say is that God had let his face shine upon me and had given me a precious gift that I hoped would continue to be a blessing to me as well as others for the rest of my life. In His grace, He chose to lift up a lowly servant girl and place her feet on higher ground. There was no mistaking it; something had truly changed in me, so much so that Mrs. Smith secretly began asking me to interpret her dreams, too.

Ruth, the woman who had prayed on her knees with me at the revival, became my Bible teacher and was able to gain Mrs. Smith's blessing on visiting for about an hour every Saturday afternoon. Mrs. Smith allowed these brief visits because she had begun to realize it was the revival meeting that had brought the amazing change in my countenance.

During her visits, Ruth and I sat outside on a concrete pad to have our Bible studies. I had innocently chosen to dust off this area to sit on as I ate my dinners outside. Who would guess a servant girl could learn so much and develop so many wonderful memories while sitting on the lid of a septic tank. Here, in this most unlikely of places, I began to learn of the wonders and truths found in God's Word.

Each week, as they sat at my feet, I would share what I had learned with the Smith children; they listened intently. It had never occurred to me that I might be a natural-born teacher, but I found that I loved teaching, and one Saturday, I told Ruth that I wanted to start a neighborhood Bible study for children. Ruth smiled at me, saying, "Louise, you are just a child yourself." She paused for a moment, thinking of how young and inexperienced I was; yet she also saw the determination in my eyes and felt the genuine passion in my heart. Ruth did not say I was too young to teach on my own, instead, she offered, "How about if I help you teach?" I was elated.

Ruth and I asked Mrs. Smith if she would allow us to use our weekly meeting times to start a Bible club for some of the local children. To my delight, she agreed, and we planned to launch the club the following Saturday. I got the word out to a few neighbors, telling them when we would be meeting.

The following Friday night came quickly; there had been no time to read the material I intended to teach the next day. During the dark, early morning hours, I awoke. My eyes simply opened, and I jumped out of bed. I reached over and grabbed the Bible study material; reading it quickly through, I was quite happy to find that the little bit of time there was to prepare was sufficient. At 4:00 AM, I dove into my usual morning chores and made breakfast for the family, excited over the opportunity the afternoon would bring.

As Saturday afternoon arrived, I was encouraged to find that not only a few neighborhood children but also a couple of Ruth's missionary friends had come. To the amazement of Ruth, the missionaries, and especially myself, I taught a compelling lesson, drawing illustrations on an old, small chalkboard.

Every Saturday thereafter, I awakened well before 4:00 AM to prepare my lesson. After leading the club for several weeks, Ruth saw that

I caught on very quickly and decided to allow me to teach on my own. For the next eight years, the club became the highlight of my life. Even Mrs. Smith listened in on occasions, and especially enjoyed hearing the children sing. In time, the ELWA national radio station invited our group to sing on "Under the Palm Tree," a weekly program hosted by Ann Matilda.

Two years earlier, at Daniel E. Howard Elementary, I had been awarded a double promotion, and was allowed to skip fifth grade; yet, as I worked through my first year of junior high school at Carver Mission Academy, a private school with a more demanding curriculum, I struggled greatly. When the day came to receive my final report card I was apprehensive, but hung on to the slim hope I had done well enough to be promoted to the eighth grade. All my hopes were dashed when I saw the word "Fail" stricken in red inside my card.

My world had ended; all hopes had vanished. My hands hung down at my sides and my eyes looked only at my feet as I walked home. *I'm dead,* I thought. How was I going to explain my deficiency to Mrs. Smith who, for the first time this year, had to pay for my education? What would become of me? I whispered under my breath, "I'm so ashamed, I've let my father down, and I've let myself down." I cried so profusely that, by the time I arrived home, I was an utter mess. I threw open the door and ran to Mrs. Smith sobbing, "I have my report card." Mrs. Smith looked up with surprise on her face asking, "Louise, what's the matter?" Through my heaving and sobbing, I managed to say, "I failed seventh grade."

Mrs. Smith looked at me with kind eyes. Placing her arm on my shoulder, she said, "Don't cry Louise. You did your best." She then removed her arm and took the report card to look it over. I could see her disappointment as she slowly shook her head from side to side, however, she still tried to encourage me by saying, "Louise, don't grieve. You have done more than well for now. I think you've learned more than enough. Some prominent members of your ethnic group haven't even reached your level of education, and they've managed to do quite well." She rattled off the names of Krahn women in prominent positions who had not gone as far as completing the sixth grade, and continued with, "You're lucky you made it to the seventh grade."

Her attempt to comfort me was not working very well; my heart's desire was to finish school. I was not at all pleased with the idea of stopping my education. Mrs. Smith said, "What God has for you will meet you and treat you well. You don't have to get a master's degree or a PhD to be considered educated."

I was stunned as she handed my report card back, saying, "We weren't able to continue paying for your education any more, anyway." Of course, Mrs. Smith still expected me to stay on as a full-time servant in exchange for room and board.

The last thing I wanted to do was to stop going to school and give up my dream of completing high school and college. I felt all of my dreams crashing down around me. I was desperate. My father had taught me to value a full and complete education because it would allow me to become self-sufficient, and I was not giving up easily. I knew I needed a plan, and I needed God's help; so I prayed, *God what should I do? I really want to finish school.*

I had just finished my prayer when an idea came rushing in, *What if I asked Ms. King if I could work for the school in exchange for my education?* I knew Ms. King, one of the school administrators, liked me and knew my circumstances at home. She just might be willing to help me. I needed more time to get my thoughts in order and determine how to best approach her. Over the next two weeks, I rehearsed my request, repeating it in my mind over and over again.

One day, after rushing through my chores, I headed over to the school to make my plea. I had such a strong desire to finish my education that I was determined to find a way. I rehearsed as I walked, kicking pebbles

from my path. I clutched the strap of my small purse, twirling it in the
air. Time was running out and I needed to have my speech ready.

I reached the school just before the administrative offices closed for
the day. Standing for a brief moment in front of the door, I said a quiet
prayer, and grabbed the doorknob. With a trembling hand, I pushed
the door open and stepped inside. I stood in the foyer of the school
for a moment, and then heard a voice say, "Louise, what are you doing
here?" I turned and saw Ms. King's pleasant smile, and immediately felt
at ease. I replied, "I came to see you." She took me by the hand, paused
for a moment, and said, "Let's go to my office."

As we walked down the hall, she lightheartedly said, "Beautiful
weather we're having today. I suppose you walked here?" I nodded
in reply. She opened the office door and held it for me saying, "Go
on inside" Once inside, I waited for her next command. I was used
to taking orders. She pointed to a wooden chair that sat next to her
desk, "Please, have a seat." She continued in a sympathetic manner,
"Louise, I know about your report card." At this, I broke down and
cried; all thoughts of a speech washed away with my tears. "Mrs. Smith
is not going to pay for any more education for me." Without a pause, I
blurted out, "I really want to finish school. Please let me graduate from
school. Please don't let my dream die, please. There is no one to pay
my tuition any longer. Only with God's help and yours can my dream
come true."

Ms. King took a deep breath and looked at me from across her desk.
She paused for a long while. My world had suddenly halted. Neither of
us moved a muscle. In my anticipation, I could hear and feel my heart
beating as I stared at my fists, tightly clenched in my lap.

She broke the silence and said, "Louise, I don't know what to say.
There isn't a way for you to continue your education here without
paying." I pleaded, "Ms. King, I see boys doing lawn work and other
jobs at the school in exchange for their education. Please let me do
something." She narrowed her eyes as she thought deeply, considering
my situation. "Louise, we don't have anything like that for you to do.

You're too small and not strong enough."

My heart sank. I wept, begging, "I will clean the entire school and mission. Please let me earn my education. I will clean toilets, scrub floors, dust—anything!" Ms. King sat quietly in her chair. She folded her hands on her desk and pondered over my pleadings. I bit my lip and began ringing my hands.

The only encouraging words she could spare were, "Louise, I will pray about this and take it up with the other board members. I can't promise you anything." With that, Ms. King stood up, walked around her desk, put her hand on my shoulder, and said, "We will pray, don't worry, everything will work out according to God's will." I looked at Ms. King, "Thank you, so much."

She opened her office door and showed me out, saying, "I will let you know what I find out. Have a nice afternoon." Knowing it would have to do, I left the school and walked home.

Several days had passed and I wondered why I had not heard from Ms. King; so I walked back on campus to find out if the school had decided anything regarding my ability to register for the seventh grade. I practically ran to Ms. King's office. I knocked on her door and heard, "Come in." As soon as she saw me, she sighed, "Oh, Louise—have a seat." With a brief smile, she looked down at her desk and straightened some papers, laying them to the side. Ms. King stood up, walked over to the window, and looked out. After some reflection, she turned around. "Louise, the board of directors believes you are too small and frail to do the type of work you suggest."

I felt faint. I buried my face in my hands. The only thing I cared about was finishing school. I raised my head, pushing the hair from my eyes, and began pleading, "I'm strong. I do all the chores for Mrs. Smith. I scrub her floors, I clean her toilets, I prepare her meals; I do everything for her! I can do the same thing for the school. Please, give me a chance."

She walked over and stood beside me and said, "Well, because you are so determined, I will take this up with the board one more time.

First, we will have to fast and pray for seven days, and at the end of that time, I will return to the board members and plead for you again." I jumped up, hugged her, and said, "I will do it. I will do anything. Thank you. Thank you, so much."

After the seven days of fasting was over, Ms. King went to the board of directors, as she had promised. She presented my plea once more, asking them to let me work for my education. I was in the habit of attending the Bible study that Ms. King taught at the ELWA churches' compound every Sunday evening. When I entered the room on the next Sunday, I saw a huge smile on Ms. King's face, as she looked my way then turned back toward the other children who were already there. I was so eager to know what happened that I shouted, "Ms. King, Ms. King!" and waved at her. As she turned back toward me, my heart leapt in the hope of hearing joyful news, but because the study was already getting underway, I was going to have to wait to speak with her privately.

I was so anxious to learn my fate that I sat on pins and needles the whole evening, waiting to hear the word, "Amen," that would signal the end of the meeting.

During the study, Ms. King looked my way as she told of a little slave girl who worked very hard for a captain's wife. She was faithful to God and faithful in her work. The little girl could not keep quiet about the goodness of God. I was sure she told this story just for me. I looked for hidden clues, and hung onto every word. Finally, the beloved word I was waiting for all evening came as Ms. King prayed and ended the prayer with, "Amen!" I shot out of my seat like a bullet and was at her side in a flash. My friends—who were familiar with my situation— crowded around me because they also wanted to hear the news.

Words tumbled from my mouth, "Ms. King… Ms. King! What did they say? Can I be a student again?" She could not hide the truth from me. Once again a smile stretched wide across her face as she said, "Oh Louise, I have good news! Come tomorrow to my office and I will tell you all about it." I screamed and jumped for joy. My friends grabbed me and hugged me and jumped up and down with me as we shouted, "Amen! Hallelujah! Praise the Lord! God is good all the time!" Tears of joy flowed like a river from my eyes, and words of elation and thankfulness from my mouth. I felt relieved—refreshed and renewed.

The next morning I jumped out of bed and finished all my chores as quickly as possible. I changed from my work clothes, put on a nicely ironed dress, and took a quick look in the mirror at the face that wore a broad smile. There was no hiding it, I was very happy today.

When I arrived at school and reached Ms. King's office, she motioned for me to come inside. I blew in like a strong wind, causing her to chuckle at my excitement. In her normally kind and cheery voice she asked, "How are you, Louise?" I answered, "I'm fine. How are you?" With complete and proper etiquette she responded, "I'm fine, thank you." I said, "Amen!" She began laughing, she was so happy for me. She said, "God is good, isn't he?" I said, "All the time." She returned an, "Amen," adding, "Louise, our fasting and prayer went well. Miss McCleary, Miss McComb, and Mr. Johnson all decided in your favor." This was remarkable news.

Although the board was reluctant, they agreed to allow me to begin working as a school janitor, a job normally reserved for boys, during a ninety-day probationary period. If I could keep up with both my janitorial responsibilities and my studies, they would accept my working at the school as full payment for my tuition. Ms. King said, "It has been decided that you will come back at 5:00 PM, Monday through Friday, to clean the premises." I could not stop thanking Ms. King and God for this opportunity. I was very willing and very happy to do anything required.

I came home and shared my good fortune with Mrs. Smith. She lifted her hands and shoulders in a slight shrug and said, "Okay, but make sure you keep up with your chores and have my meals cooked and kept warm by the time I get home from work." That was the end of her congratulations to me.

I had not allowed myself to consider how I could possibly get all my chores done for Mrs. Smith, attend classes, and clean the classrooms and offices. Each school day I arose well before dawn so I could complete my morning chores before heading off to school. At the end of the school day, around 2:30 PM, I would dash home, complete my afternoon chores, cook dinner, wrap the food to keep it warm for the Smith family, grab a quick bite to eat, and then head back, arriving at school by 5:00 PM. At school, I would spend from one to two hours cleaning blackboards, putting chalk away, closing blinds, straightening chairs, dusting, sweeping floors, and cleaning bathrooms. I then made the trek back home to begin work again, completing my evening chores and collapsing into my bed around midnight or later.

Life had been tough before for a growing, young child, but it became much more difficult. There was no time to study, and practically no time to sleep. I was living on two or three hours of sleep each night, and even that was a luxury because some nights I did not get any sleep at all. How could I continue? I hung on by a thread and, as I worked, I prayed.

For the next three months I enthusiastically completed all my after-school chores and class work to the satisfaction of the board. At the end of the probationary period, Ms. King called me into her office to congratulate me. "Louise, you've done well! It's been three months now, and your work has exceeded our expectations. I'm happy to tell you that the board has reviewed your work record and has formally accepted your request to become one of our school janitors." She paused for what seemed an eternity. "And your work will cover the cost of your school bill!" I was so happy at the news that I began to cry. I could barely speak my gratitude but managed to thank Ms. King before bolting from her office. Thoughts of the pride my father would feel at my being an educated woman were flying through my head. I was happy beyond words and my heart soared.

During the remainder of my seventh grade year, I applied myself with total focus, managing my studies in the little time left between regular household chores, after-school chores, and the few hours of sleep I was able to fit in. At year-end, I was overjoyed with my final report card; my continued diligence had paid off and I was promoted to the eighth grade. "I passed! I passed! I pa-aassed!" I sang in time to my feet as I ran and skipped all the way home, waving my report card high in the air. I hoped Mrs. Smith would be pleased, and when I arrived at home, I held out the report card, saying, "Ma, I did it, I passed!" She glanced at the card in my hand and said matter-of-factly, "That's good, Louise, now keep it up."

I knew keeping up the pace for four more years would be a formidable task, yet I was more determined than ever to work toward and complete my high school and college education.

CHAPTER 5

Presidential Palace

It was Friday evening and cousin Amos was coming over for his usual visit. I heard his footsteps as he approached the back door, so I bolted out and flew into his arms. He was dressed in his army fatigues and, as it was going to rain soon, he was wearing his raincoat. It was not raining yet so we walked over to my favorite spot and sat down on the septic tank lid.

Amos sat with his legs crossed and I made myself cozy next to him. He patted me on the head. "What are you, a septic tank kid?" We laughed until our sides hurt. It was so good to laugh; it gave me a sense of peace, security, and freedom. A cool breeze was blowing, giving evidence the rain was on its way. As we leaned over and rolled onto the soft grass, he smiled, saying, "Géesedeh, your little grassy knoll is beautiful." I trusted him deeply and basked in his love and support. He had been so faithful in visiting me almost every week since we moved to the ELWA Community. His visits always gave me something to look forward to and helped soothe my aching heart. I did not think he could ever understand just how precious his visits were to me.

I sensed that something was up because he seemed almost giddy and was particularly playful. I soon learned he was hiding a secret from me when he sang out in a childlike voice, "Géesedeh... I know something you don't know," holding the last word with a sustained vibrato. I playfully pushed him, and he fell backward on the grass and rolled onto his tummy as he turned his face away from me. I insisted he tell me.

He laughed hard, sat up, and said, "Alright, I'll give you a clue."

He knew I suffered from a bad case of impatience when it came to surprises, but he wanted to continue the suspense as long as he could. He said, "The answer is in this riddle. Someone who you do not know has a golden hand, and she may soon reach out to you, because she's of your clan." I loved riddles and word games, but this one had a deeper meaning that left me feeling totally bewildered. "Oh Amos," I cried, "please tell me. I can't stand the suspense, and I can't figure it out."

While working as a guard at the presidential palace Amos had met someone of importance. He leaned over and whispered, "Louise, I've met a woman named Sarah who works for our first lady as an interpreter. Sarah's related to us through our mothers. She is your mother's first cousin. I told her all about you, and let her know you are living with an Americo-Liberian/Congo family. I also told her that life has been very tough for you."

The sky was darkening and a few raindrops began to fall. Amos looked up, held his hand out and caught a few drops, then hurriedly said, "Louise, I can't stay long." He leaned over toward me once again and with an air of seriousness continued, "Aunt Sarah is deeply and genuinely concerned for your welfare, and wants to meet you. She also wants you to know something else. Are you ready for this? Louise, Sarah told me that you are also related to Nancy Doe, the first lady, and *she* wants to meet you, too!" I was so surprised that I did not know what to say. I sat there with my mouth open for what seemed like an eternity, but finally exclaimed, "Meet me? Are you serious!?"

"Yes!" he replied. "Sarah said she plans to visit you in two weeks, on Saturday evening, and she wants to take you to meet the first lady in person!" Amos got up, put out his hand, and helped me to my feet. I gave him a big hug and kissed his cheek. "Amos, this is so exciting! I doubt I'll be able to get any sleep for the next two weeks."

His visits were always brief because his schedule was as hectic as mine. I was always so happy to see him, yet as he would prepare to leave, my joy turned to feelings of sadness and desperation, and I would cry and beg him to take me with him. He'd reach out, pull me close to him, and say, "Géesedeh, don't worry, it will be okay. I will be back again soon… I promise."

After Amos left, I went into the house and found Mrs. Smith on the sofa in the living room reading a novel. When I shared the news with her she looked startled. "You…?" After a long pause, she added blandly, "Oh, good."

The first chance I had I ran over and told my neighbor and friend, Maggie. She had been a constant source of encouragement to me, and I knew she would be excited at the news. When I saw her, I blurted out, "Maggie, something amazing is about to happen to me. You know how the Bible says that God will open the windows of Heaven and pour out a blessing so large that there wouldn't be enough room to contain it?" I paused to take a breath, because I was talking a mile a minute. She laughed and said, "Slow down, Louise, I can't understand you."

I began again, "I just heard that I am related to the first lady!" Maggie, jumped a foot off the ground, turned me around in a circle, and said, "Louise, who told you that!?" I happily replied, "My cousin Amos told me." I told her everything Amos had shared, including the part about meeting the first lady. We laughed and danced in a circle a few times, and then talked of how this might change my life.

When the day had finally arrived I was brimming with excitement. Late in the afternoon, I saw a big, black governmental car with Liberian flags fastened to the front; it pulled up in front of the Smith's house. I was surprised to see my friend Maggie tumble out with her two nephews. The driver, who was dressed in a blue uniform, stepped out and held the door for a beautiful woman who wore a cream-colored suit. A gold necklace and several diamond rings adorned her neck and fingers. I was mesmerized as I watched her come toward the house. She ran toward me with her arms spread out like an eagle's wings. "Géesedeh," she exclaimed. I hurriedly ran down the steps and embraced Aunt Sarah.

She excitedly said, "Oh, Boahn Sophené," which is an endearing name she used to call my mother. She smiled with satisfaction. "Oh my dear, I see Boahn Sophené standing right here before me." We hugged and cried. A strange feeling swept over me. It was like having been lost in the wilderness for years, and then unexpectedly being found. My Aunt Sarah pulled me from her bosom and eagerly looked at me again. "You are such a beautiful young woman!"

I turned to Maggie and said, "How did you and your nephews manage to end up in the car with my Aunt?" Maggie smiled and answered, "They pulled up in front of my house first, and I offered to show them the way."

I opened the back door and hurried inside to notify Mrs. Smith of our visitors. The driver, who doubled as Aunt Sarah's bodyguard, followed close behind me. I called out, "Ma, someone's here to see you." I could hear Mrs. Smith from the other end of the house say, "Who's here?" I yelled back, "My aunt and her driver are here."

Mrs. Smith was dressed in a very plain housecoat, and her hair was not brushed or sculpted to her liking; so, she scurried as quickly as she could to her bedroom to make herself more presentable. The driver's head spun quickly to the side as he caught a glimpse of a frantic woman making a mad dash down the hallway.

As my Aunt Sarah entered the house behind the driver, she sensed the commotion that whirled around us. Maggie entered next, and then her nephews. The two little boys darted past everyone, and tumbled into the driver. I giggled at the sight, and at the thought that this visit was turning the Smith's house upside down.

Everyone followed me through the kitchen, into the dining room, and then onto a small landing just a few steps from the sunken living room. We all stood there, awkwardly, in single file, waiting for Mrs. Smith to emerge. We looked somewhat comical, like a group of people standing in line at a box office waiting to buy tickets to a movie. I did not dare invite them to sit in the living room without proper permission.

I looked up to see Mrs. Smith walking toward us, dressed in a beautiful African gown. She had wrapped her hair in a scarf, and looked quite elegant. Always the prefect hostess, she gracefully pointed her hand toward the living room and said, "Please, come in and have a seat." After everyone was seated, Mrs. Smith sat next to Aunt Sarah, and offered drinks by saying, "Louise, go get drinks." I lowered my head out of habit, answering, "Yes, Ma."

Every time I moved, Aunt Sarah exclaimed, "Boahn Sophené, I can't believe how much you look like your mother! If you were a little older I might have mistaken you for her." As I served the drinks, she laughed at how all of my mannerisms reminded her of my mother. As she shared stories of my early childhood with Mrs. Smith, I tried to stay close by so I could listen. Unfortunately, I had to miss a great deal of the conversation while fetching drinks and snacks.

Having served everyone's refreshments, I sat down on the carpeted step in front of my Aunt Sarah. She shared the love she had for my mother, "Louise's mother is known for her kind heart. There isn't anything she wouldn't do for anyone, even for a stranger. Because of her mother's good name, Louise will be welcomed in many homes all over Liberia."

My heart swelled within me. I was proud to be my mother's daughter. I had only wished I could honor her name by being just like her. Mrs. Smith smiled at me and said, "Louise is kind-hearted, too. She is very friendly and loves people. She wants to be a mother to everyone. She loves to play the mother's role." Aunt Sarah acknowledged those supportive words and nodded with approval.

Mrs. Smith added, "I can see everything you described about her mother in Louise as well. Louise prepares Bible studies for her Bible club every week, and she coordinates all the refreshments. It's quite an experience to watch her teach. All the children absolutely adore her."

My eyes widened because I had never heard Mrs. Smith speak of me in a complimentary way. "Monkey face" and "ugly" were the descriptions I most often heard. Hearing kind words from Mrs. Smith brought tears to my eyes. I wiped them away and basked in the joy of knowing my life was taking on a new dimension.

Aunt Sarah continued to speak about my mother saying, "Josephiné's house is always filled with people. Weary travelers, whether traveling from village to village or from neighboring countries, would be persuaded to come in and rest. In a way her home is like a local inn, yet she never charges anyone for staying with her. Josephiné is right on top of my list of remarkable women."

The conversation switched to light politics. I was not very interested in political discussions and, since I was only in the ninth grade, I completely trusted our government's leaders to make the proper decisions.

After she had visited for nearly two hours, it was time for Aunt Sarah to leave. She stood up and said, "What a lovely visit we've had. Thank you for your generous hospitality." Mrs. Smith said, "It was my pleasure. Thank you for coming."

Aunt Sarah replied, "I hope you don't mind. I made an appointment for Louise to meet with the first lady. I will send a taxi next Sunday to pick her up, and she will be back to you by the next evening." Mrs. Smith looked shocked, but agreed to let me go. She acknowledged, "By all means, what an honor for Louise." Aunt Sarah explained further why it was so important for me to meet the first lady, "You see, Louise's mother and the first lady are cousins."

I thought Mrs. Smith was going to fall over. She took a deep breath and said, "What's this, Louise… you're related to the first lady?" She laughed aloud nervously as she realized a relative of the president's family was living under her roof.

I remembered a Proverb that says, "If you trust in the Lord with your whole heart and acknowledge Him in all your ways, He will direct your paths." My paths seemed to be looking better every day. Within a week, I would be visiting my newly found relative, our country's first lady.

Soon after I arrived home from church on Sunday evening, a taxi arrived to take me to my Aunt Sarah's place where I would stay overnight prior to our Monday trip to the presidential palace. My Aunt Sarah happened to live in a townhouse complex where many other Krahn people of the Naio clan lived. Although she told me her house number, when I got out of the cab I realized I would have to hunt around to find her place.

As I walked between the townhouses in search of her house number, I heard an unfamiliar voice call out, "Lord have mercy! Géesedeh!?" I stopped in my tracks and looked around to see who might be calling my name. To my surprise, an older woman, whom I did not know, jumped out of her chair and headed straight toward me. As she neared me she exclaimed, "Géesedeh, it is you, isn't it?" By that time other women had left their porches to come see and were running, yelling, "Is it really possible Géesedeh's, here? She sure looks like Géesedeh!" Another woman shouted, "Boahn Sophené is here!" I soon found myself in a crowd of women and children who all wanted to touch me, hug me, or pat me to see if I was real.

I had stumbled upon a community where many knew me from when I was a little girl living with my mother and father. They immediately recognized me because I looked so much like my mother, a woman they all loved and adored. They were making such a commotion that people who did not know me were coming out just to see what was going on.

I found myself in the midst of a crowd chattering in the Naio dialect of the Krahn language; they bombarded me with their excited questions. "How's your Ma? How's your Pa? Where are you living now? What brought you here? Where are you going?" I understood what they were saying, but had forgotten how to speak Naio, having only spoken English since I had arrived at the Smith's home. When they realized I could no longer speak the language they felt sorry for me and said, "Oh my, she has forgotten how to speak Naio."

After things calmed down a bit, I told them, "I came here to see my Aunt Sarah, but I can't find her house number." Everyone knew my aunt, so the group swept me along in their midst. We had become a band of ten to fifteen adults and twenty or more children, skipping, talking, and touching each other in excitement.

Hearing all the noise outside, but not having any idea what was going on, Aunt Sarah opened her door and stepped out onto the front porch with her children. When she saw a large group heading her way, she wondered what in the world had happened. Just as she picked me out at the back of the crowd, a woman asked accusingly, "Sarah, why didn't you tell us that you had found Géesedeh, and that she was coming to visit?"

The enthusiastic crowd settled in as best they could on Aunt Sarah's tiny porch, with the overflow standing in the yard. For the rest of the evening everyone shared stories of their memories of my mother and me. It was exhilarating to be with people who knew me, loved me, and made me feel a part of something far bigger than I was. Everyone expressed their feelings about my mother; they all voiced how she had reached out to them, given them something, or done something special on their behalf. Meeting those whose genuine love for my mother was so apparent was a blessing; their love spilled over onto me.

It was getting late and the mothers with small children had to go home to put their children to bed. Aunt Sarah seized the opportunity and said, "Thank you all for coming and sharing in Géesedeh's visit. She's going to have a big day tomorrow and she needs to go to bed early." I looked at all the faces that had become familiar and said to them, "I'm so glad to have visited with all of you. God bless you and good night."

We went inside Aunt Sarah's home. Everything was neat and sparkling because she had her own maid and personal cook. An elaborate meal had been prepared in my honor. In spite of all the years I had lived at the Smith's home, I had never sat at their dinner table nor eaten with a fork and a knife.

Dinner was served and Aunt Sarah motioned for me to take a seat at the table. The food we were given was fit for a king, and I was amazed that the children were eating at the same table. I sat down, looked at the table settings, and thought to myself, *Oh my, what am I going to do now?* Everyone began to eat; feeling lost, I quietly sat there watching every move, wondering what to do first.

Aunt Sarah thought I was not feeling well and asked, "Louise, are you okay? You're not eating." I tried to smile and said, "Yes, I'm okay." Here I was, sitting at a formal dining room table, totally lost, used to eating my meals alone from a bowl in the back yard—not from beautiful plates like the one that sat before me. I finally chanced using a spoon. They did not seem to notice I was not using a knife and fork; either that or they were being very kind and did not want to embarrass me.

Aunt Sarah encouraged me to eat more. She said, "Louise, your skin looks dry; please eat more. You need more nutrients." Although I was hungry I was not used to so much food, and I was too shy to ask for seconds. I stuck to eating only what was on my plate, followed by the scrumptious dessert served after dinner.

Sarah filled her home with every imaginable creature comfort. Oh, how my heart ached to be a family member and not a family servant; I would have given anything to be a part of Aunt Sarah's lovely family.

When it was time for me to go to bed, Aunt Sarah kissed me goodnight. I thought I must have looked rather frail, because she looked in on me several times throughout the night, seemingly worried about my condition.

At 4:00 AM, as I woke up, I found my aunt standing over my bed. She knew I was used to getting up at this hour so she whispered in my ear, "Please, stay in bed and rest, you deserve a day off." She gently placed her hand on my forehead to soothe me.

One day of freedom could not release me from the inner chains that bound me to a life of servitude. Although I did as she asked, lying in bed for the next several hours, the word "rest" was not even a part of my vocabulary. I was not used to anyone doing things for me; I always served others.

Breakfast was finally served and joyous life was humming all through the house. As I did at dinnertime, I ate everything with a spoon; once again, the family did not say anything. After breakfast, I found myself smiling as I pulled out the dress I was to wear to the presidential palace. I held it up to my slight figure and looked at myself in the mirror. I smiled at the lovely V-necked black dress that rode just below my knees. The small cup-like sleeves made my arms appear long and slender. I slipped the dress over my head and reached for the delicate silver-ball earrings. Once I had them securely in my ears, I reached for my brush and smoothed out my hair. I let it flow straight down my back. Mainly for appearance's sake, I carried a small black purse that hung from my shoulder. In it, I had only my student ID card and a handkerchief.

As I bent down to slip on my shoes I thought, *I am about to be in the presence of the highest ruling family in Liberia. I am living a dream.*

When I met her in the living room, my Aunt Sarah looked at me as if I were her daughter. She said, "Géesedeh, how beautiful. You look lovely in that dress." I shyly responded, "Thank you." She hurriedly said, "My driver is waiting for us. Are you ready?" I nodded, barely able to hold back my excitement. "Yes, Aunt Sarah. I am." Her husband came rushing from his bedroom dressed in business attire. He had a commanding outward appearance, but I had found he had a teddy bear spirit inside. He winked at me as he passed.

Since my aunt and her husband both worked at the presidential palace, I was surprised to see two black governmental cars out front. My uncle got into the backseat of the first car while my aunt and I slipped into the backseat of the second." I thought for a moment, *What? Two cars? Why? Couldn't we all ride in one car?* My uncle's car drove ahead, and our car followed.

I shivered in the air-conditioned vehicle. I could feel my fingers going numb as I wrapped myself in my arms and looked out the window. When I saw the Liberian flags waving on the front of the car I felt both proud and humbled that this was happening to me.

I was totally lost in a trance at the wonder of it all until I heard

Aunt Sarah say, "Géesedeh ... Géesedeh! Where are you?" I looked up to see her smiling at me as she watched the wonder on my face. She continued, "Géesedeh, I am so happy that you are able to come with me today to meet the first lady. She has been longing to see you."

Was I in a dream? Had I not woken up? The frigid air coming from the air conditioner reminded me that I was truly awake. Aunt Sarah spoke tenderly, "You know, the first lady is very fond of your mother. I believe she will be able to help you a great deal. She is offering government-sponsored academic scholarships to young people who are ready for college. I know you are only in the ninth grade, but maybe she will be able to reserve one for you when the time is right." The whole idea of what was happening to me was almost too much to take in.

We drove down a divided highway that had a lovely median lined with shade trees; and I looked up to see a massive concrete and steel building that seemed to tower into the sky. In a moment, we were at a heavily guarded entrance gate, where soldiers saluted, opened the gate, and bowed to our two cars. We drove down a tree-lined drive, approaching the front of the palace. I saw three large fountains and a beautiful walkway crossing a reservoir to a concrete platform that I expected was used for large outdoor meetings and celebrations.

The building was intimidating. The massive structure and all it represented left me awestruck. In front of the building was the Liberian flag; a flag with eleven stripes and one star. The red stripes stand for courage; the white for purity. The single white star signaled Liberia's being the only sovereign African republic in 1847; the blue background represented the richness of the African continent.

A banner that read, "The love of liberty brought us here," topped the beautiful seal of Liberia mounted securely to the front of the palace entrance. Much like the original settlers of Liberia, I too had hopes and dreams for a better future.

Our drivers steered the vehicles into the entrance of an underground parking garage, and I was again amazed as we drove under the building into an area that caused the rumbling car engines to sound like African drums. Both cars stopped near an elevator. My uncle exited his car; then her driver opened Aunt Sarah's door so she, too, could get out. She patted my lap and said, "Stay right here, the driver will come around to your side and let you out."

I watched Aunt Sarah walk over to the elevator, where she waited for me. The driver politely smiled and opened my door; I stepped out. He must have known that I was an "interior child" of simple means. I thanked him kindly, but was startled when he bowed, walked backwards from my presence, and got back into the car. No one had ever bowed to me before. There was no doubt this was going to be a day filled with many wonders, starting with my first-ever ride in an elevator.

My uncle got off the elevator a couple of floors up, then Aunt Sarah punched a special code into a key pad on the elevator wall to gain access to the fifth floor where the president and his family lived. We stepped out into a beautiful, spacious living room, elegantly decorated with modern European décor.

Five men dressed in military uniforms guarded the room, one in each corner and one at the door. They bowed as they greeted my aunt and she smiled briefly at them as we entered the room. Her mind was preoccupied with me as well as the business we were about to engage in.

I scanned the room, my eyes darting here and there; the beauty was enchanting. My aunt took me over to a comfortable and handsome-looking chair, saying, "Louise, sit here and I will go tell the first lady we have arrived." She walked away, leaving me in that huge room, with the five guards. I felt a bit awkward so I sat on the edge of the chair with my back straight, afraid to lean back or touch anything. Aunt Sarah was gone long enough to allow me ample time to inspect my surroundings further.

I felt like I truly was in a palace. The room boasted its European influence with large archways and a cathedral ceiling; giving it an elevated air of opulent aristocracy. A large, crystal chandelier hung from the center of the room, lending to the grand style that pervaded the space.

Classic oil paintings, large family portraits, as well as modern art adorned the walls. Rich fabrics of varying textures, and the calming cream colors, added warmth and dimension to the room. A peach-colored Persian rug graced the marble floor between two large sofas and matching chairs and corner tables.

Each table held a large, exotic-flower-filled, crystal vase. Behind the seating area was a very large picture window, which faced the Atlantic Ocean. Sheers stretched across the window while long, flowing drapes hung to each side.

Across the room there was a curved marble bar with ten tall stools and a servant standing behind it waiting to serve. Everywhere I looked, I was amazed at what I saw.

Suddenly the first lady came into the room exclaiming loudly, "Géesedeh, baby doll, oh my, you are so beautiful!" Her smile was warming and contagious. I felt a little embarrassed by her doting over me. She joyfully said, "You look just like your mother." She did not hesitate to take me into her arms and give me a warm, robust hug. She looked at me again and said, "You have beautiful eyes, and your hair is lovely." In my heart I was thinking, *What? She's the one who is beautiful.*

She asked me many questions, and I answered each one; questions like, how long have you lived in Monrovia, what grade are you in, and how well are you doing in school? I told her that I had been living in Monrovia since I entered second grade, I was now in the ninth grade, and was doing well in school. She was heartbroken that she could not help me with a scholarship until I reached college age. She said, "I am sorry to have to leave you for a while but I have to attend to some things this afternoon. Please stay here in my suite and have lunch and dinner with your aunt. She can show you around the building and share some of its history with you. I will definitely see you again before you leave."

My Aunt Sarah and I sat and talked for a while about how amazing it was for me to meet the first lady. We moved to a beautiful dining room where we ate an exquisite meal. During lunch, Aunt Sarah showed me how to tackle a piece of steak with a knife and fork. It was not nearly as easy as it appeared.

At the end of the day, the first lady came back to say goodbye. She said, "I am sorry that I couldn't spend more time with you. State business keeps my life quite busy these days." I smiled at her. She said, "I hope you know what a blessing it is that you were chosen by your father to receive an education." She both encouraged and admonished me as she said, "Make sure your grades are perfect for the next three years so that you can be eligible to receive a presidential scholarship."

I promised her I would do my best. No one received favors just because they were related to the president. Each student had to earn, by his or her own scholastic merit, the right to consideration for a scholarship.

I was not sure how I was going to continue with my studies with the amount of work I had to do to cover the cost of my tuition. My emotions got the best of me and I broke down, telling her that my father had sent me to live with Congo people, and that my freedom had been exchanged for an education. I could tell she was saddened to learn that I was having to work so hard to earn my high school education and was sorry that she could not help me with a scholarship until I reached college.

The first lady briefly walked out of the room and returned with an envelope filled with five one hundred dollar bills. She said, "Géesedeh, I am giving you money from my private account. It is my hope that it will help eliminate some of the pain you have to endure to finish school."

I fell to the floor, grabbed her feet, and said, "Thank you, thank you. I don't know how to thank you for your kindness." A bit surprised, she bent down, lifted me up, and said, "Oh no, no, get up. You don't have to bow down to me." With concern in her eyes she continued, "God can do anything. I was once just a soldier's wife and today, look at me; I am the first lady of Liberia. God is full of surprises. Study hard."

She then added, "You don't need to thank me. Your mother's love for me and my husband has gone before you; you need to thank your mother." She smiled and said, "Your mother is a true hero. Anyone who knows your mother would agree with me."

She reminded me to do my best in school, exhorting, "I want you to study, study, study. The next time I see you I want you to be qualified to receive the presidential scholarship." She turned and said, "Sarah, please call for the car and make sure Louise gets home safely." We hugged goodbye.

As we rode back to Aunt Sarah's, I marveled at the past twenty-four hours and thanked God for his favor. Aunt Sarah called a taxi for me; we hugged and she said, "We had a great time together, didn't we?" I responded, "Aunt Sarah, it was the greatest day of my life, and I will never forget it."

When I got home, I gave the five hundred dollars to Mrs. Smith and asked her to keep it for me. I told her she could keep what she thought she needed. With some of the money, I bought gifts for the Smith's children.

About a year after my visit at the presidential palace, I was delighted when one Friday afternoon my friend Maggie advised me that her older brother George Boley, who was the minister of education, knew of several academic scholarships offered by the ministry. Maggie suggested I speak with George to find out more. The next Saturday I had the opportunity to meet with Maggie's brother. After I explained my financial situation, he recommended I meet with Charles Gaye Breeze, the deputy minister of education. When I heard Charles' name I said to Maggie, "That name sure sounds familiar. When I was a little girl, still living in Grand Gedeh, I knew a man named Charles Gaye Breeze who was my mother's cousin." At George's suggestion, I went to the Ministry of Education in downtown Monrovia the following Monday.

When I met Mr. Breeze he said, "You are Louise Barton? It's nice to meet you." His warm greeting made me feel right at home. He looked just like the Charles Gaye Breeze I had known as a child. The funny thing was he had not aged a day and actually looked a little younger. I responded, "It is my pleasure to meet you, sir. Excuse me for asking, but when I was very young I knew a Charles Gaye Breeze in Grand Gedeh; he was my mother's cousin. Would that be you?"

An astonished look washed over his face and he said, "What? Who is your mother?" I was more than delighted to tell him, "My mother is Josephiné Barton." His eyes sparkled with joy as he asked, "You are Josephiné Barton's daughter? Little Géesedeh Barton?" I giggled and answered, "Yes." He threw his arms up in the air in complete and total surprise, cleared his throat and said, "To answer your question, I am Charles Gaye Breeze, Junior; you amaze me that you remember my father. My mother and your mother were very close friends."

He laughed and leaned back in his chair. "I can't believe this. Little Géesedeh is sitting in my office." He closed his eyes, breathed deeply, smiled, and shook his head slowly from side to side. When he opened his eyes, he smiled at me and said, "Louise, your mother is a very fine woman, and I now see your mother in your face. Are you living with your mother here in Monrovia?" My eyes dropped and my countenance fell. I looked at my folded hands in my lap for a moment and sadly shook my head, "No, I am living with the Smith family. They are so kind to help me with my education."

He knew what kind of sacrifices underprivileged families in Liberia had to make in order to procure an education for their children. I did not share any details of my situation except for my strong desire to finish school and my fear that I may not be able to continue my education due to my long work hours. I pleaded, "Sir, I need a scholarship that will help lessen my burden so I can spend more time studying. I also plan to further my education by attending college."

He said, "Louise Barton, I can tell you are a good student. You are very articulate, your English is very good, and your determination will take you a long way. College will go well with you, and I believe you will go far in life. I am so proud of you. I'll get in touch with the administrative board at Carver Mission to get your grades and, I assure you, everything will be all right."

The Ministry of Education awarded the academic scholarship just in time for me to begin my eleventh grade. They paid Carver Mission directly, with a little allowance to cover the cost of my school supplies, some clothing, and my graduation gown. Although I still did a little cleaning for the school to earn some money, were it not for the scholarship I would not have made it. I had lost the physical strength to carry on.

At about the same time, on a day like all the rest, I heard an oddly familiar voice coming from the kitchen. *Could that be Solo?* I stepped around the doorway and saw his face. Although it had been five years since he had left me without saying goodbye, I couldn't keep the buried emotions of sadness and disappointment from surfacing. Dismayed, I stood there speechless. After a moment, Solo broke the silence with, "Louise, our father needs to see a doctor in Bomi Hills and he's on his way from Grand Gedeh. He'll be here Saturday and wants to visit!"

I had not seen my father since I first arrived at the Smith's home, and it had been nearly a decade since his gentle eyes and warm embrace had comforted me. With tears brimming, I thanked my brother for the heartwarming news.

I watched Solo head down the same road, just as he had years earlier. This time he would be returning in a few days with our father, and I was elated. I was so excited that I had a new spring in my step as I went about my daily chores. The days flew by quickly, and before I knew it, Saturday had arrived.

CHAPTER 6

Unexpected Visitor

My father traveled all the way from Grand Gedeh in the same manner as I had almost ten years earlier; in a beat up, old mini-bus, crowded with other travelers and all their bags of clothing, boxes of food, caged livestock, and chickens held on laps. I chuckled, cringing at the memory of my trip as an innocent and trusting child clinging to a fawn and to the hope of a bright and happy future.

Saturday arrived and I bounced out of bed at the usual hour of 4:00 AM, rushing through all of my morning chores; the air smelled much sweeter than other days. I was thrilled at the thought of seeing my beloved father again. I kept peeking out of the windows throughout the day to see if he had arrived.

In the afternoon, as I glanced out the window, I saw two men winding their way up the lane. I strained to see their faces in the distance and could tell one of them was a strong, younger man. The other was older, bent slightly forward, and walked with a cane. I thought, *This cannot be my father, weak, old, and bent.*

My heart skipped a beat when I recognized the younger man as my brother Solo; I realized the older, worn-out man must be my father. A lump filled my throat and tears burned my eyes because my father was no longer the strong and robust man I remembered; I could clearly see that the years had taken their toll on him. He had become a gaunt, slender man bent over with pain; his well-worn face disclosed his suffering.

He wore an elegant, traditional African gown with matching pants;

delicate designs masterfully stitched onto the fabric with a shimmering, peach-colored thread ornately embellishing them. The hat of a village chieftain adorned his head and he bore the appearance of an aging African king.

It was a delight to see my father's face, an aged version of the same loving and kind countenance that had visited me all these years in my dreams. The memory of the promise he made to visit me often, as I left the village many years ago, intruded on my happiness as I wondered, *Why did he not come to see me sooner?* I decided not to ask, as heart-felt tears welled up in my eyes until I could barely see. I clumsily pushed open the door, stumbled down the steps, and ran at full speed across the yard toward my father.

When he saw me running toward him he abruptly stopped walking, straightened up a bit, leaned his cane against his leg and, with a warm and inviting smile, stretched out his open arms. With tears running down my face I sobbed, "Papa, Papa!" I fell into his arms, leaning my head onto his breast. My own chest heaved as I continued to chant, "Papa, oh Papa."

I was flooded with joy and sadness; joy at seeing my beloved father and holding him in my arms again, and sadness at all the years of separation I had endured. The emotions flowed over me and I wept, holding on tightly for fear of losing him again. He stroked my head and my hair, and cooed in my ear, "Oh, Géesedeh, Géesedeh, my little girl. It will be okay." His voice quivered as tears streaked down his face and fell on his gown.

"Géesedeh, my little chestnut, don't cry." His soothing voice calmed my frazzled and love-starved soul. Our embrace cancelled out the years, the distance, and the pain.

I lifted my head from his chest and peered into his wonderful eyes. It was like looking into a magical looking glass and being spirited back to the days when life seemed so perfect and happiness knew no limits. I was loved and adored. I kept looking into his enormous brown eyes, a trait all of his children also carried as a badge of honor; people who recognized us would often say, "You must be Charles Barton's child."

Solo also had tears streaming down his cheeks as he participated in our emotional exchange and the healing taking place. When I was finally able to get control of myself, father picked up his cane and said, "Shall we?" He pointed his cane toward the house, and I placed my arm in his as I led him to the back yard. Solo ran ahead and grabbed some chairs for us to sit on. He placed the chairs under the tree in the back yard and said, "Papa, here, sit down and rest." My father sat down and placed his cane against the chair.

Mrs. Smith looked out the window and saw that my father had arrived. Noticing we were sitting near the septic tank in the back yard she opened the back door and said, "Hello, Mr. Barton, please come and sit in the front yard." She meant to honor my father with this kind and generous gesture. He looked up at me with a twinkle in his eye, and smiled at Mrs. Smith.

After we resettled in the front yard, my father and Mrs. Smith struck up a pleasant conversation regarding my father's health, his trip to Monrovia, and other pertinent matters. My father expressed his gratitude to Mrs. Smith for caring for me all these years. He truly meant it when he said, "I am eternally grateful for all you have done for my daughter. She looks good, and my heart is pleased to see that you've been a good mother to her." Mrs. Smith asked, "Would you like to have a cold soft drink?" My father nodded his assent and Mrs. Smith disappeared into the house.

I automatically stooped down and offered to remove my father's shoes, just as I did for all of Mrs. Smith's guests. I kept my eyes lowered and my head slightly bowed. The thought of sitting never entered my mind, and if it had, I would not have dared. I had definitely changed over the years. Instead of finding me a carefree, confident young woman, my father found himself in the presence of a well-trained servant—reserved, broken, and humbled. He leaned over and quietly whispered to me in the Naio dialect of the Krahn language; although I understood most of his words, I was not able to respond in Naio, having lost the ability to speak the language.

Mrs. Smith returned with the cold drink. They picked up their conversation as I stood to the side and listened. Mrs. Smith realized I was not sitting down, or joining in the conversation. Somewhat embarrassed, she said, "Louise, sit and talk with your father." This was awkward for me, sitting and not serving. I felt very much out of place.

Since it had been some time since he left the Smith's home, Solo disappeared into the house to say hello to the children. Having spent most of his childhood as a servant of Mrs. Smith, he felt like a big brother to them; from the excited voices and laughter inside the house, it was clear they were very happy to see him.

Solo must have told the children that our father was outside, because they all tumbled out the door nearly knocking their mother over. Mrs. Smith introduced her children to my father one by one. They were not at all shy about what they thought, for they loudly proclaimed, "Look, Louise, your old man's wearing your eyes." My father laughed aloud because it was true; there was no hiding it.

I grabbed his hand and said, "Papa, tell me everything. How are all my brothers, sisters, and mothers?" He said, "Everyone is doing well. You should know that your mother has never forgotten you. Her family and friends from the Ivory Coast bring words of love and blessing from your mother whenever they come through the village."

My father tried several times to speak to me in Naio so he could share things with me in confidence, but he soon realized I wasn't responding because I could no longer speak the language. It brought tears to his eyes knowing that, in addition to time and distance having first separated us, language did so as well.

He also noticed the luster of my youth had been lost, and I appeared trampled on and frail. He was very sad to see me like this. He leaned over and whispered to me, "Géesedeh, I am so sorry I didn't let you go to live with your mother. Please forgive me; I tried to do right by you." He then gave me a kiss on the cheek. As my father looked at my thin and boney frame, he stammered, "Are you being treated well?" I knew he was deeply concerned for me. He had given me up so long ago in the hope of bettering my life. I did not want to worry him, so, to put his mind and heart at ease, I replied, "Yes, I am well."

He shared that he had been working on his farm for many years. He said, "Louise, talking about farms has reminded me of a relative of yours, an uncle who owns a large plantation. It just occurred to me that he lives right here in Monrovia. His name is Siah Willie Nyoun and he is related to your mother." The thought of having another relative who lived nearby excited me. I repeated the name, "Nyoun," memorizing it so I might later see if I could locate him.

I noticed a cataract hindered the vision of one of my father's eyes, making it difficult for him to get around; it was for this reason he had traveled to Monrovia. I was very worried for him, and asked, "Papa will you lose your sight?" He replied, "Louise, I will be fine. I've scheduled eye surgery at the hospital in Bomi Hills, where your brother Tye lives. After the surgery, I will recuperate at his home. Maybe you can come for a visit." The thought of visiting with Tye, my affectionate older brother who used to look after me when I was a child, made my heart skip a beat. Even though Bomi Hills was only a two to three hour drive north, I had not seen Tye since I left the village to live with Mrs. Smith. In spite of the invitation, I did not have much hope of Mrs. Smith allowing me to visit.

My father could not stay for long, and our time grew short. In somewhat broken English he said, "Your mother's blessings are still here with you." He smiled and said, "My blessings are still here with you, too." I choked down the tears and committed the moment to memory, etching his words in my mind. He looked at me tenderly saying, "My little Géesedeh, don't give up. We will see each other again." His eyes glistened with tears as he smiled and said, "You look just like your beautiful mother."

With that, he stood up, cleared his throat, and leaned heavily on his cane. Solo also rose to assist him. I knew he had to go, but could not stop myself from pleading with him, "No, don't leave. Not now. Please,

I need you." He gave me one last hug and said, "See if you can come and see me at the hospital." I have no doubt he looked pleadingly at Mrs. Smith, who by that time was standing behind me.

I watched as he and Solo disappeared down the lane, and wondered if I would ever see him again. My heart was broken into a million pieces, and I could not stop myself from weeping as they left. *Oh Lord, I thought, can you possibly mend my broken heart?*

My father's visit was such a blessing, yet seeing him again, and then watching him leave, took a major toll on me. For the next five days, I was only a shell of my former self. Mrs. Smith obviously noticed that the little joy I once had, had totally vanished; and it touched her heart to see that the light seemed to have gone out in my life.

Much to my surprise, the Friday following my father's visit, Mrs. Smith said, "Louise, last Saturday, when Solo and your father were here, Solo said he would be traveling up to Bomi Hills to visit your father a week after his surgery." With a slight grin she continued, "I've been thinking, now that you're out of school for Easter break, and you have a week free before your classes begin, why don't you take five days off and head over to Solo's home. You can go with him when he heads up to visit your father." My jaw dropped a little, and I joyfully responded, "Thank you, Ma!" I could not believe my ears. I did not dare say a word out of fear she might change her mind.

I quickly ran to my room, packed my bags, ran out the door, and walked two minutes to an area down the road where I could hail a taxi. In under an hour I arrived where Solo lived. I knew he would be home that day preparing for his trip to Bomi Hills.

When I arrived, Solo was very surprised to see me; he never expected Mrs. Smith would allow me to take time off to join him. He was nearly ready to go and, in a few minutes, we took a local taxi to a downtown terminal. There we hired another taxi for the two-hour ride to Tye's place. I was so excited about the opportunity to see my father again and spend time with my brother, Tye, that I could barely control my emotions. I wanted to laugh and cry at the same time.

When we arrived, Tye came out in his dental smock and apron, having come home early from his dental assistant's job. He reached out to shake hands with Solo and drew him close. The two brothers embraced and jovially patted each other on the back. Unaware I would be coming, Tye jumped back when he noticed me standing behind Solo. With a broad smile and a surprised tone, he shouted, "Géesedeh?" I nodded my head, burst into uncontrollable tears, and collapsed as my knees gave way under me.

Tye bent down on one knee, gently hugging me and rocking me in his arms. He helped me to my feet and pulled me a little away to get a better look. "Géesedeh! What? When you stand up, I see your Ma stand up." He could not have said any sweeter words to me. "Look at your hair—it's so pretty! Oh, Géesedeh, you've grown up! You're a beautiful woman now."

Over the years, the wind had tossed over twenty siblings and me in all directions, robbing us of the opportunity to enjoy each other's company. On this day, three of us gathered once again.

Tye's four-year-old son, feeling a bit left out, came over and yanked on his father's sleeve. Looking at me shyly, he cupped his tiny little hands around his father's ear and whispered, "Papa, pick me up." Tye picked him up and stood facing me. I straightened my skirt, smoothed out the wrinkles, and got back on my feet.

During all the commotion, Tye's lovely wife had come out with their two-year-old daughter on her hip. Tye turned to her and said, "Saywon Oretha, this is my little sister Louise." She smiled at me and gave me a big hug. I noticed more children hiding behind her and peering at me with their big brown eyes. I asked one little girl, "What's your name?" She shyly turned her face away, and did not answer. Saywon said, "Her name is Chinese Girl." I giggled and said, "Hello, Chinese Girl. What an interesting name you have." I leaned over and said hello to all their children as each one squirmed away from my reach. I decided it would be best to wait for them to come to me, so I backed away and just smiled.

A stucco concrete-block house stood before us. We were invited inside and Tye and Saywon showed us their small but tidy home. We bent down to get through a shorter than normal front door and ended up in a tiny, sparsely furnished living room. A coffee table and four stuffed chairs were at its center and off in one corner was a tiny dining area with a bamboo table and three bamboo chairs.

Chinese Girl hurried into the bedroom where my father was resting. From around the corner we heard her little voice, "Grandpa, Grandpa, one boy is here to see you, and one girl is here to see you, and their eyes look like you." She quickly ran back into the living room to take another peek at us, turned and ran back to the bedroom, and jumped up on grandpa's bed. Tye nodded toward the bedroom, indicating we could go in. We entered the room in time to see father struggling to sit up.

The scent of his homemade bed of old rice sacks sewn together and filled with dried grass, sitting on a bamboo frame, reminded me of when I was a child in the village in Grand Gedeh. The surprise of seeing me in the doorway brought him to tears. Saywon pleaded, "Please don't cry Papa; your eye bandage will get wet." I sat beside him, hugged him and whispered, "I love you so much, Papa." Father whispered, "My little ebony angel has come to see me!" Solo squeezed in and hugged him, too. It was truly a miracle that I had this precious gift of five days with my father and brothers.

Because my father only spoke in Naio, I had to strain to understand what he was saying. He asked Saywon to translate his Naio into English. He went on, "Your mother prays for you every day that God will give you long life and keep you safe everywhere you go." His words were like a fresh flowing spring. I covered my eyes with my hands, leaned on my father's chest, and said, "Papa, I love her, too." Papa's chest heaved with grief, because he missed her as much as I did. His grief mingled with mine, and in spite of our warnings, his tears had soaked his eye bandage.

Saywon, who had been cooking prior to our arrival, asked, "Is anyone hungry?" We eagerly sat down to lunch and the children began to warm up to Solo and me. A beautiful six-year-old girl with sparkling eyes boldly touched my long hair, and asked sweetly, "Aunt Louise, do you want something to drink?" I nodded yes. She brought me an ice cold drink and ran back to her mother's side. Each day of my five-day visit, I spent a little more time with her. By the time I left, she was sitting in my lap and letting me tell her stories.

Their oldest child—a seven-year-old boy—was slower to trust us than the other children were. He watched as the little ones took turns sitting on our laps; before long, though, he too learned to trust us. Their four-year-old was the bravest of them all. He had a head full of thick, curly brown hair and was happy all the time. Whenever he smiled, his little white teeth glistened like newly strung pearls.

Chinese Girl, the two-year-old, cried a lot and always wanted to be with her mother. The only time she walked away from her mother was to be with her special grandpa. She bonded with him very quickly, much to my father's delight. He called her, "My little chocolate baby."

As I looked at this lovely family, I remembered my dream of the devastation and conflict God had given me a glimpse of when He warned me, "War is coming and will be like the ocean rushing through the streets of Monrovia and its surrounding areas." I pushed the thoughts as far away as I could.

After lunch, Tye said, "Louise and Solo, I want to show you around town." We took a short walk to downtown Bomi Hills, a delightfully beautiful, hilltop town with breathtaking views. We could see mountains, valleys, and thick, rich forest in all directions. We walked past the lumber company and sawmill, where pallets of exotic hardwood lumber were waiting for shipment all over the world. Tye said, "Some of America's homes are built from our finest lumber." I thought, *Wow, this lumber is shipped to America?*

The five days with Tye, his family, and my father flew by in a blur;

yet in that short timeframe I had dug in firm roots and I did not want to leave. It was refreshing being loved and so well treated. I did not know what to make of it. One thing I did know was that freedom felt good; and I longed for it to continue.

Our last day arrived, the sky turned dark and a heavy rain fell as if the heavens cried with us and matched our gloomy spirits. My father, who was in tears over my departure, was so broken-hearted that no one could comfort him. The thought of losing me again cut him so deeply that he refused to say goodbye. I hugged him and said, "I love you, Papa. I hope to be with you again soon."

CHAPTER 7

Death to All Krahns

It was Christmas Eve of 1989, and a major rebellion against Samuel K. Doe, the first indigenous president of Liberia and a member of the Krahn tribe, was brewing. Many years before, a vivid dream forewarned me of coming terror—like an unrestrained ocean roaring through the streets of Monrovia.

I had graduated from high school at age seventeen with high honors, and was attending college at the University of Liberia. Whisperings of war made their way around campus for some time, yet everyone felt that, no matter what happened, government troops would be able to hold back the tide, just as they had done in the past. Regardless of what trouble might be brewing in the countryside, the inhabitants of Monrovia felt safe continuing their preparations for Christmas.

Mrs. Smith had invited a number of friends over to join her for a Christmas Eve dinner. As I prepared to serve the meal, she strolled over to the radio and turned it on. Christmas music filled the air. Mrs. Smith smiled at her dinner guests and said, "Now it feels more like Christmas."

I was in the kitchen at the time; even from there, I could hear the sudden firmness and concerned tone of the British Broadcasting Corporation (BBC) announcer's voice as he interrupted the music. All the merry-making and chatter going on in the living room came to an abrupt halt, and Mrs. Smith ran over to the radio to turn up the volume. The BBC announcer said, "Rebel forces have entered Liberia from the Ivory Coast and are heading toward Monrovia." At the time,

I did not know what a rebel was; I learned very quickly, however. One of Mrs. Smith's guests explained, "Rebels are rebellious, disgruntled people who fight to bring down the government." He also shared why he felt this was happening to our country.

While trying to fathom the meaning of what he was saying, I realized the man had stopped talking. He quizzically looked at me, and then turned his gaze toward Mrs. Smith. Her eyes narrowed as she looked my way. She bit her lip and furrowed her brow as if in deep thought.

Immediately after dinner, Mrs. Smith's guests excused themselves and headed home. Mrs. Smith spent the rest of the evening on the phone; several times, I heard her mention "Krahn;" this confused and scared me.

The next day Mrs. Smith was especially tense and I could tell she was very uncomfortable having a Krahn servant in her home. As time went by, she unleashed her temper on me more often and for the smallest of things.

Six uncomfortable months crawled by. The whole city agonized over the news that rebel forces were nearing Monrovia. Neighbors spoke of leaving. American and British citizens began evacuating.

Since the president of Liberia was a member of the Krahn tribe, most Krahns had felt safe. Samuel Doe had assumed power via a military coup in 1980, toppling an Americo–Liberian-led government that had ruled the country since its founding in 1847. Doe's Armed Forces of Liberia (AFL) had begun their attempt to combat the National Patriot Front of Liberia (NPFL), which was a rebel group led by Charles G. Taylor, a former governmental minister who had previously fled the country after accusations of embezzling national funds. Suddenly, my Krahn descent put me, as well as the Smith family, by association, at significant risk. The once whispered rumors had become shouted truths. War was upon us. Hatred toward Krahns escalated; and we heard phrases like, "The boys are coming for those Krahn dogs!" in the streets. Mrs. Smith was worried about the safety of her family; most of her friends and relatives were fleeing the capital.

One morning, in the midst of all the turbulence, Mrs. Smith informed me that one of her daughters reported having caught me stealing perfume. Mrs. Smith angrily accused me, "Louise, you stole my perfume! And are using it!" I pleaded, "No, Ma, I didn't take your perfume." Visibly shaking she screamed, "Don't lie to me, my daughter told me that she smelled my perfume on you." I was shocked at the accusation, and begged her to believe me. I offered to let her smell my clothes, and before she could protest I ran to my closet and grabbed the clothes I had worn the day before, saying, "Here, you can smell these, too." She reached out, ripped the clothes from my hands, quickly smelled them, and threw them back at me.

She looked at me with anger in her eyes and shouted at me with a quiver in her voice, "It does not matter whether or not I can smell perfume on your clothes. I can not and will not have a thief living in my house!" I dropped down, holding onto her feet and begging, "Please, Ma, don't throw me out. I have no place to go." She pointed her finger at the door and screamed, "Get your things and get out!" I could not do or say anything that might change her mind. I cried as I pushed myself up from the floor and retreated to where I kept my few belongings. This was the first time anyone had ever accused me of stealing anything from the Smith family.

Mrs. Smith's daughter had never accused me of anything before. We had always been friends, and she had been my advocate, even pleading my case in years past. She had often come to my rescue in order to protect me. I thought, *Why is she doing this to me?*

I stumbled out the front door and collapsed on the porch, begging for mercy. Mrs. Smith, who was standing at the door, did not listen to my pleas. I continued to scream and beg, "Ma, I have no place to go!" I sobbed and begged with all my heart, "Please, don't throw me out. You are the only family I have. If you leave Monrovia, please take me with you. Please, please!" I was frightened and had no place to go.

She waved both hands in the air. "Go and find somebody. Just go. You can't stay here anymore." She turned away from me, saying nothing, and closed the door. I had no place to go because most of our neighbors had already fled the city. How was I going to survive in the midst of civil war where those of my ethnic background were being hunted down like vermin? I looked toward the house I once considered home and to the door that separated me from safety. I shook my head from side to side in disbelief; the Smith family had abandoned me.

I knew my cousin Amos, who worked as a guard at the presidential palace, could not leave his post, and would not be able to help me flee the city. I also knew that my brother Solo, who shared an apartment in Monrovia with other young men, had no source of transportation. As I wondered what to do next, I remembered my uncle named Siah Willie Nyoun, whom my father had mentioned to me during his visit. I had later learned that he worked at the Ministry of Lands, Mines & Energy in Monrovia and had dropped in on him for a brief visit at his office the year before. With nowhere else to go, I flagged down a taxicab and headed for Capitol Hill.

I was quite shaken and nervous by the time the taxi arrived at the Ministry building. I noticed my uncle, having completed his workday, was heading out to his car. With teary eyes, I ran up to him and said, "Oh, Uncle Nyoun, please help me." He said, "What has happened Géesedeh? What are you doing out here at a time like this? It's no time for you to be on the streets." I burst out with all that had happened; he had no time to respond during my deluge, but held me close, whispering, "Don't worry. Everything will be all right."

Uncle Nyoun led me to his old, rusty, brown pickup truck and we drove to his home, where he invited me to have dinner with the family. As we ate, I learned they were planning to pack all they could in the pickup truck and head out of Monrovia for Sierra Leone in the morning. Confident Liberian forces would soon crush the rebellion; they expected to be able to return in a few weeks. My uncle assured me, "I am certain I can convince Mrs. Smith to keep you on until all this rebel stuff blows over."

After dinner, Uncle Nyoun, his wife Betty, and I crowded into their truck and drove to Mrs. Smith's home. When we arrived, my uncle got out and headed straight for the front door, with Betty right behind him. A look of solid determination covered Mrs. Smith's face when she answered their knocking. It was clear my uncle was in for a battle. Expecting Mrs. Smith to close it, he placed one foot on the threshold, and put one hand on the doorframe while holding the door open with his other hand. "Mrs. Smith, I am Mr. Nyoun, this is my wife. May we please come in and speak with you about Louise?"

Mrs. Smith replied, "No, you may not." He smiled and continued, "Please, Mrs. Smith, Louise has been a good and faithful servant for many years. If she has done something wrong, have mercy on her, and forgive her." With a stern, unflinching look, Mrs. Smith said, "Louise is no longer welcome here. She stole perfume from me and I won't have a thief in my house. That is my final word on the subject."

He continued to beg her. "Mrs. Smith, you can't kick Louise out, our country is under siege. Please forgive Louise. It is a time of tribulation, and too dangerous for her to be on the streets. Please allow Louise to stay with you." Mrs. Smith continued insisting that she was not about to have someone who had stolen perfume stay in her home. I protested that I had not stolen any perfume, and pointed out once again that my clothes did not smell of perfume. It appeared nothing would budge Mrs. Smith.

My uncle and his wife were convinced I would be safer in her home than running with them and their family, so they made one last attempt at convincing Mrs. Smith to take me back in by offering to buy her two bottles of the perfume she claimed I had stolen, if she would just allow me to stay. If she preferred, they would buy three bottles. All their pleading was ignored. Mrs. Smith pointed to the belongings I had brought up from the truck, and said with cold sternness, "Take Louise, and her things, and leave."

Uncle Nyoun resigned himself to the fact Mrs. Smith could not be moved. He shook his head and stated, "I will take Louise with me; and

wherever I go, she will go; whatever I eat, she will eat; wherever I lay
my head down, she will lay her head down; wherever I die, she will die;
and wherever I am buried, she will be buried."

He thanked Mrs. Smith for taking care of me for all these years.
He asked God to bless her and keep her family safe. After gathering
all of my earthly belongings, he nodded for me to follow him back
to the truck. He had hoped Mrs. Smith would listen to reason and
offer me a safe haven. Instead, I would be traveling with him and his
family as they fled Monrovia. I wept bitterly, feeling as if I had lost
everything. All hope faded, vanished into thin air. As we drove away,
I glanced back and saw Mrs. Smith still standing there, stone-faced.
Her children were beside her, stunned and motionless; sadness painted
on their faces.

I stayed the night with Uncle Nyoun and his family and, the next
morning, I helped them pack the truck for the trip out of the city. We
drove away with my uncle and his wife in the cab. I rode in the back
of the truck with ten of his children who ranged in ages from nine to
twenty-two; we were all crammed together alongside cans of gasoline
and other critical supplies. We had weighted the truck down so much
that it leaned to one side, and its tires bulged under the burden.

There was no time to waste, by then the war was upon us. I saw
why my uncle had hoped Mrs. Smith would take me back in; we were
putting ourselves at great risk as we traveled out of the city and into the
countryside.

Before heading to Sierra Leone my Uncle Nyoun needed to stop at
a diamond-mining village he owned, named Marbon Nyoun, that was
a short walk from Zingbaku. He wanted to ensure those who worked
for him were safe and to arrange for continued management of the
operation while he was away. Although he owned a diamond-mining
operation, he, as most others, made very little money at it.

When he told me we would be traveling through Bomi Hills on our way to Marbon Nyoun, I pleaded with him to allow my brother Tye and his family to come with us. Although it would be nearly impossible to get anything else in the truck, he agreed, "We will make room for them somehow, don't worry." We were unaware that the entire country had already exploded with rebel violence and there were no safe havens for Krahns.

We arrived two and a half hours after leaving Monrovia, but were too late to save Tye and his family. The day before, rebels had swept through the town and killed every member of the Krahn tribe they could get their hands on.

When I asked some people on a street corner if they knew my brother, the dental assistant, their horrified looks immediately told me that something terrible had happened. Some began crying and sobbing. I immediately lost the strength to stand and grabbed my uncle's arm to keep from falling.

Uncle Nyoun asked about the circumstances. The witnesses pulled at their hair and wrung their hands as they told us of Tye's capture, torture, and murder by the rebels. They said he had tried to avoid being singled out by using the local dialect; however, someone pointed him out as Krahn, and told the rebels he was a dental assistant. With that news, the rebels yanked out all of his teeth, one by one, with a pair of pliers, causing his head to swell up like a basketball. I became sick to my stomach.

One man continued, "We all wanted to help him, but there was nothing we could do. The more Tye pleaded with the rebels for mercy, the more they brutalized him. After several hours of begging for his life, they flogged him with barbed wire until his skin had peeled from his body and he was drenched in his own blood. The more he cried out, the crueler they became."

A woman added, "The rebel who beat your brother was not satisfied. He grabbed Tye's hand..." She began to sob as she continued, "...and yanked out every fingernail by its roots. He then pulled out each toenail, one by one. Everyone in the town could hear his screams.

After his torture they drug him to the Bomi Hills police station, which had already been overrun by the rebels, where they cut off his head, and stuck it on a post as a warning to other Krahn people."

We learned that Tye's wife was able to escape with two of their four children. The other two had been kidnapped. I could not believe my wonderful brother had been so mercilessly tortured and murdered. I staggered, almost passing out, and became hysterical with grief and panic. I did not want to stay another minute in Bomi Hills and pleaded with my uncle to take us away immediately. He and his wife agreed we should leave.

We all got back into the old, beat-up pickup truck and headed to Marbon Nyoun. During the hour-and-a-half drive, I could not get the thoughts of Tye's death out of my head no matter how hard I tried. I kept hearing the town's people describing his torture. I cringed at the images in my mind of what he had endured in the final minutes of his life.

When the thirteen of us arrived at Marbon Nyoun, no one family could take us all in; the villagers divided us into smaller groups and gave us shelter until we were ready to leave. Once inside the protection of four walls, I did not want to go back outside. I thought to myself, *Where can we hide? Where can we go? Will we survive this ordeal or end up like my brother Tye and his family?*

Emotionally and physically drained, all I could do was cry. I did so the rest of the afternoon, and most of the evening. As I finally lay down to sleep, I comforted myself with the Psalmists' words, "I lift up my eyes to the hills. From where does my help come? My help comes from the LORD, who made heaven and earth. He will not let your foot be moved; He who keeps you will not slumber." Meditating on the thought that God does not slumber afforded me a few hours of sleep.

I was startled awake when I heard a door slam. Immediately sitting straight up, I looked toward the door and saw Uncle Nyoun standing with bags of food and other supplies in his arms, embarrassed that the wind had unexpectedly yanked the door from his hand as he struggled with the load. My uncle was our rock. He was our provider, our strength, and the one we all depended on. We looked to him for security and reassurance. God was with him each step of the way. With twelve precious souls in his care, his burden was tremendous. I was so very happy to be a part of his family. I prayed that God would protect them and give my uncle wisdom as he navigated us through this war-torn country.

Unsure where to go next, we stayed in the town for three days. On the morning of the third day, we heard women and children screaming. People frantically scattered in all directions. Some were running for shelter, some were desperately calling for their children, and others were already fleeing.

Uncle Nyoun rushed out into the madness that filled the streets, grabbed a man who was rushing past him, and said, "What's happening?" Jerking out of my uncle's grasp, the man kept running. My uncle ran out into the middle of the road and yelled, "What's going on?" Someone screamed back, "The rebels are coming, and we are all going to die."

My uncle turned to us and said, "Gather your things. We're leaving! Now!" We scrambled into the overloaded truck as quickly as we could and he stomped on the accelerator. With everything occurring in slow motion, fear spread like molten lava, engulfing us. My heart raced and adrenalin rushed through my veins.

People clutched at us, trying to hang onto the sides of our truck. Mothers and fathers begged us to take their children. We would gladly have taken them all with us, so it tore our hearts apart knowing it was impossible. It was terrible to drive away and not be able to assist these terrified villagers who knew the rebels were approaching.

We raced down a dirt road, threading our way through the middle of the rain forest. We all sat in silence, aware of our rapidly beating hearts and listening to the rumble of the old engine and thump of the rubber tires on the road. In a few minutes, we heard the loud roar of a large truck, raucous laughter, and blaring music heading our way from around the curve ahead.

Uncle Nyoun quickly steered off the road. We bumped and thrashed through heavily wooded briars and bushes, bouncing to a dead stop a few feet before a large palm tree. He hissed at us to get out of the truck and run behind him into the bush. His quick thinking, and God's grace, had gotten us off the road just before the truck, filled with rebel soldiers, turned the corner. As we shrank down into the underbrush, we could hear the truck round the bend and screech to a stop. Grinding its gears into reverse, it backed up.

Holding our breath, for what seemed like an eternity, we were relieved when the truck changed gears and sped away. Although things were quiet, we did not know if any rebel soldiers had gotten out and might be making their way toward us, so we remained still for nearly two hours. When my uncle finally felt it was safe for us to return to the truck, we were happy to find there were no rebels in sight. We all piled back into the truck and he backed up onto the dirt road. Wasting no time, we again headed for the Liberian–Sierra Leone border, crossing at the Mano River Bridge. We raced along the highway so fast that our bottoms and arms were soon bruised from bouncing in the truck bed, banging into the metal and into each other like rag dolls.

We soon found ourselves driving past large groups of frightened people fleeing on foot. After an hour, we came to a clearing; a small village spread before us. We stopped and got out of the truck. Having lost their trust of strangers, the villagers were on guard when we approached. They were greatly relieved when they recognized my uncle. They offered us a place to sit and rest and proceeded to tell us stories of the atrocities that had occurred in nearby villages since the rebellion began.

Living in Monrovia had sheltered us from the raw reality of what was happening all over the country. All we had heard was propaganda telling us that government forces had pushed back the rebels, and the entire rebellion was under control. Being outside the capital and in the countryside, we quickly learned that it was far from the truth.

The truth was that rebel forces were committing mass murders of Krahns, Mandingos, government workers, and government sympathizers—or any person they suspected of being one. In actuality, anyone was fair game, because neither Krahn nor Mandingo has characteristics, physical or otherwise, that would easily differentiate him or her from anyone else.

To be certain they got them all, drug-crazed rebel soldiers, including children as young as six and seven, high on brown-brown (cocaine cut with gunpowder) were mowing down entire villages in a single swath. The wicked concoction, which was standard issue, sped up their metabolisms, made them frantic, greatly increased their endurance, and caused them to be more aggressive. Turned into fearless and ruthless killers, they often slaughtered fleeing civilians simply because they did not like their faces. They were, without a doubt, capable of the worst acts human beings could perform on each other.

We learned that rebel children would casually stroll into a village, innocently asking for food. Suddenly, they would savagely stab, slice, and shoot anything that breathed. They forced people to dance, laugh, and clap while watching the rebels butcher their relatives or friends alive. Other rebels would follow and burn the village to the ground. Some of those who escaped met their death in the bush at the hands of other rebels, or were killed by wild animals.

As the traumatized villagers reported more terrifying stories, I plugged my ears and silently screamed, *Enough, enough, enough!* I had to turn away because I could not bear hearing any more. I thought to myself, *When will this torment end?* I feared that, if I should survive this living nightmare, the memories would haunt me forever.

Uncle Nyoun told what we had seen in Bomi Hills, and that, while in Marbon Nyoun, we had learned the rebels were coming this way. He urged them to flee for their lives.

We jumped back into the truck and continued our dash to Bo Waterside, which straddles the Mano River on the Liberian–Sierra Leonean border, and was about seven hours away. It was not long before we found ourselves amidst the growing horde of humanity traveling on foot in the same direction. So many people were pushing and shoving their way along the narrow road that it was difficult to drive through them. We saw women carrying goods on their heads and children on their backs, men carrying heavy loads, and older children trying to stay by their sides. They were all fleeing from villages attacked and burned by the rebels.

As we arrived in the small town of Bo Waterside, Liberia, the sun was directly overhead, and we struggled in the intense heat. Suddenly, one of my cousins yelled, "Look Daddy, I see the checkpoint!" I could see a grim smile of relief on my uncle's face. He tightened his hold on the steering wheel as he steered determinedly toward the first checkpoint we must pass through on the Liberian side of the Mano River Bridge. I thought, *Once we're across the border we'll all be safe.*

Those who were on foot began to run for joy. Nursing women held their babies tightly and began to sprint. Men hugged each other and yelled, "We made it!" Women danced, sang, and thanked God for bringing them to freedom. We hugged each other at the thought that we had finally made it to safety.

As we approached the Liberian checkpoint, we found ourselves immersed in a sea of humanity, surrounded by hundreds of hungry, scared, and tired Liberian refugees who waited in line for immigrations officers to register them and allow them to cross the Mano River Bridge into Sierra Leone.

Things were at a near standstill because an elderly immigrations officer, who did not seem to understand the danger, was taking his time processing the refugees. Panicking refugees screamed, "Hurry up, hurry up, the rebels are coming!" The massive crowd continued to swell as more of the fear-driven mob shouted, "Rebels are coming; we need to get across the bridge!"

Finally, I heard a female immigrations officer bark, "Get these people across the bridge!" The officer gave her a startled and questioning look. The woman looked at him sternly and, stressing each word, blasted, "I said get these people through the border—immediately!"

It was true—the rebels were coming, and would overtake the Liberian side of the border within several hours. We understood that anyone not across by then would be slaughtered. Governmental employees, such as border guards, would be prime targets. Realizing their own lives were in danger, the immigrations officers speeded up the registration process and we were soon driving across the Mano River Bridge.

With people filling in every square inch of the bridge, we could have crossed much faster on foot. We spent more time sitting still than driving, and a simple river crossing that would normally have taken us less than a minute took hours. Thousands of feet filled the roadway and bridge, hurriedly shuffling in one direction—away from the terror of rebel forces. Everything looked surreal. The water in the river calmly moved down stream toward its final destination, just as the sea of humanity moved toward theirs.

Once across the bridge and into Bo Waterside, Sierra Leone, we arrived at a second immigrations checkpoint where we awaited registration as refugees. The Sierra Leonean officials were just as slow as the Liberian officials had been, and it was near sundown by the time they finally admitted us into the country.

After being processed, the immigration officials ordered us to head to the Red Cross Registration and Medical Center situated just a few hundred feet from the checkpoint. The Red Cross Center stood out in stark contrast to its green, forest surroundings. When we saw the bright white, cement-block walls and the large red cross, we felt we had reached the gates of Heaven. Inside, the medical staff offered us hope and healing to mend our broken spirits and bodies.

The staff directed us to the UNHCR (United Nations High Commissioner for Refugees) offices, which had been set up soon after the onset of civil war. UNHCR personnel gave each of us humanitarian supplies such as tarpaulins, blankets, toiletries, and bottled water.

After having replenished our supplies, we piled back into the truck and continued down the road a few minutes more to a nearby town named Malema.

CHAPTER 8

No President, No Capital

Recent rainstorms made the road to Malema difficult for driving. Red mud, ridged and rippled, covered the road and we were jolted, forward and back, up and down, as the truck's tires jounced in and out of potholes of varying depth. Drenched refugees trudged along the narrow, tree-lined road, partially protected from the sun by huge branches that hung dripping overhead. Monkeys chattered from the dark branches above while birds chirped and sang as they flitted from limb to limb. Striped ground squirrels darted in front of us, avoiding the puddles, and seemed oblivious to our approaching vehicle. Were it not for the rebels at our heels we would have found this scene one of idyllic charm.

We arrived to find that many Liberians had already settled in this predominately Muslim town. Malema was normally home to around 3,000 people; it and other surrounding villages had since swollen to over 20,000. Thankfully, the town chiefs had given their consent for refugees to remain. Many kind Malema residents opened their homes, allowing us to stay in extra rooms; others gave permission to build mud huts on their land.

Uncle Nyoun knew many people in Malema, including the chief of the village, and he was confident he could find our family a place to lodge. As he parked the truck, we were surprised by an excited group that quickly surrounded us, chanting, "Louise, Louise!" Some of my cousins, whom I had not seen since I left village life in Grand Gedeh, left Liberia a few months earlier at the start of the civil war and recognized me. They came running over to the truck. They knew I had moved to Monrovia and thought I might not have survived. Overjoyed at seeing each other, we hugged. I was told heart-wrenching stories of friends and family who were not so fortunate and were known to have been killed in the early weeks of the uprising.

My uncle promptly secured a place for us, knowing we would be in Malema until the rebel crisis was over. We spent the afternoon settling in and getting to know our new surroundings.

The next morning, we awoke to the jubilant sounds of children running and laughing, and the morning birds welcoming the day. For the moment, life seemed normal and, in a short time, we found ourselves feeling deeply connected to this small community.

Three days after our arrival, I ran into a nephew of mine named Richard. Richard was the son of one of my older sisters, and I knew him from Grand Gedeh. After moving to Monrovia, I had learned from my cousin Amos that Richard was living there, too; before the war broke out, we had met at his place of employment. He had escaped the capital at about the same time I did, arriving in Malema with his wife, Edith, and Gmaa, his young niece. Gmaa's parents, who were poor farmers in Grand Gedeh, had sent her to live with Richard so she could receive a good education, much as my father had done for me.

Gmaa was a very sweet little girl who had beautiful, thick, jet-black hair. During the months we were together, I grew to love her. I saw myself in her, and she seemed to see her mother in me as she followed me around like a little lamb. During play times I helped keep an eye on her.

With over five times more refugees than local residents, the religious leader of the village (the *Imam*) generously allowed the Malema Community Center, which had previously been dedicated to town meetings, Islamic education, and religious gatherings, to also be used for Christian purposes. We held church services there on Sundays, choir rehearsals on Saturdays, and prayer meetings on Friday evenings.

During one church service, a voice that resonated richly through the room enchanted me. It seemed to glide along the aisles and between the seats as a bird would on the breeze, and I searched for the owner of the voice. There he was, a very tall man, looking toward Heaven while singing, "His Eyes Are On the Sparrow," a song I knew very well. He sang all the verses, and as his voice faded away on the last note, I thought, *A man who has a voice like that must be a man who really knows and loves God.* The service was over and I left feeling refreshed and filled with joy.

In the evenings, we ate our meals together as one large community and enjoyed cultural drumming and dancing. These daily encounters created a sense of normalcy for us. I made various acquaintances and met Asata, the sister to the man with the beautiful voice. I became fast friends with the Imam's daughter, Abimatu. She was studying the Koran and spoke English quite well. We spent hours discussing the similarities and differences of our faiths.

Being just across the border from Liberia, we all realized that the rebels could attack us at any time, day or night. Abimatu was scared, and asked me how we as Christians kept our faith so strong. I said, "Abimatu, life hasn't been easy for me, but even in the rough times, the sad times, and the lonely and fearful times, God has been with me. He has never left me. He doesn't always take us out of trouble, but He does go through the trouble with us."

One day, I encountered a group of Armed Forces of Liberia (AFL) soldiers dressed in civilian clothing. They talked about how National Patriotic Front of Liberia (NPFL) rebel forces had swarmed into Monrovia and taken over the capital. In spite of their putting up a valiant fight, the AFL soldiers were overpowered and they retreated to avoid inevitable death.

As they spoke of their fallen comrades, I heard them mention my cousin Amos' name, saying he had been killed while defending the presidential palace. I forced my fist against my teeth to hold back cries of anguish as my mind flashed on his smiling face, his encouraging eyes, and his delightful laugh.

I grieved for weeks, knowing I would never see him again. During those dark days I thought of the good times we had shared. He was a faithful cousin and friend to an innocent little village girl who struggled as a servant; the one bright and shining star I had in my life was gone. As I mourned for Amos I thought, *Oh, Lord, how I will miss him.*

The man who sang so splendidly at church was much older than I was, but a friendship had blossomed between us and I had grown to consider him as close as a brother. I so grieved for the loss of Amos that I could not bear the pain alone. I ran to my friend who comforted me the best he could. He soothed my sadness and, even though I knew he had previously committed himself to another woman, I was captivated and, regrettably, we found ourselves swept into an intimate moment.

On September 9, 1990, two months after the rebels had swarmed into Monrovia and taken over the capital, Prince Y. Johnson, the leader of the Independent National Patriotic Front of Liberia (INPFL), a break-away faction of the NPFL, captured Liberian President Samuel Doe. Having no mercy for Doe, Johnson and his men interrogated, tortured, and brutally killed the president—all the while videotaping the grue-some details. They made their videotape public to prove Doe was dead. Doe's blood-curdling screams and the repugnant images shocked the entire world.

Street battles erupted; remnants of the Armed Forces of Liberia who were still loyal to the slain president fought fiercely against the rebel forces. A correspondent in Monrovia for the British Broadcasting Corporation reported hearing Government soldiers shout, "No presi-dent, no capital!" and "No Doe, no Liberia!" In an apparent effort at leaving nothing behind for their enemies, they drenched homes and stores with gasoline and set them ablaze.

Many civilians were caught in the crossfire. Their blood flowed into the gutters; their bodies lay rotting in the streets. The Island Clinic, Monrovia's only working hospital, reported that malaria and gunshot wounds had become the two leading causes of death.

Total chaos and destruction had engulfed the nation; no more law and no more order. Liberia had rapidly become a land where "might makes right;" ransacking, hijacking, raping, and killing defined its new way of life.

Because Samuel Doe had been a member of the native ethnic Krahn tribe, all across Liberia, and especially in Monrovia, Krahn tribe members became prime targets for the rebels. Unfortunately, the violence being dealt out in Liberia soon spread into neighboring countries like Sierra Leone, where Krahns, Mandingos, and government officials were hunted down—and when found, were gunned down or hacked to death. Mock trials were held in deep forests, on street corners, in beer drinking stalls, and on beachfronts. Some people were tried in their own homes and executed on the spot.

Just a few months before, government-run TV and radio stations had assured us the Liberian army was on top of the situation and would soon quell the rebellion. With Samuel Doe dead, and the capital of Liberia in the hands of the rebels, it was clear that we would be refugees indefinitely.

Malema was about two hours walking distance from Bo Waterside, the border town where we had first visited the Red Cross Center and the UN offices. On Saturdays, Bo Waterside featured a large, outdoor market where vendors sold crafts, produce, and other goods; and we traveled there each weekend to barter for much-needed supplies. I occasionally rode with Uncle Nyoun in his truck as he aided Malema merchants by carrying their goods to the market; however, on most weekends, I chose to enjoy a good walk with my friends.

I looked forward to these outings on market days. The sights and sounds were overwhelming, yet invigorating. Vendors, with tables covered in merchandise, hollered for shoppers to stop and buy from them as they sat under umbrellas stuck in buckets to shade them from the fierce, noonday sun. They laid blankets neatly on the ground and placed baskets of herbs and produce on them. Live chickens clucked in cages, and freshly slaughtered goats hung upside down by their feet from makeshift awnings.

One Saturday at the market, I ran into former neighbors from Monrovia ELWA who had been there when the rebels invaded. Realizing no place in the city was safe, they had fled to Sierra Leone and planned to stay out of Liberia until law and order could be restored. They told me that a group of rebels, upon hearing Mrs. Smith had a Krahn girl living there, had raided her home and demanded that the "Krahn bitch" be produced immediately or she and her children would be killed. As they knocked her children around, showing they were serious, Mrs. Smith admitted I had lived there. She pleaded that I was only renting a room, and had left months before. They let her and her children live because other neighbors confirmed that I no longer lived there.

Not being satisfied with eliminating all of the Krahns and Mandingos they could get their hands on in Liberia, the rebels were intent on pursuing us across the border. To our surprise and horror, Sierra Leonean governmental security guards were allowing rebels to cross over from Liberia to sell their looted goods at the market. One could safely assume anything they sold had been stolen, and most of their goods had come off the bodies or out of the homes of those they had killed. I was repulsed at the thought of trading with murderers, or in any way aiding their cause.

Not long after I heard about what had happened to Mrs. Smith's family, I went to the market with my cousin Wacchen Anita Nyoun and several of our friends. We had brought along some of our Red Cross staple foods so we could barter for other necessities. I was bargaining with one of the vendors when Wacchen Anita came running over to me, grabbed my sleeve, and said, "Louise, you have to come see this beautiful dress I found! Hurry!" I completed my transaction and turned to follow Wacchen Anita. I was shocked to see her eyeing a yellow dress wrapped in clear plastic, held up by a rebel boy who was yelling, "Buy your own thing! Buy your own thing!"

He did not mind telling the truth, that he had stolen this item and everything else he was selling. I could not believe Wacchen Anita would consider trading with him. I certainly knew her father would not be happy if he found out.

I did not trust the boy, nor did I want to go near him; so I kept my distance until Wacchen Anita looked back and noticed I was not following her. She walked over to me and said, "It's okay, he's harmless, Louise. Just come and look at the dress, I need your opinion." I said, "You know he's a rebel. What are you thinking!?"

I reluctantly walked over and took a quick peek at the dress. I was careful not to look the boy in the eyes. She was right; the dress was beautiful. "Yes, the dress is lovely," I said. That is all it took. Wacchen Anita haggled with him, and he was happy with the trade. He tried to sell wedding bands to her also, but she turned away quickly. The thought of buying wedding bands offended her because the rebel had more than likely murdered the previous owners for them. Yet she refused to let herself think of how the boy had acquired the dress as she cradled it admiringly in her arms.

Many of the refugees tried to tell the Bo Waterside police and the Sierra Leonean guards that they were risking all our safety by allowing the rebels free access to the market. Their response was, "You have nothing to worry about. They're harmless. They're not here with guns. They only want to make trades, and that benefits everyone." This type of reasoning was purely insane. The police and guards knew the rebels were selling spoils of war.

During the two-hour walk back to Malema, Wacchen Anita kept eyeing her prized possession. She could hardly wait to get home to tear it from its wrapping and try it on. Once we got home, she hurried to her room and called me and the other girls to watch her unwrap the dress. Wacchen Anita carefully laid the package on her bed, tore open the plastic, lifted the dress to shake out the wrinkles, and instantly let out a blood-curdling scream as the dress sailed into the air.

We all screamed with her as we looked on in horror. The once cherished dress lay discarded on her bed; dried blood thickly encrusted the neck.

Wacchen Anita crumpled on the floor and sobbed violently. Not wanting anyone else to see it, I grabbed the dress, ran into the woods, and threw it into the bushes. The thought of market day was forever stained, just as the dress had been; the sight of the bloodied collar was burned into our minds. We were sick to our stomachs and wounded in spirit; we vowed never to trade with rebels again.

I had far greater worries than the dress I had just discarded in the woods. I placed my hand on my abdomen. Although I was not showing yet, I was pregnant at age eighteen and decidedly rueful over bringing a new life into this world. My nerves were close to unraveling. Motherhood before marriage, and in this environment, was not something I could be pleased over; so I had not told a soul, neither friends nor family, of the trouble I was facing. I knew the time was coming when I would have to share my secret with my uncle and the thought tormented me.

Visions of the blood-stained dress recaptured my thoughts and my mind turned to a few months ago at the Christmas Eve dinner at Mrs. Smith's home, when we heard on the radio that rebel forces had entered Liberia and were heading toward Monrovia. Since that time I had learned that on December 24, 1989, a band of Libyan-trained rebels led by Charles G. Taylor, Samuel Doe's former procurement chief, invaded Liberia from the Ivory Coast. The group called themselves the National Patriotic Front of Liberia (NPFL). By Christmas afternoon, Taylor had announced to the world on BBC Radio that his forces had entered the country to overthrow what he called, "the corrupt and dictatorial regime" of President Samuel K. Doe.

Many politicians and Liberian citizens hailed the rebels' actions, because they promised milk and honey for the suffering people of

Liberia and assured them that the evil visited upon them by President Doe was going to end. What resulted, however, was a horrible reign of terror over the peaceful inhabitants of the country.

One of the most disturbing aspects of the conflict was how Charles Taylor's NPFL recruited children. Some of them were so small that the guns they carried were bigger than they were. The NPFL drugged them, trained them in killing techniques, and sent them into the battlefield where they took on names such as Babykiller, Castrator, and Ballcrusher. Adult rebels who marched the children into battle, fed them cocktails of amphetamines, cocaine, and gunpowder daily. The drugs helped ensure they could maim and murder without any feelings, turning them into killing machines.

To make matters worse, Charles Taylor also trained and supplied a Sierra Leone-focused rebel group known as the Revolutionary United Front (RUF) as a means of destabilizing the country. Corporal Foday Sankoh, a man who, like Taylor, had trained in insurgency warfare in Libya, led the RUF rebels. At one point, the RUF included up to 23,000 children, many of whom were made to murder their own parents.

The RUF forces, which had been in earlier skirmishes with UN forces in Sierra Leone, sought refuge in Liberia. They were simply biding their time as their ranks swelled with Liberian mercenaries who shared with them their tradition of raping and maiming civilians as a military tactic.

Some of these same rebels began crossing the Mano River in canoes, successfully passing through two checkpoints. When the soldiers had said, "They only want to make trades, and that benefits everyone," they were speaking of the benefits of trading rice and other food items for the diamonds, cigarettes, and alcohol the rebels carried.

Refugees noticed the regular exchanges between the soldiers and the rebels, and warned them they were playing with fire and were putting us all at risk. The soldiers insisted that these innocent-looking children were harmless, and we had nothing over which to worry.

At one point, when a group of young Malema boys organized a

soccer team that included Sierra Leonean soldiers, the soldiers insisted that they allow rebel boys to participate. When the teams formed, rebel boys were allowed to dress in soccer uniforms alongside local boys.

When my uncle saw this, he raged at the rebel boys, "We know you are only playing to take advantage of us, and you are really here to kill us." When they pretended to be friends with their fellow soccer players my uncle approached the soldiers and said, "We don't want our young people playing with rebels. They cannot be trusted!" The soldiers, who had developed a loose and friendly relationship with the rebel boys by smoking and drinking with them, scoffed at Uncle Nyoun.

Other refugees also warned, saying, "What you're doing is not good. Rebel boys will strike without warning. They may seem friendly now, but they will cut our throats! In broad daylight, or at night, it won't matter. One day, they will come and kill all of us." All our warnings went unheeded.

CHAPTER 9

Unleashed Horror

Rumors of a possible RUF rebel invasion of Sierra Leone began circulating in early March 1991. If true, Malema would be one of the first towns invaded as the flux of RUF rebels from Liberia surged into Sierra Leone.

One Sunday, near the end of March, the rebel boys began to complain to the soldiers that they were not receiving sufficient goods in exchange for the loot they were bringing in, and they accused the soldiers of cheating them. After the rebels complained to the border commander, they delivered a hand-scribbled, barely legible letter to the soldiers, "We are coming for you and our diamonds. Your heads will roll. Watch for us. We are coming back soon." Most of the soldiers were Muslims, and a few ran to tell the Imam of the rebel threat. He immediately called for a meeting of the elders.

The staggering news of the likely invasion quickly spread all over town. A breathless local resident suddenly interrupted our church meeting by running in and shouting, "The rebels are coming. They plan to kill us all." This brought us to our knees and we prayed for God's almighty protection.

Many of the villagers found the news hard to believe and tried to convince us that the checkpoints were secure. We countered, "The soldiers allowed themselves to be bribed and they let the rebel boys sell in the market and play in soccer games on our field. The rebels roamed free among us, and they know who we are and where we live. That was their plan all along."

We should have left Malema that very day. However, we had been there for over nine months and were lulled into complacency by the encouragement of those assuring us the Sierra Leonean soldiers would easily fight back any rebel invasion. What's more, where would we go? How would we get food, water, and other essential supplies that were already available to us in Malema?

I was still only in my first trimester, but I grew so frightened one evening that I told my secret to Asata. She looked at me in despair, "Oh, Louise. There's so much you don't know about my brother." As my heart fell, I asked, "What do you mean?" She spoke after a pause, saying, "He is an angry man and can suddenly lose his temper. He has a violent nature, and beat our mother and the girlfriend he is living with." I was shocked. Asata continued to enlighten me regarding her brother's issues. Heartbroken, I broke into sobs, fearing what lay ahead.

In this state, I broke the news of my pregnancy to my uncle. He was very compassionate and encouraged me not to worry; he and his family would continue caring for me. His unmitigated love and compassion toward me was much more than I deserved. The Nyoun family blessed me beyond reason, and I thanked God for uniting us.

At 4:00 AM, on April 3, 1991, and while the father of my baby was away on business in the town of Bo, we were jolted from our sleep by loud reports coming from behind the house. At first, it sounded like heavy rain hitting the water retention drum, but turned out to be gunfire. As we ran out to see what was going on, we saw people scattering in all directions; a band of rebels ran behind and encircled them.

Children wielding AK-47s and teenagers dressed in party wigs, tattered wedding gowns, and rainbow-colored, feathered boas filled the town. A macabre scene had become our world—gruesomely horrifying, ghastly in appearance. These doped-up, dressed-up, messed-up rebels, performing their dance of death, believed their cross-dressing would both terrify their victims and confuse their enemies' bullets because they were assuming two identities at the same time; they also believed they were magically protected by their rebel tattoos and the voodoo talismans that hung about their necks.

The RUF rebels had quickly overrun and killed the Sierra Leonean soldiers; those we had been encouraged to believe would more than adequately protect us from an invasion. In a matter of minutes, rebels were marching around the town, shouting for everyone to get out of their houses.

Fearing we would be one of the first families to be attacked because of my uncle's outbursts on the soccer field, he yelled, "Everyone out now! Follow me and stay on the main road. Don't take the jungle paths; take the main road. Run, run, run!"

We ran as hard and as fast as we could, without looking back. Had we not obeyed his command and had, instead, tried to flee into the forest we would have been ambushed by the concealed rebels in the underbrush; mowed down by their gunfire—exactly as others who avoided the main road were.

We ran with a throng of other barefoot and scantily clad people who had made their way from Bo Waterside, the border town the rebels had attacked first. The people were exhausted, screaming and crying; some of them held dying loved ones. In a panic, I realized I had lost my uncle and his family. I was one of the hundreds of terrified refugees who were running for their lives in a storm of bullets.

We were all running in the direction of the next town, Zimmi, which was over two days away on foot. Before long, we found ourselves overrun by wild-eyed child rebels who had either caught up with the throng or jumped out of the bushes from the side of the road.

Those who did not have guns would slash at anyone who ran past them. They used knives, machetes, and any other instruments they had in their possession. It was clear that most of them were running purely on the drugs that pumped through their veins. Those who did have guns fired into the crowd with AK-47s and M-16s. People dropped all around me, and I found myself jumping over their heaped bodies; piles of the dead and dying littered the road. Screams, moans, and final utterances of pain filled the air, as did the sounds of the cheers, chortlings, and intimidating threats of the maniacal rebels.

A little while later, I caught up with a man who, while carrying a child on his back, was pushing his ailing mother in a wheelbarrow. His pregnant wife and four small children straggled along behind. Exhausted, his legs and arms were violently shaking; his strength was spent. His mother knew it, and she was insisting that he leave her behind. She begged him, "You must leave me. You will die with me if you don't." Shaking his head no, the man pushed forward. She screamed out in desperation, "Son, please—I love you. You must leave me. Save your wife and children. Don't let my grandbabies die!" He screamed back, "No, Ma, I can't leave you here!" His wife tugged at his arm; she knew her mother-in-law was right.

As the heartbroken family wailed, the son lovingly pushed the wheelbarrow under a shade tree on the side of the road. Tears gushed from his eyes as he held his mother's frail body. She tightly wrapped her arms around his neck. She was a Krahn mother, and blessed her son just as my mother had blessed me, "May your strength be used to save your family. May you live long to see your childrens' children." She urged him to go. He gathered his family and ran, but kept looking back toward his beloved mother until he could no longer see her.

The child rebels had become wild and ravenous creatures, fearful monsters. Putting their hands into the open cavities of those they had shot, they would smear the blood on their own faces and rub it through their matted hair.

Sounds of magazine rounds and screams from the injured and dying filled our world. I came upon a woman who had collapsed and fallen onto her side. She had gone into labor prematurely and given birth to a baby right there on the road. Both the baby and the mother were dead. The woman's horrified and frightened husband held onto his two-year-old son. He screamed for help, but no one could stop to assist him because rocket-propelled grenades (RPGs) had begun to explode all around us. Pathetically, he and his crying child ran for safety, having no idea where safety might be.

We did not want to run barefoot into the brush, but with RPGs shrieking past us, we had no other choice. Unseen branches yanked wads of hair from my head as RPGs screamed past, lighting up the forest. Trees split in two and fell across escaping refugees.

We darted under branches and behind trees and bushes. I burrowed down in the underbrush, lying flat on my stomach. Rebels, who had heard noises from the brush, pointed their rifles and shot in our direction. They did not care who they killed, and often killed their own comrades this way.

Still thinking someone was hiding in the brush, one rebel yelled out, "You little shits!" Another rebel tried a more persuasive tone, coaxing, "Safe zone! This place is safe for you. Come on out." A couple of young, naive children who had lost their parents in the scramble, headed out. Without so much as a pause, bloodthirsty rebels, grinning and snarling, slashed their throats.

I did not dare move or breathe, and kept my hands over my mouth to help ensure no screams would escape. The rest of us stayed hidden in the underbrush until we felt the rebels had left the area.

We soon stumbled into a band of child rebels, and I thought I had seen my last day alive. Many of the refugees called out, "Hello brother, hello sister," while others tried to bring a semblance of humanity to the situation by saying, "Hello there, Danny," or "It's good to see you, Becky." They did not know these children, but hoped calling out names would help them see us as humans, not animals ready for the slaughter.

The friendly greetings had the intended effect, and one of the rebels, covered in blood and grime, looked at our small band and said, "It's not safe for you here. Run for your lives. I don't want to kill you. I want to kill the soldiers." Not hesitating, we ran, completely oblivious to our surroundings.

We ran, none of us thinking about the other dangers that might be lurking in the rainforest. Wild animals could kill us, but we were more concerned with the rebel soldiers who surely would.

Our small group of refugees traveled like this for the rest of the day, and into the night—watching for rebels at every turn. Wracked with fear and with my heart pounding so loudly in my chest that I was sure any rebels nearby could hear it, I made my way. We had soon amassed a large assemblage of men, women, and children who had also left the main road and were traveling through the safety of the forest. In the lead were four young brothers who seemed to know their way through the jungle terrain.

As we made our way, we tried to unburden ourselves by telling stories of the atrocities we had witnessed. I was distressed and sickened to hear that pregnant women had become sport for rebel boys. They placed bets on the sex of the unborn child while ripping the unborn baby from the mother's womb to find out which rebel had guessed correctly. They left the mother to die and tossed the baby to the side like refuse.

I also heard of how, in Bo Waterside, a group of rebels murdered a family by gleefully telling the parents they would see their children again in Heaven. They stripped and shot dead the parents in front of their children. I was hoping to hear that the children were set free or escaped, but was sickened to hear they were forcibly tied up in a large rice sack and thrown into a crocodile-infested river. Those who witnessed this horrible nightmare said the river ran red with the children's blood, and they could still hear the children's screams as they begged for help. Feeling deep sadness and pain, I moaned, "Oh, Africa, Africa!"

Unable to bear any more horror, we walked in silence for quite some time. Then, one young boy broke the silence by telling us about his favorite music, sports, and foods, and other trivial topics. The light-hearted conversation served as a temporary distraction from our desperate situation.

As the sun was coming up, we were thrilled to come upon a village. We were confident the kind villagers would share a little food and water to help us continue on our journey. Much to our horror, we found we had stumbled into an angry hornet's nest of rebels who swarmed out of the huts. They had thrown the bodies of the former villagers into piles and staked several heads on sticks as silent threats.

People continued to stream out of the bushes and into the clearing, unaware of the terror into which they were heading. Refugee children trembled, and women fainted. Some of us dropped to the ground, while others frantically ran back toward the protection of the forest. Machine gun fire mowed down many who ran. Rebels ordered those left standing and lying on the ground to stay still or be killed.

The rebels herded us as bullets kicked up dust around the feet of those who attempted to run. Mothers fell on top of their children to guard them from stray rounds. Our tormenters gleefully pranced about like young colts. They had spun a web and had entangled us. If we moved an inch, they would shoot us.

Wanting to single out and kill all Krahn and Mandingo people, they tried to herd us into groups based on our ethnicity. That task turned out to be impossible because no one wanted to step forward for shooting. Frustrated, a rebel woman took command and gathered all of the children into a group, pushing them away from their parents. Rebels beat down mothers who tried to keep their children by their sides.

The first little boy questioned was about four years old. The rebel woman held out her hand with a smile, asking him his name, where he lived, and where he and his family would go on vacation, knowing this information would reveal his ethnic tribe. He looked up with his big brown eyes, took her hand, and told her what she wanted to know. She said, "You're so cute. Your mother must really adore you."

The woman escorted him out of sight, and brought him back with a cookie in his hand. The child ran over to his mother. The rebel looked directly into his trembling mother's eyes and sweetly said, "Oh, that's your mother. Good, do you have any other family here with you?" The boy naively smiled and walked over to his grandmother and hugged her leg. "Good. Anyone else?" He looked back at his uncle and pointed.

"Are there any others?" The boy shook his head and answered, "No." He smiled longingly at his cookie.

The rebel woman nodded at a young man with matted hair, a blood-smeared face, and eyes that failed to display any semblance of humanity. He sauntered over, shrugged his machine gun off his shoulder, pointed toward the little boy and his family, and yelled, "You, and you, and you, and you ... over there." He pointed his rifle in the direction he wanted the family to go.

The mother pleaded and fell at the feet of the rebel soldier. She begged and held onto his boots. With disgust, he kicked her in the mouth, and her blood spurted and splattered on her son's face. The little boy screamed and looked up in shock as the cookie dropped from his fingers.

In an annoyed tone, the rebel said, "It's not me that kills you, it's your own child that kills you." He yelled again and pointed, "Move over here!" The little boy's uncle lifted up the mother from the ground, took the little boy by the hand, and walked them over to where the rebel had pointed.

Heartlessly, the rebel lifted his machine gun and let a barrage of bullets tear through the bodies of these four, innocent and helpless souls. They fell like stalks of wheat at one swing of the scythe.

Everyone in the crowd shook with terror and we began to scatter and run for cover. The rebels quickly shot their rifles into the air and yelled for all of us to get back to where we were. The rebel woman continued to hand out cookies to the children one by one, and her minions continued to mow down the wheat.

I broke out in feverish sweats and chills. My teeth became loose from their violent chattering. Fear emptied the bladder and bowels of some of the refugees standing near me.

The fearless rebels tormented the terrified crowd of refugees with their AK-47 rifles and sharp knives. Shoving their hands in our faces to show us their wooden voodoo rings they said, "These rings have special voodoo powers, and when they're near a member of the Krahn or Mandingo tribe they get hot and burn our skin!"

One rebel boy thrust his closed fist at unsuspecting people, screaming, "It's getting warmer!" Reaching me, he shouted, "Oh, oh, it's burning me!" as he opened his fist and frantically shook his hand in the air. He announced to the others, "Hey, I've got a firecracker over here!" He looked me straight in the eyes and said slowly and pointedly, "Today could be your lucky day." I begged for mercy as he laughed hysterically.

Another rebel boy boasted loudly, "Our voodoo magic and our voodoo spells protect us from bullets. We cannot be shot and killed because bullets bounce off us as if they were made of rubber, and bayonets break like twigs." He continued, "One time a soldier aimed his AK-47 at me and all the bullets that struck my body bounced off me and fell to the ground and did me no harm. That soldier wished he hadn't met up with me. Do you know what I did to him? I sliced him into a million pieces!" He picked up and twirled the good luck charm he had hanging on his necklace and said, "This is his trigger finger."

At one point, the rebel boy with the trigger finger necklace playfully skipped over to where twin, teenaged girls were holding each other. The boy danced around the two girls as they trembled in fear and tried to turn away from him and his taunting.

"My finger is burning hot and you two are going to die." He was sure they were Mandingo girls because of their ebony skin. The twins were dragged behind the hut. Their screams for mercy pierced our hearts for we knew there was no one to rescue them. When the rebels had run out of strength, they forced the girls to stand naked along the side of the road, and shot them down. Two delicate and beautiful, ebony girls were dead.

Another rebel danced his way through the crowd and stopped abruptly in front of the four young brothers I had been following down the trail earlier. As he shoved his voodoo ring in their faces he said, "My ring is getting hot again." He quickly pulled his hand away, shook it violently in the air, and said, "Ouch! I got a hot one over here."

Two other rebels came running over to check it out. They shoved their voodoo rings toward the boys and they all danced and joyfully proclaimed, "Oh yeah, they're hot for sure!"

I had become faint and thought I would vomit. One of the rebel boys who came over tilted his head from side to side as if noticing something about the brothers. His eyes narrowed and he looked straight into the oldest boy's eyes and growled, "Don't I know you?"

The boy froze with fear and could not respond. The rebel reached out his hand with the ring and joyfully chanted, "Yes, yes, yes. You are a Krahn. A dirty rotten Krahn dog. My ring never lies. I recognize you from school." He turned and looked at the other three boys and said with a wicked smile, "What do we have here? Did we hit the jackpot? Are these your brothers?" The youngest of the four cried; he had soiled his pants. I had followed this family through the forest and we had shared our joys, hopes, and fears with each other. I shook violently as they were forcibly ushered out of the group.

The oldest boy, shot in the head, collapsed to the ground. The youngest ran to his side and was blasted with bullets. The other two fell under waves of gunfire. That wretched scene was committed to my memory as if branded there by a hot iron.

A rebel yelled, "Give me six feet," as he motioned for the crowd to move back. He felt six feet would give him ample clearance and, before I could blink my eyes, I saw bullets rip through the entire family he had ousted from the throng.

One of the rebel executioners took out a sharp machete and with one sweeping blow beheaded the father. Grabbing the head by the hair, he brought it over to me and told me to hold it and dance with it in celebration. When I refused, he hammered me with his fists until I passed out.

While I lay on the ground in a heap I dreamed of my mother— when she had blessed me with rice and water, saying, "May your life be full. May success follow you. May you live very long to see every strand of hair on your head be as white as these grains of rice, and may many years lie before you. Blessings will flow from above, and you will be strong and great."

A rifle fired near my head, and the resulting loud ringing in my ears jolted me back to consciousness. I gasped, realizing I was again in hell. I wanted to yell out, "We are all of the same race—the human race," but I bit my tongue, thinking, *Dear Lord, how can anyone commit such atrocities?* Why are they so intent on killing us, and how can they derive such pleasure from it? As I got to my feet, I saw a multitude still standing. The dead had been dragged and dumped on the growing pile of human carnage. The stack of bodies resembled a grotesque and twisted, rag-doll sculpture.

The rebels told one crippled old man he could go. He did not move at first because he was not sure he had heard right. A rebel woman yelled in his ear, "I said, go!" The old man ran and stumbled down the path. He had only run a few yards when the same rebel woman lifted her rifle, took aim, and shot him in the back. His body tumbled onto the pile. She turned toward her rebel comrade and gave him a high five.

The rebel boy with the wooden ring, the one who had killed the four brothers, came bounding toward me. I quickly looked down at my feet hoping he would pass me by. I could smell his rotten breath as he belched in my face and snarled, "What's your name?" I did not want to answer because my name would give me away. "You're on reconnaissance," he accused. I nearly passed out when the butt of his AK-47 slammed into my jaw. The force drove me to the ground. Blood spurted and dripped from my mouth. I reached up and found my lips split; my jaw was hanging to the side, and my teeth had been broken and shattered.

I screamed in anguish. My pain fueled his fury, and he violently kicked me in the face and sides, yelling, "Get up, bitch! What's your name?" I mumbled through the blood, "My name is Louise Géesedeh."

He immediately recognized Géesedeh as a Krahn name. He laughed and called for his rebel buddies to come see the Krahn bitch he had just caught. With a leering smile, he leaned over me and cursed with his vile breath, "Bitch, this is your lucky day."

He dragged me by my hair, his buddies helped by kicking and shoving me, until they had me pinned down behind a tree. Once they had ripped my clothes from me and I was completely naked, five vile and ferocious rebel beasts raped me. Their breath reeked of decaying gums and the weight of their rancid bodies crushed me.

There was not a thread of humanity in the hearts or minds of my torturers. They were utterly depraved and given over to their perversions. I was completely ravaged, destroyed within and without—broken.

In the end, viciously and brutally, they had murdered all of the Krahns in the group, but me. They ordered me to tell all other Krahns that what I had witnessed and experienced was the exact fate awaiting them; but for them, there would be no mercy.

I got up and gathered what was left of my clothes. Like a zombie, I stumbled and dragged myself along the well-worn footpath that wound through the forest, into the unknown.

A short way down the path, a young Sierra Leonean woman saw me and came out of the bushes to help me. It turned out that she was a woman I had exchanged smiles with earlier in the day who had somehow taken another path through the jungle. She touched my shoulder and comforted me, saying, "You're going to be all right." I broke down in uncontrollable sobs and crumpled to the ground. She said, "You're going to live."

Soon others came to my aide, gathered me into their arms, and carried me to a spot where they could attend to my crushed body. They gently laid me down and a woman tore a small corner from her *lappa* to help bind my wounds. Another woman used drinking water combined with salt to help clean my wounds and stop the bleeding.

One woman wandered off into the woods looking for healing leaves that she had learned about as a child. Returning with a handful, she knelt down next to me and crushed the leaves in her palm. She said, "These leaves help prevent infections and reduce pain." She leaned toward me kindly, "This will help you." She tenderly put the remedy on the wounds in my mouth and I immediately felt relief from the pain.

She helped me up and let me lean on her. We could not rest any longer, for we heard the loud blasts of explosions behind us. For the next three hours we kept walking until we came to rest at an abandoned, five-hut village. Those who had helped me along the way, now carefully placed me under the shade of a tree.

I leaned my crippled body against the trunk, and slipped into another more peaceful world—halfway in and out of consciousness—as my helpers brought wet rags and wiped my face. Their gentleness toward me helped soothe some of the pain that wracked my body and my mind. After a brief rest in the little village, we got back on the path and continued our long walk to Zimmi.

For some time, we were able to travel in the semi-cloaking cover of the forest; however, since many refugees had fled into the woods, the rebels set the forest on fire, forcing us back onto the nakedness of the main road, where the noonday sun exposed us to the additional danger of dehydration and heat stroke.

After all that I had witnessed over the past twenty-four hours, I had no doubt my uncle as well as his family had been killed, and I thought for certain I would never see them again.

CHAPTER 10

Death March

We ran out of the woods, away from the fire and onto the main road, just in time to see hundreds of other refugees scattering to the sides of the road as Red Cross, UNHCR, and UNICEF vehicles honked and drove through the crowd.

It would have been wonderful if they had come along to aid us; however, they were also trying to escape the terror that lay behind us. Their worried faces and somber voices disclosed their concerns. Some of the relief volunteers leaned from the windows, crying out, "Follow us. Don't give up. We will meet you at the next town. Keep going."

Every vehicle was crammed to capacity, leaving no room to give a much-needed ride to any of the refugees. I could tell by their eyes that they were very afraid for us and wished they could help in some way. The best they could do was head to the next town, set up a station, and wait for us to arrive on foot.

By that time, we had all been on the run and without sleep for two days. The long, hot journey was taking its toll, and our numbers were slowly diminishing. We had no food, no water, and no energy. Those who could, slowly marched onward with blistered and bleeding feet. Many, however, expired under the strain or simply had neither strength nor motivation to go on and sat down to die.

In hot, humid, tropical climates, a healthy person can expire in less than three days without water. Walking in the open sun can cut that time in half. The survival time for children and the elderly is even less. Those remaining had survived this long by drinking small amounts of water found in the dirty creeks and puddles along the way.

My lips were cracked and my tongue cleaved to the roof of my mouth. My sinuses and throat were so raw that I could feel the air scrape its way down my esophagus and into my lungs. I did not have enough saliva to speak and I avoided breathing through my mouth. Calling out to God in silent prayer was the only thing that quieted my pain and the anguish of my incredible thirst.

In about an hour, the town of Zimmi was in sight and we slowly shuffled on as I thought to myself, *You're almost there. Just one more step. You're almost there. Just one more step.*

Much to our disappointment and adding to our desperation, we arrived just in time to see the Red Cross volunteers and aid workers from other relief agencies packing and getting ready to leave. Everyone else in town had already evacuated because of the danger posed by the advancing rebels. What we had thought would be a relief station was turning into a ghost town.

Those who had enough money to pay for transportation snatched up the few seats available on commercial vehicles that were there from nearby towns. The rest of us had little hope of survival, as we had to fend for ourselves.

I heard hundreds of voices screaming, wailing, and crying out for mercy. "We have no food. We have no water. We are dying. We can't keep going. Please! Help us! Take our children!"

The relief agency personnel looked at us with sadness as they hung their heads, shaking them in despair. They knew that a large number of the hundreds of fleeing refugees they were leaving behind would die on the nearly twenty-mile journey to Potoru, the next closest town. As the crowd of refugees cried out, some of the same vehicles we had seen on the road earlier left us in their dismal dust once more.

I prayed, *Oh God, please carry us, please help us.* Finding water, food, and shelter had become a chimerical dream, an elusive hope. Many were too dehydrated and weak to carry on, and Zimmi became their final stop.

A woman sitting on the ground with her hands and arms stretched toward the sky, moaned pleadingly, and cried uncontrollably. She had come from Bo Waterside, the town where we used to shop in the local market. Just before the rebels arrived, she had stepped out to use the outside bathroom. She rushed back when she heard the gunfire and found her home riddled with bullets and her husband and children dead. Now, she cried hysterically, "Look at me! I don't have children no more—what do I have to live for?" Although I had no words to comfort her, I leaned over, put my arms around her, and cradled her. Other refugees came to her aid and we were able to get her on her feet and moving again.

Realizing we could not survive any longer in the hot sun, many of us decided to return to the shelter of the forest to continue our journey. I thought, *Which is worse, venomous snakes and underbrush ripping the already blistered and oozing sores on our feet, or being sandwiched between an unforgiving orb of fire overhead and the stovetop-surfaced road?*

We walked all day with no food or water other than the little moisture and fiber we could obtain from the leaves of unknown plants. Starvation and dehydration hounded us and slowed our pace so much that we were afraid the advancing rebels would overtake us.

We were still hundreds strong when, by mid-afternoon, we reached the Moa River, where, for the first time on our grueling journey, we were able to drink all the fresh water we wanted. We still had no food, but were no longer in danger of perishing from dehydration.

God had blessed us and we had reached the river at one of the few points where a ferry service operated, transporting cars and people across the river.

Sierra Leonean soldiers, aware of the fact that rebels were closing in, had been assigned to guard the ferry, a large wooden barge capable of carrying up to a hundred people and a few automobiles at the same time across the river. The barge was pulled by hand via rope lines that stretched across the wide expanse of water.

A group of about ten strong men, positioned on each side of the river, pulled the barge across. After loading the ferry to capacity, it was ready to move; a conductor blew into a long bamboo horn to signal the men on the other side of the river to begin pulling. As they pulled, they chanted to create a strong and steady rhythm.

Aware of the danger approaching, and with hundreds of refugees' lives in the balance, the team managing the ferry decided to overload the barge each trip so they could get as many people across the rapidly flowing river as possible. In addition, they normally closed the barge at around 5:30 PM, today would be no exception because the men pulling the barge across would be worn out and those pulling the barge to the east side of the river would be facing the same dangers as the refugees if they waited until the rebels caught up with us.

With more cars and people on board than they had ever allowed, they pulled the barge across the river as quickly as possible. Even after several trips and having transporting hundreds of people across the river, hundreds more remained on the eastern shore, pleading to get across before the rebels arrived. It was nearly 5:30 PM, however, and the operators knew they could only pull the barge across one more time.

Worried I might not be able to cross the river that evening, I tried to jump aboard the last barge to cross as it pulled away from the shore. Others jumped as well and made it onto the boat. In my weakened condition, I fell short. Still trying to grasp at the vessel, a man standing on the bank pulled me from the water. As he pulled me back to shore, he warned me, "Please, don't go on that thing, it is way too overloaded. It's a disaster waiting to happen."

He was right. They had overloaded the barge more than ever for this last, desperate load. There were over a hundred people on board, packed inside of, on top of, and around a number of cars and buses. As the ferry reached the middle of the fast-moving river, it started to take on water. The men on the western shore continued their pulling and chanting.

Moments later, we heard a horrifically loud screech and pop as the rope line snapped, leaving the barge at the mercy of the river. Within seconds, the overloaded barge tilted on its side and dumped its precious cargo into the treacherous current. All of the vehicles plunged to the bottom with their trapped occupants inside. Those not in vehicles screamed out for their loved ones, as the strong current swept them down river. We looked on in wretched horror as over one hundred people perished. We could do nothing for them.

I will never forget how that man grabbed me, holding me back from my attempt to climb onboard the doomed ferry. He was like an angel of God, sent to save me from a watery grave.

As the sun began to set, we heard machine gun fire in the distance; our stomachs knotted and heaved. The owners of the few small canoes left on the eastern shore hastily offered rides to as many refugees as they could carry, and I was fortunate to be asked on board. After having just witnessed a multitude perishing in the raging waters, the thought of crossing the massive expanse in a small canoe terrified me; yet staying to face the rebels would mean certain death.

As two strong men paddled the boat out into the powerful current, I kept my eyes on the shore, praying that advancing rebels would not reach the riverside and pick us off with their rifles. When we reached the middle of the river the canoe rocked and rolled from side to side. I bent forward, held onto my knees, and squeezed them tightly, as if that would keep me from falling out. The horror of those who had just died flashed into my mind, and I wondered, *Will our lives be required as well?* The sounds of approaching gunfire caused the men to paddle even faster and my spirit urged us onward. When the canoe finally reached the shore, we hastily struggled out and began running. I ridiculed myself for thinking I had ever been mistreated or had ever experienced exhaustion as a servant girl back in Monrovia.

Those days were from another life, one very long ago. I had started out as a little village girl and spent a large portion of my life as a servant girl. I had become a tired, hungry, refugee girl. As I picked up the pace, I thought, *Will I ever be a free girl?*

I looked up and found I was running beside the kind woman who helped me after the rebels had beaten and abused me. I thanked God for her compassion and companionship. We ran and walked non-stop all night long and throughout the next day. We reached the next town twenty-four hours after crossing the Moa River, having had no sleep, no food, and no water. I was delirious, running on nothing but fright and nervous energy.

We discovered after arriving at Potoru that the local residents and foreign aid workers had fled, heading to Gondama, the next town beyond. That we had arrived at yet another ghost town was almost beyond bearing. How could we go on with neither food nor adequate water? Learning that reaching Gondama would require another three days on foot crushed me.

Even though we kept one step ahead of the advancing rebels, we remained one overwhelmingly large step behind the life-giving aid we so desperately needed. Much to our relief, some local villagers who had worked alongside the foreign aid workers decided to risk their own lives and stay behind to provide us with aid. In addition, the Red Cross medical staff had left behind a couple of briefcases of critical medical supplies such as rubbing alcohol, bandages, and pain relievers.

The locals' courageous acts of selflessness deeply touched our hearts as they compassionately tended to our wounds and supplied us with life-giving water and food they had prepared. Hundreds of worn, battered, and near-dead refugees cried out, "Thank you, so much. Bless you. May God give you long life." They hugged us, cried with us, and became one with us—as if they were our own mothers, fathers, brothers, and sisters.

The villagers who had listened to their hearts and put their own lives in jeopardy to care for those less fortunate amazed me. At the same time, I was deeply aware of the sharp contrast playing out on the dusty roads and deep woods of western Africa. The RUF and NPFL rebels showed how low humankind could stoop when it abandons all morality. To satisfy some inner urge, these depraved and lawless men, women, and children were hunting us down. Much worse than animals that hunt for food, they seemed deranged and rabid; their aim was to destroy us.

Even though the rebels' relentless march of destruction was sure to overtake us if we did not begin the three-day journey to Gondama soon, we had no choice but to stop for food and rest before attempting the trip. A kind villager served me some food on a makeshift plate fashioned out of banana leaves, saying the idea for the "plate" had come from one of the refugees.

As I shuffled along with my food, looking for a place to sit down in the crowd, I anguished over the thousands of faces surrounding me. Families that had managed to stay together huddled closely, eating from their banana leaves. I saw one such family sitting off to the side under the shade of a tree. The fear-worn father was dressed in nothing but a pair of tattered briefs, and the deep lines etched into his children's faces betrayed the tragedies they had witnessed and endured.

Still in a daze from lack of food, water, and sleep, I was drawn to them. I thought I might be able to sit with them and not have to eat alone. I walked a little closer and stood at their feet. The man looked up slowly and, when our eyes met, I gasped, crying, "Uncle Nyoun?!"

He did not recognize me because of my rifle-injured, badly disfigured face. "It's me—Louise." My uncle and his family immediately stopped eating, jumping up to hug me. We cried together as we held onto each other. I heard my uncle say, "Louise, Louise! We thought you were dead." We wept long and hard, yet shed few tears because of the severe dehydration.

I was overjoyed at God's grace in keeping me, as well as my unborn child, alive and at the miracle of being reunited with my uncle and his family. We did not have much, but at least we had each other—and we promised not to be separated again. It was difficult for me to see with my severely swollen and infected face; I would need to depend on my uncle and family to keep me within their sight.

In addition, the pain from my face and jaw injuries made it very difficult for me to eat and drink. I was unable to chew, and swallowing was nearly impossible. The best I could do was to soften my food with water, and mull it around in my mouth until I managed to swallow it, bit by bit. Not being able to hold back my excitement over finding my family, I managed a bit of lighter conversation with the children who, when I commented that we were eating on unusual plates, were quite pleased to tell me it had been their father's idea.

We had barely finished our food when word began to circulate that the rebels were approaching. Thousands of refugees frantically dropped their banana leaf plates and rushed back onto the road toward Gondama. There were so many of us on the road that the best we could accomplish was a fast shuffle as we hurried along, shoulder to shoulder, pushing against those in front of us.

In this fashion, we faced a three-day journey to Gondama, without provisions of any kind. I thought, *How can any of us possibly travel that far and live for three more days in this condition, in these elements, without provisions?*

As the days dragged on, the story repeated itself. More and more refugees, especially the infirm and the elderly, succumbed to dehydration and exhaustion, falling down at the side of the road to die. Babies continued to die in their mothers' arms, causing the mothers to give up in despair, deciding that the journey and living to see another day was beyond bearing; and their efforts ceased.

By the third day, fly-covered carcasses and dying refugees littered the road, and the smell is one I will never forget. I continued my silent chant: *One more step to safety, just one more step, just one more step.*

At the end of our three-day journey, we finally reached Gondama, where we again hoped to find food, water, medical treatment, and much-needed rest. As we approached the town we could hear Sierra Leonean soldiers shouting, "Men and boys, step out of line," as the mass of humanity split down the middle. They directed the men and boys to the left, and women and girls to the right.

My uncle was herded into formation and a rugged-looking soldier with an AK-47 rifle shouted, "Everyone, drop your clothes. Everything off! Do it!" He pointed to the men's group, and then swung around and pointed to the women. The tone of his voice and the stern look on his face made it clear he was deadly serious.

We were too weak and stunned to argue. As we began to take off our ragged clothing, an open truck containing naked captives held at gunpoint slowly drove through our broken assemblage. Huddled in the back of the truck, terrified prisoners were crying imploringly, begging for their lives.

This made no sense at all and we looked at each other's confused faces. We had come to Gondama expecting critically needed aid; instead, we were screamed at, stripped naked, and left in fear of what was coming. Allied forces were publicly humiliating battered and beaten people who had little hope for their next breath.

Apprehensive over what the soldiers might do to me, I kept my eyes focused on the ground, hazarding only slight glances out of the corner of my swollen eyes. As we all stood there naked, with gaunt faces and bodies reduced to skin hanging on bones, it should have been immediately obvious that we were refugees, not rebels, and that we posed no risk to the Sierra Leonean soldiers.

For unbearable hours, the ill-tempered soldiers examined our emaciated bodies, checking us for marks, tattoos, or other telltale signs—such as impressions left on legs by military boots—that would indicate we were actually rebels masquerading as refugees. They spent the majority of the time examining the males, with a special focus on young boys. All the while, mothers and fathers were pleading with the soldiers to leave their young sons alone. It was an appalling scene.

The soldiers violently yanked one boy off his feet and threw him into the back of the truck because he had made some small tattoos on his arms while playing with his friends at school. His panicked screams mixed with his mother's high-pitched wailings. They quickly beat her to the ground along with any other parents who tried to interfere.

This inhumane scene was played out repeatedly until the truck was full of helpless boys, falsely accused of being rebels. They reached out toward us, pleading for us to help them. As they begged, the soldiers in the truck hammered their outstretched arms and hands down. Their appeals of innocence rang in my ears.

Truckloads of the accused were taken to a local cemetery, told to get out of the truck and, when they ran, were leveled by machine gun fire. They had no trial, and received no mercy. We had fought so hard to make it this far only to find ourselves in a pit of wretchedness.

They were right to be cautious, because a few rebels had infiltrated groups of refugees, mercilessly killing Sierra Leonean soldiers. Unfortunately, they were overly cautious, killing an untold number of innocent refugee boys.

Once the pitiful dance with death was over, they allowed those of us who remained standing to pick up our clothes and put them back on. They directed us to the lawn of the Gondama Community Center, which the Red Cross had taken over.

Sierra Leonean nurses dressed in Red Cross uniforms hurried through the crowd of refugees in search of the worst of the wounded. When my uncle saw them, he yelled out, "Over here, over here!" A nurse headed in our direction. When she saw me she gasped, and promptly pulled me out of the crowd to receive immediate medical attention.

The swelling and infection had badly disfigured my face and I could see the fear in her eyes as she took me by the arm and guided me into the building. Once inside, they removed my scant and ragged clothing and washed the dried blood from my face and body. After the staff had cleaned and bandaged my wounds, they dressed me in a medical gown.

Soon, nurses and aides were hovering over me, asking a few routine

questions. One asked me if I was pregnant. A nurse promptly wiped an
alcohol swab on my hip and gave me a shot. Another nurse leaned over
my face and looked kindly into my eyes. She smiled at me and said,
"Don't worry; your baby is fine. You're going to be okay." She swabbed
my mouth with an anesthetic, numbing it so she could further assess
the damage without causing me additional pain.

My body did not feel like mine anymore; it was a beaten and brutalized shell. I had been violated in every possible way a person could be.
The shame I carried was unbearable, and the anger and hatred I felt for
those who had inflicted such pain on me was beyond expression. The
medical staff ordered venereal disease and HIV tests when they learned
of my rape and beating by the band of rebels several days earlier. When
the test results came back negative, I was happy to know I was disease-
free. So many women who suffered rape also suffered from resulting
life-threatening, sexually transmitted diseases.

For eight days, I lay on a Red Cross cot in a space partitioned by cur-
tains. Whenever I was lucky enough to drift off for a moment, every little
noise, even the quiet closing of a door, would jar me awake, causing my
heart to race. I was an exhausted, battered, and nervous wreck; restless,
filled with fear, and suffering from vivid dreams of what had happened.
As waves of pain hit me, the scenes would begin replaying in my head. I
was a captive audience with no way of escaping the memories.

My uncle and his family visited me often, filling me with their love
and compassion. Christian refugees would come every day to encourage,
sing with, and pray for the ill and injured. I gained strength from their
solid faith in a loving and all-powerful God. Sometimes they would
share stories about the power of forgiveness. At the time, I honestly did
not know how to forgive. My only thought was, *Why me, God?*

Many people came to the center in search of family members and
friends they had lost in the havoc. One morning, a woman who had
been coming to the center every day in search of her lost son, surveyed
a frail body she found lying beneath a clean white sheet. She cried out
so loudly that the medical staff came running to the bedside, fearing

someone had just lost a loved one. Instead they witnessed a mother and son reunited in an unyielding embrace.

The rebel forces continued their advance, and in the early afternoon of our eighth day in Gondama, UN and Red Cross officials announced mandatory evacuation. They told us to relocate to a place called Seminary, a suburb of the town of Bo, where a Christian college was located. They had set up a new camp there and believed the Sierra Leonean soldiers would be better able to protect us at that location.

Red Cross vehicles were called into action to transport the most severely ill and injured. I turned down the ride offered to me. There were around 20,000 refugees in Gondama and I could not bear the thought of losing my uncle and his family again. I preferred the risk of walking with my injuries to the risk of losing touch with my family.

The throng streamed onto the road for the five-hour march to Seminary. It was good to see the thousands of refugees saved from the brink of death had a chance at surviving this conflict. Although we were no longer starved and dehydrated, our clothing had worn out and we had to dress in Red Cross handouts, whether the garment was the right gender and size or not. We were a shabby group. My uncle ended up with nothing but a vastly undersized, women's, black bathing suit bottom that was so tight he waddled, wincing in pain with every step.

After transporting the ill and injured, the Red Cross sent vehicles out to pick up the infirm, elderly, mothers with young children, and any others who were struggling. Before sundown, we were all crowded onto the grounds of the college at Seminary. Earlier arrivals and those who still required medical attention had taken up any space available in the buildings. My uncle and some of the other refugees had tarps they could place on the ground on which to lay. Those who did not have tarps had to sleep on the bare grass and dirt.

Although officials had told us we would be safer at this location, and the Red Cross was still treating the sick and injured in their indoor

clinic, there was no food, no running water, no toilets, and no electricity. Over twenty thousand refugees fended for themselves. Hungry
and thirsty, we discovered that a few muddy creek beds were our only
source of water. Edible vegetation available in the surrounding area,
discarded food in garbage cans, and a little produce set aside by vendors
in the outdoor market in the town of Bo who took pity on us, were our
only sources of food.

Overall, we were a very resourceful group. For example, we used
empty cans we found in garbage dumps as cooking pots. In addition,
we would eat most anything to stay alive. I even saw whole families
eating unused toilet paper they had found, after soaking the paper first
for easy swallowing. They did this to prevent a serious condition of
starvation known as intestinal wall collapse.

In these wretched and unhealthy conditions, communicable diseases such as cholera, tuberculosis, and malaria became rampant. Then,
if starvation or disease did not kill us, venomous snakes and scorpions
gave it their best shot, especially at night. One dark and moonless night
a mother who was lying near us desperately screamed, "Oh God! My
baby has been bitten by a snake!" In an instant, nearly a hundred people
were on their feet, jumping up and down, and stomping the ground at
a snake they could not see.

Moments like these would force me to consider my own unborn
child, and wonder how I could possibly provide for a baby in an environment like this. As fears rose up in my chest, I comforted myself with
Uncle Nyoun's promise to take care of me.

The daily 6:00 PM and 9:00 PM rounds of the soldiers hunting
for more rebels reduced our numbers. They would command whole
groups of refugees, "Get up! Everyone get up. Stand up!" We would
stand stiff as boards as they shined flashlights in our faces. The soldiers
would call out several people, screaming, "I know you. You're a rebel,"
only to hear, "I'm innocent. No, please. I'm innocent. Please don't take
me away!"

Just as in Gondama, the soldiers would beat suspects, throw them into the back of trucks and cars, drive them to the local cemetery, and shoot them. Growing tired of that, the soldiers decided to let the suspects go and simply run them down with their trucks. We knew what had happened when the trucks returned for their next load of suspects with human blood splattered over the hood and front bumpers. Those whose relatives had been snatched from their grasp wept and wailed all night long.

It took the UNHCR almost two weeks to begin distributing badly needed relief supplies such as food and clean water. Before long, however, our condition became so deplorable that rumors had it we would relocate to a more sanitary and safer area.

It was around this time that the father of my baby, who had traveled to Bo ahead of us on business and had missed the attack on Malema, found me. He seemed distraught and said, "My family is gone. I've looked everywhere for them." He meant his girlfriend and her child, which was not his. He had been unable to find them, and feared the rebels had killed them as they fled Malema with the rest of us. I felt a tremendous compassion for him, and wanted to offer comfort in his time of woe. We prayed and I encouraged him to talk and rid himself of his pain.

As we talked, our conversation came around to the pregnancy and the responsibilities it was bringing. He told me he could offer the baby and me a better life, and that he had distant relatives who lived in Bo who would be happy to give me a place to stay. He wanted to help, and his genuine kindness touched my spirit. I did not want to leave my family, but decided to discuss the subject with my uncle; he was convinced it would be better for me, and my unborn child, if I were not sleeping out on the ground. Reluctantly, I left those I loved standing beside their tarps.

The father of my baby and I walked about five miles to the Villa Restaurant in Bo, on Mahei Boima Road. It was well known for its fine food and live music. There, he introduced me to his relatives, George and Tete Naphas, who were the owners. They extended a warm welcome, inviting me into their home that was attached to the restaurant. George, Tete, and George's sisters Sophie and Florence, who also lived there, became my extended family, and treated me like a queen. Every morning they brought fresh water for drinking and bathing and a delicious breakfast from some of the fine foods served in the restaurant. Their thoughtfulness and considerations for my needs helped soothe the ache I wrestled with in my heart over having forsaken my family.

I had only been in my new home for two days when Uncle Nyoun and his family came to tell me the UNHCR had said they, and all the other refugees, must leave Seminary and travel to Waterloo, another refugee camp. Waterloo was over eighty miles away, and the UNHCR somehow expected them to make the arduous journey on foot with only the meager rations they could carry. I knew the torturous journey would take them at least a week. I was shocked to learn that the UNHCR expected all the refugees to walk to the refugee camp. My uncle was more concerned about how I would fare with their leaving me behind, but George and Tete promised him they would take very good care of me. My uncle and cousins hugged me, and we wept, not knowing if we would see each other again. With tears in his eyes, my uncle turned to George and Tete, and said, "I don't want to leave Louise, especially with her being pregnant. I refused to leave her in Liberia, yet I must now leave her behind. I am so thankful that you are willing to take care of her."

I did not tell my uncle that I had become very afraid of the father of my child and that I was planning to run away after the baby was born. Even though there was no relationship between us, the man had become very jealous and accused me of being with other men. He would sometimes drop me to the floor with a swift, backhanded slap. He did not live at the Villa, but I knew I was at risk of his attacking me whenever he came. On occasions, he would grab me, pull my shirt up to his nose, and imagine he smelled cologne so he could accuse me of being with someone else. I felt ashamed at the situation in which I found myself. In spite of this torment, the love and support of George, Tete, and his sisters, who were unaware of his outbursts, continued to ensure my life in the Villa was pleasant. I had to admit things could be worse; I could be dead on the side of the road trying to make the eighty-mile trek to Waterloo with the other refugees.

CHAPTER 11

Nightmare

Several months after Uncle Nyoun, his family, and thousands of other refugees headed from Seminary to the Waterloo refugee camp, I met a Liberian woman named Janet who had also fled to Sierra Leone to escape the Liberian civil war. She had visited the Villa Restaurant in the past on an earlier trip to the country, and was dropping by to see her friends, George and Tete. When they told her someone from Liberia was living with them, Janet said she would love to meet me. I was delighted to greet a fellow Liberian. When she realized I was pregnant, she offered to stay to help me with the delivery. The Naphas generously offered for her and her son to move in until my baby was born. We quickly became close, like sisters. Having Janet in my life made every day a little brighter.

The day I went into labor I was at home with Tete and her younger sister Satta; unfortunately, Janet was away, visiting friends. Tete and I walked to the local maternity clinic that Sister Eleanor Gbonda owned, where I had been going for regular checkups. Sister Gbonda was there, and after she helped me get settled in she turned me over to Theresa, a new midwife-in-training. Prior to heading out to run an errand, Sister Gbonda told me she should be back soon, and that in her absence Theresa would be assisting me with the delivery. Not long thereafter, my son was born.

Immediately after the birth, the room fell silent, and I was surprised not to hear my baby's cry. The midwife began briskly rubbing the baby in an attempt to make him breathe, with no success. She then placed a tube in his nose to see if his airway was blocked. In a panic, I sat up, reached out with my hands, and wailed, "What's wrong with my baby?" Teresa was too busy to answer, so I continued with my helpless supplications. After long minutes of trying to revive him, she sorrowfully announced, "He's dead." I thought I, too, would die, and then fell back onto the bed in a faint.

I kept asking myself, *What went wrong? The baby seemed perfectly fine up to the moment he was born.* In spite of all my questions, no one had any answers. Tete, who had attended the birth with me, was also in shock, and turned her gaze from my lifeless baby to me. She brushed away the droplets of sweat from my brow and kissed my cheek. I knew she was trying to comfort me, but I had already fallen into a deep depression.

A few minutes later, Tete's sister Satta arrived to see the baby, and was heartbroken to find the baby dead, and everyone in the room in tears. Seeing that I was inconsolable, she assisted Theresa with gently washing the baby, and then wrapped him in a soft, new blanket. Just then, Sister Eleanor Gbonda, the owner of the clinic, came in. When she heard that my baby had died, she said, "Oh my Lord! This young refugee girl, who has traveled so far, and has suffered so much, has now been burdened with the death of her own baby. The trauma of being a refugee on the run must have been too much strain for the little boy."

Moments later, the baby's father, having heard I was in labor, came sprinting in. He immediately realized something terrible had happened. Rushing to my bedside, he could see from the tears running down my cheeks that things had not gone well. His glance fell on the tiny bundle, his baby boy, and he cried out, "Why God, oh why?!" He wept uncontrollably at the loss of his son. I could feel his heaving sobs as he held onto the headboard of the bed and bowed his head in grief.

I stayed in the clinic overnight; a night that felt like an eternity. In the morning, the midwife allowed me to go home with Tete. I was heartbroken when I saw the small crib sitting next to my bed. I picked up a pair of booties and a little shirt, and looked at them. A wave of grief, so oppressive that the clothing dropped from my fingers, crumpled me to the floor. My heart was breaking, and I wished I could reach in and rip it from my chest; the pain was too great for me to bear.

Within a couple of weeks of my son's death, my cousin Wacchen Anita Nyoun decided to travel from the Waterloo refugee camp to Bo to see my baby and me. When she arrived and saw my flat stomach she excitedly asked, "Louise, where's your baby?" My bottom lip began to tremble, but I managed to say, "Oh, Wacchen Anita, he's dead." She kneeled at my feet and cried. I stooped down to comfort her and we ended up crying in each other's arms. Finally, Wacchen Anita stood and lifted me off the floor; we sat together on the sofa to talk.

I was shocked to learn that one week after their arrival in Waterloo, Uncle Nyoun and Wacchen Anita's siblings had decided to take the UN up on an offer of free transportation by boat for any who wished to repatriate to Monrovia. Liberia was still in the midst of civil war, and Monrovia was not a safe place to be, especially for Krahn tribe members. Even so, my uncle said he would prefer to travel back home and take his chances in Monrovia than live in a camp where the conditions were so atrocious that the UN provided wheelbarrows for transporting the daily dead to the shallow graves they had dug nearby.

I gave Wacchen Anita a stunned look as she shared the news. She said, "I would have gone back with him, but I decided to stay in Freetown with my boyfriend." I knew that must have been a difficult decision for her, and a difficult one for her father to accept as well.

Wacchen Anita knew I had only stayed behind in Bo because I was pregnant. With my son being stillborn, I did not have any further ties to his father, so she urged me to leave right away and return with her to Waterloo where, she said, I could obtain a college education. Grabbing both my hands, she pleaded, "Louise, please come with me. You can start all over again. You can follow your dreams and finish your education. It will give you a chance."

The baby's father interrupted us as he dropped by the Villa and came into the room. Wacchen Anita stood up, greeted him warmly, and shared with him the good news that I could receive an education if I would travel back with her to the Waterloo camp. Realizing it was time for her to go and that I would need to talk it over with him, Wacchen Anita said, "Louise, you are very smart and you deserve to finish your education." She then bid farewell and reiterated her request for me to come to Waterloo.

As soon as Wacchen Anita was out of earshot, the baby's father bellowed, "I don't want to live in the Waterloo Refugee camp! What kind of life would that give us? Wacchen Anita is only interested in taking you away from me." As he threatened me with raised fists, he yelled, "She is only interested in getting you involved with another man!"

I had developed a routine of visiting my baby's gravesite every Friday and, as much as I wanted to go to Waterloo and secure my education, I became saddened by the thought of moving away from where I could visit with him. At the same time, I felt sorry for my baby's father and was not sure if it would be right to abandon him, as he was still mourning the death of our child and the loss of his family. I continued my stay at the Villa for a few more weeks in order to recover from the birth. I found that he had searched for and found a place where the two of us could stay together. Feeling pressed into it, and like I had no other choice, I left the Villa and moved in with him, where he subjected me to more frequent accusations and beatings. Were it not for my desire to stay near my baby's grave, I would have taken Wacchen Anita's advice and headed for the Waterloo camp.

Aware I wanted to continue my education, my "boyfriend," as I began to refer to him, registered me for the seamstress course at St. Mary's Vocational School where, as one of only three Liberian refugees to do so, I received a scholarship. Margaret Foday and Grace Gee were the other two Liberians, and I was excited to find that they too had grown up in Grand Gedeh. We had many things in common and felt right at home with each other. Margaret, who was especially sympathetic to my situation, introduced me to her parents, Michael and Irene Foday, and then advised me to let her or her parents know if I ever needed anything. I also befriended a lovely Sierra Leonean woman named Lucia Coker. Her name, which means "light," fit her perfectly; the brightness of her countenance helped me overcome the deep sadness and loneliness I was feeling. She would sit for hours, if necessary, and kindly listen to the stories of my struggles, and share hers with me.

Classes were just what I needed to divert my attention from the death of my son. I thrived on learning, yet becoming a seamstress was not what I had in mind; so, after three months of seamstress training, I spoke with Sister Immaculata Gallachet, the department head for secretarial education, and asked if I could transfer to her department. She approved my transfer, and became my new instructor. I found her very nurturing and looked forward to her classes. Finding out that her stay in Bo had ended and she would be returning to Ireland saddened me. She handed her classes over to Rosetta Dembe, another teacher who was very kind to me and to my Liberian friends.

Just as much as I looked forward to each day at school, I dreaded each evening and weekend at the apartment, since I never knew when my boyfriend might explode into a rage of jealousy. He had traded his once beautiful voice for the angry, condemning outbursts he showered on me, and I had become a guarded and frightened woman.

I came home from class one day about a year after my baby's death and, as usual, went about straightening the apartment before my boyfriend returned from work. I noticed it was 5:00 PM, and silently prayed, *Oh Lord, he'll be home soon. Please fill his heart and this home with peace.* As I was straightening the bed, I picked up my bed pillow and gave it a good shake, fluffing it with both hands and laying it down again. When I did the same with his, I jumped back with a scream as a large, sharpened, kitchen knife tumble from the pillowcase and dropped to the floor, narrowly missing my foot. A freshly folded piece of paper fluttered after it.

After a brief pause, I dropped the pillow on the bed, picked up the paper, and unfolded it to discover its contents. My hands trembled as I read a note penned in my boyfriend's hand and signed by him that read, "Don't worry or feel sorry for us. We are happy now and are on the 'other side' with our son. I have ended all of our suffering and sadness with a knife. We are happy now and at peace with ourselves and with each other. This is my grave, and this is Louise's grave."

I was horror-stricken. My vision blurred in my confusion. As I crumpled the paper into a ball and trembled with fear, I cried out, "Oh dear God, protect me!" Recalling Margaret's sincere offer to assist me if I ever needed anything, I grabbed a plastic bag and shoved in a change of clothes; then, wrapping the knife in a shirt, I dropped it and the telltale note in as well.

Realizing my boyfriend's intention was to kill us both, I did not want to chance running into him coming home, so I tossed the plastic bag and my bed pillow out the back window and climbed through, dropping into the back yard. I threw the plastic bag over the barbed wire fence, installed to deter thieves, laid my pillow over the top, and climbed over. Even with the pillow in place, the barbed wire tore through my clothes and I received injuries in several places. As soon as my feet touched the ground, I grabbed my belongings and ran to Margaret's house, about five miles away.

Fortunately, Margaret was home when I arrived. I was out of breath and could barely speak; she was shocked to see my tear-stained face and my bloody, torn clothing. Assuming my boyfriend had beaten me, she quickly ushered me in and led me to a chair. My hands trembled and tears streamed down my face as I pulled out the knife and crumpled letter. Through my sobs, I told the story of how I had found them and she began reading the horrifying note. Her mouth dropped open, her eyes widened, and she cried out, "Oh my God, Louise! We must get you to the police station. They can help you." After cleaning my wounds, she and her family walked with me to the station a mile away.

When we arrived, we were directed to the third floor of the building.

After making the climb, Margaret marched right up to the counter and told the officer on duty, which happened to be the chief of police, that my boyfriend had threatened my life, and I needed their help. I handed him the knife and the letter, and told him how I had found them. His brow furrowed and he shook his head in dismay as he read the hand-written note. He looked up and said, "There are a few questions I need answers to so I can send police officers to arrest the man who wrote this letter." Once the chief of police had my boyfriend's name and the location of the place he worked, he immediately dispatched four officers to apprehend him.

Thinking I could head back to Margaret's, I thanked the chief, got up, and headed toward the door. He stopped me, saying kindly, "I'm sorry, Louise, but I need you to stay so you can be here when we bring him in and question him. We need to get to the bottom of this and find out what's going on so we can decide how to deal with your boyfriend."

Within a few minutes, the officers were back with him in tow. All they had told him was that they needed him to come down to the police station so they could ask him a few questions about something. I could see the shock on his face when my boyfriend, who was too tall for the doorway, leaned over to come in and realized I was there. Before he could speak, the chief picked up the letter, held the writing toward him, and said, "Did you write this suicide note?"

He admitted to writing the letter, but retorted, "So what? She and I are leaving now!" As he started to head my way, reaching to grab my arm, the chief of police shouted, "Stay right where you are! I will shoot you down if you try to take her from here!" I shouted out, "Wait, no, I don't want to see anyone shot!" The chief turned to me and ordered, "Be quiet!"

In an instant, my boyfriend lurched around the counter, grabbing the chief of police by the neck in a stranglehold, and began pressing him toward the window a few feet away, apparently planning to toss him out and down the three stories to the ground. Five other police officers rushed him, tackling him to the floor. They held him down while the chief rubbed his bruised neck and angrily shouted, "If you attack me again, I WILL kill you!" Pointing at me, he said, "And I will NOT permit you to kill this woman."

After waiting for my boyfriend to calm down, the chief said, "You have done enough to her, and I don't want you causing any further harm, or putting her through any more pain. I'm keeping the knife and this note as evidence, and if you promise to leave Louise alone, and allow her to go home with the Foday family this evening, I will not put you in jail tonight." My boyfriend gave a disgruntled nod. The chief continued, "This is a very serious matter, and I need both of you to appear at a hearing tomorrow morning in the town meeting hall. We will decide then how to best deal with the situation." I waited for my boyfriend to leave, thanked the chief of police and the other police officers, and headed home with the Foday family.

The next morning, the Foday family, anxious to support me in any way they could, accompanied me to the meeting hall. When we arrived, the chief of police, as well as the officers who had brought my boyfriend in to the police station the afternoon before, greeted me with pleasant looks and hellos. They gave me reassuring nods and I accepted their encouragement.

When my boyfriend arrived, I was surprised to see he had brought along an entourage of character witnesses. They turned out to be extended family members and friends of his, most of whom I had never met. As they passed by, they gave me evil, threatening stares, making their disapproval quite plain. I had no idea what he had told them; however, I was sure it was not the truth.

Soon a band of Sierra Leonean soldiers arrived, sliding in around my boyfriend and his family. Some of them slapped him on the back in friendly greetings, while others let me know with their snorts and sideways glances that they were not at all pleased with the situation. Obviously, he had led them to believe he was the victim in this case.

The chief of police made his way to the front of the room and, amid some grumbling from many in the audience, began, "I want to thank you for coming to this hearing. We will decide the correct course of action to take in regard to the evidence Louise Barton brought to the police station late yesterday. For those of you who don't know the details, this young lady came into the police station yesterday afternoon with a note and a knife in her hand." At that, everyone became silent and began listening intently.

He held the note in one hand and brandished the knife in the air with the other, while nodding toward my boyfriend. "Louise found this note, and this knife, hidden in this gentleman's bed pillow as she was straightening their bed. In her distress, she ran to a friend's house, injuring herself in the process on a barbed wire fence that blocked her path. She and her friend's family all came down to the police station to show us what Louise had found. Here's what the note, which her boyfriend has already admitted to writing, says." With that, he read out the condemning words for all to hear. "In addition, and as you can see," he pointed with the knife at the signature, "he signed at the bottom of the note. He placed the knife in the pillowcase and the note along with it. There is no question that Louise's boyfriend had every intention of killing her, and then killing himself."

A low rumble of voices filled the room and exclamations rolled through the crowd as the chief paused for effect. The news obviously stunned my boyfriend's family members; those who had been giving me the evil eye became confused and turned their condemning gazes from me, shaking their heads. They aimed glaring looks of disgust toward him. The chief of police seized the moment and topped his case with, "When my officers brought him into the station for questioning, he attacked and tried to strangle me. It took five other officers to subdue him. This is a violent man who, in this very note, has threatened the life of another person. So, we have decided that Louise needs to remain in the protection and safety of Mr. Foday's home."

One of the soldiers immediately jumped up from his seat and shouted, "No, no, she needs to go with this man!" The chief of police retorted, "Look, he intended to kill her." The soldier fired back, "Her own family left her in the care of this man, so she has to go back with him. No harm was actually committed; the note just says he wanted to." Voices buzzed with disapproval over what the soldier was suggesting. The chief insisted, "She cannot go home with this man, because he made it clear in this note that he intends to kill her."

"Intending to kill her and killing her are two different things. It's not a crime to think of doing someone harm, is it? Since she is not a Sierra Leonean citizen, and is causing so much trouble, she should be deported. Turn her over to us and we will make sure she leaves our country."

Knowing the Sierra Leonean soldiers wielded more authority than local police did, and that I could soon find myself at their mercy, I prayed silently, *Please God, don't let the soldiers dominate this hearing and have their way. Please protect me and allow me to go home with the Foday family.*

The chief of police responded, "She is not just a visitor in Sierra Leone, she is a refugee, and you can't deport her simply because someone else wants to harm her." Knowing he did not have the authority to countermand the Sierra Leonean army's wishes, but also knowing he was in the right, the chief of police framed a look of solid determination on his face and brought an end to the hearing with a firm, "Louise will NOT be deported, and she will NOT go home with this man! She will go home with, and will remain with, the Foday family."

The soldiers decided to stand down. As they slowly cleared out of the room, along with my boyfriend and his extended family members, the chief of police came up to me and said, "Louise, I am so sorry you had to go through all this, but I'm glad you came to us right away." He reached into his pocket, took out a small roll of money, and handed it to me saying, "Please, take this to help cover expenses since you are now out on your own. Take my advice. Do not ever consider going back to that man." Thanking him for his kindness, I followed the Foday family to their home, where I also thanked God for protecting me from deportation.

Within a few days, my boyfriend stood in the street outside of the Foday's home with a threatening look on his face. Margaret and her family began shouting and yelling, "Louise, he's standing outside— let's run to the police station." When he heard all the commotion, he left. The next evening, while I was out on the porch, he came back, stood in the street, and called out to me, saying, "Louise. Louise. Come home with me. Let's go. Let's go!" I was terrified, and shouted out, "Mr. Foday, he's back!" Mr. Foday came running out onto the porch, and my boyfriend left.

The next time I saw George and Tete they told me they had confronted my boyfriend, asking, "Why would you want to kill Louise?" They said he felt sorry for me and told them, "I want us to be with the baby on the other side. This way she won't be lonely for the baby." George had told my boyfriend, "You may be sad at the loss of your baby, however, that gives you no right to take Louise's life. If you want to kill yourself, then go ahead, but don't even think about harming Louise." I decided to tell them my plan of making my way to Waterloo to pursue my education there. This saddened them further, and knowing this was likely our last visit together, we clung to each other before saying our goodbyes.

Although I did not want to leave my son's grave, with the increasing number of visits and continued risk that my boyfriend might harm me, it was clear I needed to leave for my own safety. The morning I told Margaret and her parents of my plans to travel to Waterloo and join the other refugees in the Waterloo refugee camp, they were very sad. They did agree it would be best for me, though, and told me of some friends they had there, suggesting I contact them when I arrived.

Once again, I packed my belongings in a plastic bag. Hugging the Foday family goodbye, I walked down to the bus station, where I purchased a ticket with the money the police officer had given me and took the next bus to the Waterloo refugee camp. It took nearly five hours to make the trip. When the bus arrived, I went to the UNHCR office to register, but found they had already closed for the day. When I asked a group of refugees, who were still hanging around outside the office, if they knew of the family the Foday's had asked me to look for, one old man said, "Yeah, they live at AK-47." I thought for sure he was teasing me, so I replied, "What? That's the name of a rifle." He then explained to me how the huts in the camp were numbered, and sure enough, AK-47 was a legitimate number. I shuddered at the thought of living at a place with that number, and wondered why the officials had not chosen to skip it when assigning hut numbers.

In the gathering dark, I followed the directions the group had given me and eventually found the address. The Foday's friends greeted me warmly and offered for me to share their hut for a few days. The hut was so tiny it would only hold the belongings of a few people and then provide room to lie down at night.

In spite of what my cousin Wacchen Anita had told me about the conditions at the camp, conditions that had caused my uncle and the rest of her family to return to Liberia before it was safe to do so, I was shocked at what I saw in the next morning's light as I stepped out of the hut. The place looked like an old, abandoned industrial site. Poorly constructed makeshift huts filled its expanse, and a horrid stench filled the air. Many refugees wandered around, seemingly in a daze, having no place to go. In the evening, as I surveyed the landscape, I noticed a man pass by who looked familiar. I was not sure if I knew him, so I did not say anything; yet when he passed by again I asked some people if his name might be Moses. They said, "Yes, that's his name," so I shouted out, "Moses!" He turned, and recognizing me, cried out, "Géesedeh!"

Moses was a forty-year-old man whom I had met in Malema when I was pregnant, and he immediately asked about my baby. When I tearfully told him my baby had died, he offered his condolences. To lighten the conversation, he quickly changed the subject, sharing the news, "Hey Louise, some of your family members are here." I said,

"What? Who?" He joyfully told me, "Your cousin Alfred Gbarzayee," is here, and Edith is here, too." My heart swelled with the thought of seeing them. Moses paused, and then continued, "Unfortunately, Edith's husband, Richard, is dead, and the little girl they were watching out for is missing." Right there on the ground, I sat down and wept. When he knelt down and cradled me in his arms, I moaned, "Moses, life is too painful. There is just too much pain." With sorrow in his voice, he said, "I'm sorry, Géesedeh, I didn't mean to hurt you."

He helped me to my feet, and listened to my story of how I ended up coming to Waterloo. When I had finished my story he offered, "Would you like me to take you to Edith's house?" I replied, "Yes, absolutely!"

When Edith saw me, she screamed and grabbed my arms. After a short pause for hugs she said, "Oh, Géesedeh, Richard is dead!" She told me the tragic story of how, before her arrival in Waterloo, Richard had joined a Liberian paramilitary outfit, which formed out of desperation to help fight the rebel forces in Sierra Leone. Richard, who had training in first aid, had become a battlefield medic. In a heroic attempt to care for wounded comrades on the front lines, he had been caught in the crossfire and killed.

While shaking her head despairingly, she groaned, "I've not only lost Richard, but I've also lost Gmaa." I nodded and watched her forlorn face. She continued, "Before Richard died, when we were all fleeing Malema with thousands of other refugees, little Gmaa let go of his hand. I heard him yell, 'Oh God! Gmaa! I've lost Gmaa!' We both turned to find her, but she had been swept away by the ocean of people."

Edith's voice faded away as she choked on the tears brought on by her misery. Her shoulders shook violently. Having lost both her husband and niece was tearing her apart. My tears mingled with hers, as her loss became mine. She shook her head in grief and, after reflecting for a moment, a confused and puzzled look wrinkled her brow. She remembered the last time she had seen me I was pregnant, and now it was evident that I was not. She cautiously asked me, "Where's your baby?" She saw the answer well up in my eyes, and we held onto each other until we could not cry any longer.

Taking a deep breath, Edith undertook the retelling of how my uncle and the rest of his family had found the conditions in the Waterloo camp intolerable, and had returned to Liberia during the UNHCR's first voluntary repatriation. My cousin Alfred, who had been quietly listening nearby, cleared his throat and, as soon as I saw him, I jumped up, giving him a warm embrace.

Alfred (who most everyone affectionately called "white man" because he was so organized) and Edith, launched into telling me of their week-long, eighty-mile trek on foot as they and thousands of others endured the "death march" from Bo to Waterloo—a journey I may not have survived. They told me they had no food or water except for what they carried; dehydration, starvation, and death were their relentless and oppressive tormenters on the arduous journey. They walked about six hours a day on blistering hot blacktop pavement, with the scorching sun burning them from above. Previously able-bodied men, who had carried elderly and sick on their backs for much of the journey, were no longer strong enough to do so. After laying their relatives or friends on the side of the road, the men made the awful choice between waiting with them as they died, possibly dying with them, or suffering the anguish of leaving them behind. They said that many people sat down with a parent, spouse, or friend, choosing to die with them.

After seven onerous days on the road, those who made it to Waterloo thought their struggles were over. They saw the United Nations flag in the center of the compound—a banner of hope and a warning to would-be intruders that the area was under the UN's protection. When they arrived, there were no houses; there was no food, no water, and nothing to sleep on other than the ground. Until they were able to construct huts, the refugees, again, shared their earthen beds with scorpions and snakes. During the day, those who had the strength traveled miles into dense forest in search of water and plants to eat.

About a week after their arrival, Alfred and Edith told me, critical supplies finally began to arrive; yet with everyone on starvation rations because there were so many to feed, many refugees began stealing food from each other. In addition, locals were stealing UNHCR-provided food rations from needy refugees, whom they considered easy targets.

Not long after I arrived in the camp, one woman with a newborn baby had all her allotted food stolen while she left her hut to fetch water. Even though we tried to share our meager portions with her, she succumbed, dying from lack of adequate nutrition. A woman, who had recently lost her own child, voluntarily took the baby.

There were thousands of us in the Waterloo refugee camp, and our numbers continued to grow as the rebel onslaughts displaced more and more people from their homes. I was appalled to witness the continued suffering of those herded into the camp.

One man walked by me, and I was stunned to see that the back of his head was gaping open from where he had been struck with a cutlass. When I saw the inside of his head was visible, I wondered how he could possibly be living or walking around in that condition.

I saw other refugees in similar condition. One young woman who came to the camp had both hands chopped off by rebels when they attacked her village. The UNHCR paid female refugees to help her with her daily needs. Even worse was the young boy I met who was blind because rebel soldiers had poured molten plastic onto his eyes as they told him they were putting in eye drops. Horrors like these were committed as the child rebels attempted to out-do each other in the severity of their tortures.

Because there was little privacy, I was frightened to bathe alone in the camp, and with no law enforcement, many women were victims of gang rape. It was clear that our world had unraveled. We were a lost, displaced people and our surroundings were destroying our humanity.

During the years I spent at Waterloo in this despicable condition, I saw parents sell their own children for life-sustaining supplies. Some sold their children to people wanting to adopt them with the hope they would possibly find a better life elsewhere. A baby could bring in as much as twenty US dollars, which was a great deal of money to us. Some parents sold their young girls as wives for as little as a dollar-fifty. Those parents who kept their children lived in fear every day, knowing disease could strike them down or they might be stolen and sold.

CHAPTER 12

Arrested and Flogged

I had been at the Waterloo refugee camp for several years, and as the years dragged by, I wondered when the Liberian and Sierra Leonean civil wars, which were holding me captive, would end. Countless lows punctuated my dreary existence; yet, by God's grace, I also experienced many highs. Cultural performances graced the camp almost every evening. During these events, members of different tribes gathered to entertain with their drumming and dancing; it became a friendly competition. Others recited poems or sang. It was always a special treat when the children performed; their innocence put smiles on the toughest of faces and softened many hearts.

I was overjoyed the day Janet found me. It seemed so long ago that we had met at the Villa, while I was living with George and Tete. She had recently moved to Freetown, the capital of Sierra Leone, to live with her boyfriend who taught at Albert Academy, a high school founded in October of 1904, and named after Reverend Ira E. Albert, an American missionary.

Janet had heard that I left Bo and relocated to the Waterloo refugee camp. In hopes of locating me, she took a bus to the camp and asked a UNHCR official to look up my name. He directed her to the section of the camp where I lived, "Louise Barton, yes, she lives in Area Q." I was standing outside my makeshift hut when I heard a woman call out, "Louise, is that you?"

Hearing someone call my name, I looked up and was startled to see Janet standing there. I could not believe it! I ran over, gave her a big hug, and twirled her around. This sweet woman, a fellow Liberian refugee, had ridden a bus eighteen miles to the Waterloo camp UNHCR office just to see me.

We spent three wonderful days together; we shared stories about our lives since fleeing Liberia and spoke about that which God had helped us through. I was happy to find out that Lucia, who I had also met in Bo when I was attending classes at St. Mary's Vocational School, was living on Fort Street in Freetown, just around the corner from Janet. When it was time for her to leave, Janet said, "I am so glad to know you, Louise; you are a wonderful person. I will come as often as I can. Please come visit me in Freetown."

One beautiful, sunny day in May, when I was twenty, I did just that. I decided to take a bus into Freetown and surprise Janet and Lucia, so I scraped together the money required for bus fare to Freetown and back. When I arrived at the gate of the Albert Academy, a young man named Mustapha, the school's gatekeeper, took great pleasure in giving me a hard time about gaining entry. I shrugged it off and took it all in stride, even joking back, because I knew from Janet that he was related to her. He finally let me in, and directed me to Janet's apartment.

Janet squealed when she saw me. She rushed over and we exchanged warm hugs. After a long conversation I mentioned wanting to visit Lucia. Janet told me she lived just outside the school compound and gave me directions.

As I departed, I bid farewell to Mustapha, who responded in Creole, "We go see again, when God spare our lives." What he meant was, "We shall meet again, if God spares our lives." A chill went down my spine. I nodded to him while thinking, *Why would he say that? I surely do hope we see each other again.*

As I walked to Lucia's house, the warmth of the sun washed over me and erased the discomfort Mustapha's comment had caused. Lucia spotted me from her upstairs window and greeted me with a delighted, "Louise!" She rushed downstairs, flung open the front door, laughing, "Louise, you've surprised me." She reached out to hug me. As our eyes locked and our arms stretched out to greet each other, I received a sharp smack on my back. A look of terror came across Lucia's face and her eyes widened in panic.

I slowly turned and saw a pistol inches away, pointed directly at my forehead. I fell to my knees and covered my head with my hands. I heard screaming but did not know if it was mine. The Sierra Leonean police officer growled, "You are under arrest for cooking for rebel soldiers!" I protested that I was a refugee, and would never aid the rebels. He retorted caustically, "Someone told us they saw you cooking!" Instead of handcuffing me and taking me in a police car, he threw a rope over my head, wrapping it around my neck, and yanked it tight. This cut off most of my breath and caused my temples to throb and my ears to ring.

A crowd of people came over to see what all the commotion and screaming was about. The next thing I knew, the mob had caught me up in a frenzy of hatred that Lucia was powerless to stop. They pummeled me with their fists. The endless kicking and punching, which the officer had initiated and participated in, nearly killed me. One last time I managed to scream, "Please, don't kill me. I'm not a rebel. I am innocent!" It was no use; they ignored my pleas. The thought washed over me that this was most certainly my last day. Experience had taught me that once a person has been accused of being a rebel, or of aiding rebels, he or she is dead.

Someone suddenly yelled, "Back off!" The crowd parted and another police officer strolled over to me. Instead of coming to my aid, he ripped off my clothes and tied me up with ropes so tight that the blood stopped circulating in my arms and legs. Loud boos and jeers came from the homicidal mob and angry onlookers threw stones and whatever objects they could pick up. An angry woman ran across the road and struck me on my back with a shovel. The officers allowed the crowd to claw at me, beat me, spit on me, and throw filthy water on me.

The crowd continued to grow as the word of a captured rebel spread through Freetown like an out-of-control blaze. I heard a loud fury of voices chanting, "Kill her! Kill her!" Thoughts of Jesus began tumbling through my mind; when he was falsely accused of treason and an angry crowd called out, "Crucify him! Crucify him!" I was powerless and felt myself slipping away.

I cannot explain the feeling I had at that moment other than my spirit was leaving my body. I simply gave myself up for dead and knew this was the end. I was like a piece of raw meat the rabble was violently dragging, tossing, and kicking around. Another officer grabbed more rope and tied me onto the back of his motorcycle. As we traveled through the streets, my arms and legs dangled and dragged on the pavement.

The vexed crowd chased alongside us and continued to chant, "Kill the rebel! Kill her!" Lucia ran alongside, too. Poor Lucia had to hide her tears because if anyone thought she was with me they would surely lynch her. The battering crowd followed us all the way to the police station in central Freetown on Pademba Road by the historic Cotton Tree, around which the founders had built the town. I was brought before the chief of police.

The officer dispassionately threw me off the motorcycle, in the direction of the door to the police station. My blood ran and clotted over my naked body while the ropes remained securely tied in place. Prior to facing the chief of police for my interrogation, I tried to speak to the officer who was dragging me in. The moment I uttered a sound a violent kick landed under my cheekbone and he yelled, "Shut your dirty mouth!" Blood gushed from my mouth and my right eye was blinded.

The officer propelled me into the Criminal Investigation Department, where I found myself facing the chief of police. Apparently embarrassed by my nakedness, he ordered the officers to get me dressed. I stood there waiting while the chief of police turned his back to me. He stood tall, as straight as a tree, with his hands neatly folded behind his back. Hearing the noise outside, he placed his hands on either side of the window, and leaned, straight-armed, against the frame, staring out at the angry mob as it continued to grow. His body blocked the rays of the sun, casting a cross-shaped shadow forebodingly across my feet.

Standing there, shaking, in severe pain, and with no hope of escape, it was all I could do to maintain my composure. Soon an officer returned with a handful of dirty clothing and threw it at me. He removed the ropes and, nearly collapsing, I leaned down to pick up the torn dress. I stepped into it as quickly as I could; when I had finished, the chief of police turned to face me.

He looked at me and saw the blood still issuing from my face. He winced briefly, and the furrows in his brow deepened. Putting his hand to his forehead, he cleared his throat, sighed deeply, and sternly asked, "What's your name?"

I could barely stand, and my voice was weak and shaky. I was not sure if he could understand me. I tasted blood as I swallowed and nearly choked, but managed to reply, "Louise Barton." Without hesitation and with the ease of a seasoned interrogator he said, "Are you a Sierra Leonean?" I shook my head no, "No, I am a Liberian citizen, and I am a refugee here in your country."

He fired off an endless barrage of questions. My agony was so great that I could hardly concentrate. I was innocent, and all I wanted was to go back to the refugee camp. His booming voice interrupted as my mind began to wander, "Which part of Liberia are you from?" I tried to breathe deeply, but found that my ribs had been broken. I gasped, "I am from Eastern Liberia, and I belong to the Krahn tribe."

The chief of police hurled condemning words as he shouted, "So, you're here to cook for rebel soldiers?" I was shocked at the accusation and shook my head doggedly, "No, no, I am from the Krahn ethnic group, the same as President Samuel K. Doe. I am related to his wife, Nancy Doe." He looked at me incredulously, as if he did not believe a word I was saying. I did not let him think too long about it, for I was afraid he would have me thrown out to the wolves still clambering in the street for my life. The curses and threats had become a loud roar as the crowd grew outside his window.

I continued, "Please sir, I am innocent. The rebels are hunting down the Krahn tribe and they are killing us off as fast as they can. How could I cook for rebels who want to kill me? I run *from* rebels. I don't run *to* them."

The chief listened more closely to me. He said, "Anyone may speak a little Krahn and still be a rebel. Can you speak Krahn fluently?" My heart fell; I had spent so many years away from my family while living in Monrovia. *Oh my God,* I thought, *I can understand it, but I can't speak it well.* I had been using the language lately to converse with other Krahn in the refugee camp and I could only hope to convince my interrogator. The chief of police looked at the police officer who was standing at attention behind me. "Go. Get an interpreter and bring him to my office," he ordered. "We will soon see who is a rebel," he said as he pierced me with a pointed look and lifted one eyebrow. Turning away from me, he watched out the window.

My nerves were shattered. A loud knock on the door shot through me, giving me another dose of adrenalin, which caused my heart to bang painfully in my broken chest. As I sucked in air, I felt faint and my knees began to buckle. Ignoring this, the chief greeted the interpreter and said, "Thank you for coming, this shouldn't take long. We have a woman here. She is accused of being a rebel. Tell me if she speaks Krahn fluently. The interpreter saw my horrid condition and kindly asked me in Krahn, "Are you a rebel?" I prayed to God that my rusty Krahn would not leave him thinking that I actually was.

I responded to him in Krahn, "I am innocent. I am from the Krahn tribe. My father gave me as a servant when I was very young in exchange for my education. My father is a Liberian soldier, and my mother is related to the first lady of Liberia. I am Krahn, and my family has suffered many deaths at the hands of the rebels."

The interpreter smiled and said, "Sir, this lady is *not* a rebel. She truly belongs to the Krahn tribe." The chief's chest filled with air, and a great sigh left his lips. The deep furrow in his brow softened a little. He and the interpreter had one last test for me. The interpreter pointed to the photographs on the wall and said, "You see these photographs? They are of Liberian government officials and heads of various rebel factions in your country. As I point to each picture, I want you to identify the individuals."

His finger landed on the first face, and I said, "That's Samuel Bull." Sliding his finger across the picture to the next face, he looked at me and I said, "That's Roosevelt Johnson." This continued only for a few more seconds until the chief raised his voice and said, "Stop!" He turned to the interpreter and said in Creole, "Dis woman not to rebel. Dis na the Krahn people rebel de fin. Dis na Doe fambo. Not to rebel!" I understood him to say, "This woman is not a rebel. This woman belongs to the Krahn tribe that rebels are looking for. This is Doe family, not a rebel!"

At this point, the chief of police, his face still hard, slipped his hand into his pocket and handed me some Sierra Leonean currency to cover the cost of my transportation back to the Waterloo refugee camp. Embarrassment kept him from extending an apology, but I did not care. I yearned for freedom and the seclusion of the camp.

The chief ordered the police officer at the door to release me. As we walked down the hall together, he stopped and looked me square in the eyes and said, "You have a very long life. Most times, we don't even bring people here to be interrogated. In fact, this is the first time we ever did. On any other day, we would have taken you to the beach and finished you there. God's divine hand must be on your life."

He escorted me to the front door and faced yet another problem; an angry mob, numbering in the hundreds, wanting to tear me to pieces and hang my body in the center of town, waited for me. If I were to step outside, they would kill me instantly. The officer shoved me back inside and closed the door. As I waited inside, I clung to what sanity I still possessed and prayed for my protection as he located a megaphone and walked outside to address the unruly mass that had gathered to witness and assist in my lynching. I heard him say, "Good afternoon." After clearing his throat he continued, "You came to see a rebel brought to justice." A loud roar of approval arose from the crowd. He went on, "But, what you have seen instead is an innocent person falsely accused."

That is when another officer opened the door and took me outside. I stood in front of the crowd, feeling humiliated and frightened. The officer with the megaphone pointed at me saying, "This woman, who stands before you today, is innocent—just like yourselves. She is not a rebel." I could hear a moan of disappointment from the crowd. He went on, "You do not want to shed innocent blood. Too much has been shed already."

I could see the disappointment on their faces. A few people who were standing in the front turned and yelled at a young man who stood nearby. "Not everyone you see is a rebel! This woman is not a rebel. She is innocent. You could have caused her to die for no good reason!"

The entire crowd turned to look at the man who had turned me in. I was shocked and nearly collapsed. It was Mustapha, the gatekeeper at the Albert Academy. He had padded his pockets with reward money for turning me in. I later learned from Janet that Mustapha had assumed I was on a reconnaissance mission because of my Liberian accent. She later chided him for turning in someone who was her friend, and who had spent time visiting, asking, "Why would you think a rebel would be coming to visit me?"

The crowd broke up and the people dispersed. A police officer that had not been involved in my beating walked with me for a few blocks and flagged down a taxi. He seemed to be sincerely concerned for my safety, so, after he opened the door for me to get in the back, he rode in the front with the driver, directing him to the bus station. Once at the station he darted out of the cab and stopped the bus for Waterloo, as it was about to leave. He came back to the cab, paid the driver, and led me to the bus. As I boarded he said, "Be well. Take care of yourself, okay?"

I found my way to a seat and realized all eyes were riveted on me. Some passengers were confused by my appearance, but others looked at me with sadness and compassion, shaking their heads and looking away to give me privacy in my pain. They did not have to say a word for we were all pawns in this hideous game of war.

When I arrived back at the camp, I snuck in the back way. As I neared my hut, however, a small group saw me and gathered around. They were stunned to see my condition and asked what had happened. When I described my arrest, flogging, and interrogation, they were appalled.

Once inside my hut, I warmed a pot of water over a small fire, and daubed at the dried blood, pouring warm water over my body from a cup. I put on a clean dress and headed over to the camp's Red Cross clinic, where the attendants cleaned and dressed my wounds, and gave me a shot of penicillin to help ward off infection. Bruised and shaken from the battering, I felt very fortunate to be alive.

A week later, while I was still healing from my wounds, I was asked to speak at a meeting held under a tent that was used for large gatherings. I still looked badly beaten and winced when I spoke. Everyone listened raptly as I shared my story of false accusations and despicable treatment. I told of the police stripping me naked and tying me with ropes so tightly that they cut off circulation in my limbs. I spoke of the angry mob's pelting me with stones and beating me with their fists; and how the police had dragged me through the streets on the back of a motorcycle and kicked me in the mouth when I tried to speak.

Seeing what had happened to me in Freetown caused other refugees who traveled into the capital to be concerned for their safety. After the meeting, a few of us penned a letter to the UNHCR regarding the Geneva Refugee Convention, which defines the rights of refugees and the responsibilities of the host countries, in the hope of preventing further attacks like this on innocent people.

A handsome young man walked up to me after the meeting. He held out his hand to shake mine. I was attracted to his sincerity and, when

I took his hand, I felt an unmistakable peace. I had seen him around camp but had not spoken to him before. "Hi, my name is Abel." He looked at me with a great deal of concern in his eyes. "Good speech. I am sorry to hear what happened to you. Your survival is evidence that God is watching over you." I shook his hand and looked down, saying, "Thank you. I agree, it's only by God's grace that I am here today to tell my story." Abel nodded, "God spared your life, and I am glad for that."

Others, coming to shake my hand and share their sorrow over what happened to me, interrupted our conversation. I looked back at Abel and noticed that he had not moved or taken his eyes off me. I smiled, and hoped we would get to know each other.

CHAPTER 13

Torrential Downpour

Abel and I began to spend time with each other, and our friend-ship grew. I shared with him how my father had instilled in me a passion for education, and how I earnestly desired to fulfill his dream that I graduate from college. With Abel's encouragement, I applied for admission to Fourah Bay College, the first Western-style university in West Africa, which was founded February 18, 1827, in Freetown. Upon passing the college entrance exam, I was accepted as a student in the Library Science program. Being back in school gave me hope in the midst of extreme destitution. As I began my first semester, I applied for a scholarship, but learned that university scholarships were only available to refugees who had completed a full year of study. Unable to afford the tuition on my own, I had to withdraw from the university at the completion of my first semester.

My cousin Alfred received a trade school scholarship and began studying auto mechanics at the Government Trade Center at Ferry Junction in Freetown. One afternoon he came rushing through the camp like a whirlwind. All of us who happened to be home gathered around to hear his story. With enthusiasm he said, "I was on my way back from class today, on the bus from Freetown to Waterloo, when the bus stopped to pick up passengers at the Fourah Bay College Junction. I wasn't paying attention to anything in particular when I glanced out the window and saw a girl selling "ground peas," our name for peanuts, from a basket she carried on her head. Her slim figure, and the way she stood, reminded me of my sister Cecelia when she was a teenager.

When she reached up to grab a bag of peanuts for a customer, I caught a full view of her face. There was no doubt about it; she looked just like her mother, Cecelia."

He explained how he had remembered back a few years when his sister's daughter, Gmaa, had slipped away from her uncle Richard as they escaped Malema. Realizing who she might be, he yelled her name out the window, "Gmaa!" The young girl had reached to balance the basket and turned her head in the direction of his voice. Not seeing anyone, she turned away. He said he jumped out of his seat, nearly tripping over the person sitting next to him on the aisle, and yelled for the bus driver to wait as the bus began to pull away from the curb. Alfred yelled again, "Please wait," as he staggered down the aisle between legs and feet. The bus jerked to a stop and Alfred hurtled down its steps onto the sidewalk.

We were all waiting anxiously to find out if the girl was really Gmaa. I urged him on in his story-telling and Alfred continued by saying he had then walked up and asked for a bag of peanuts. We all laughed. I thought I would surely have run up and grabbed her shoulders and screamed right in her face. Why had he not said who he was? Well, he said that he did not want to frighten or startle her by telling who he was just yet, so he hummed a traditional village tune instead. The girl seemed to recognize it, so Alfred seized the opportunity to start a conversation and ask her name. "My name's Evelyn," she had told him. He knew right then he had found her; Evelyn was her birth name while Gmaa was her nickname. Gmaa said, "You look familiar. Do I know you? Have we met before?" He answered, "Yes, many years ago."

Alfred asked Gmaa if she remembered going to school in Monrovia while living with her mother's brother, Uncle Richard. She responded, "Yes, I do remember. How do you know about that?" He told her he had met her there, and just wondered if she was the same girl.

Alfred said Gmaa seemed happy to meet someone who knew her from her past and, inviting him to come meet her family, told him she lived just up the road, pointing up the hill toward Fourah Bay College Junction.

Since she had sold her last bag of peanuts—to Alfred—it was time for her to head home, and he walked her part of the way in order to identify which house she lived in. He said he would see her later, and walked back down to catch the next bus to the Waterloo camp.

By this time, we were all jumping up and down, full of suggestions, and begging to know what he planned to do next. I grabbed his hands as he told that he planned on catching the first bus back to Freetown in the morning and heading straight to the UNHCR main office to meet with the protection officer. He said he would let the officer know he had found Gmaa, who had been under the protection of the UNHCR as a Liberian refugee at the time her family had lost her. UNHCR protection officers generally have degrees in law or international law, and work closely with local authorities to help ensure that countries establish and maintain refugees' legal rights. The UNHCR keeps comprehensive records on all refugees, and they had obtained Gmaa's records from the Red Cross who had registered her while she was in Malema.

The next morning, Alfred headed off, taking along Richard's wife, Edith, who had been grieving over Gmaa ever since she had been lost. The wait seemed interminable for those of us left to ponder what would happen, but we stayed busy with our usual routines and later in the day Alfred and Edith arrived back at the camp with Gmaa. We were so overjoyed to see her. She was even more beautiful than when I had first met her in Malema—and she still had the same thick, jet-black hair.

Alfred boomed out over our excited voices that the UNHCR protection officer had located Gmaa's records. We all shushed each other and gathered close to hear him. "They found a photo of her taken before she had been lost," he said. Realizing Alfred might need some help convincing the family Gmaa was living with of her familial relationship to him, the officer had sent a UNHCR staff member along and asked a member of the Sierra Leonean Security Forces to join them as well.

When the small entourage arrived at Gmaa's house, the family had claimed they were her biological parents. They were not keen on the idea of letting her leave because she was helping provide extra income. To make matters worse, they had already arranged for Gmaa to be married to a Sierra Leonean man, and, perhaps, were anticipating a payment to finalize the agreement. Alfred said that when he showed them the photograph of Gmaa as a young girl, and asked all those present to compare her features with his, no one could deny the resemblance. Alfred happily relayed to us that the authorities insisted Gmaa go with him so he could reunite her with her mother.

We all shook our heads in dismay as the story came out that the family had actually purchased Gmaa from someone who had found her those seven years earlier. Children separated from their true families, and sold like this, often became servant children. The family finally admitted to this and the man said, "The people who sold her to us assured us she was an orphan. We meant her no harm."

Through all this, Gmaa remained silent and shyly watched our faces. I wondered at what emotions and thoughts were washing through her mind and smiled at her to remind her of the love we had shared and to let her know it was going to be all right.

Alfred, with the aid of the UNHCR, managed to get word to Cecelia, Gmaa's mother, that he had found her daughter, still alive and well—and that he would bring her to Liberia as soon as possible. All this time, poor Cecelia had assumed her only child had been killed in the war. I could only imagine the magnitude of the relief that must have struck her heart on hearing of this splendid miracle.

One evening in December of 1994, soon after Gmaa's arrival, a terrifying dream awakened me. In my dream, I saw a large celebration in the center of Freetown. The crowd was dancing and laughing. No one seemed to notice, however, when the joyful drumbeat changed to a frenzied battle cry. I frantically tried to warn the merrymakers that they must leave, as they were in grave danger, and that an onslaught of rebel forces was approaching. I watched as those who heeded my warnings survived and those who did not fell in the massacre. The terror I felt wrenched me awake and I feared that, just as the flooded streets of Monrovia had been, this was another premonition of actual events to come.

I told my family and friends of the horrors I had seen in my dream. Those who knew me well knew of my gift of dream visions and of my ability to interpret dreams; they were very concerned over what I had received the night before. Unfortunately, as refugees, we had nowhere to run.

Word of my vivid dream, supported by rumors of advancing rebel forces, quickly spread throughout the camp. An ominous cloud enveloped us and it became more apparent just how uncertain our existence was. We shuddered at the threat of another ghastly rebel attack. Waterloo and Freetown are located on a peninsula, and the only way out, other than heading right into advancing rebel forces, was by plane or by boat. I did not have sufficient funds for either, so in spite of the warning I had given to others, I remained stranded with no way out.

I also told many I knew in Freetown, and word spread quickly that a young lady who heard from God had issued a warning of a coming rebel attack. After hearing of my dream, many made plans to leave Freetown, trusting that God had given a warning that they should heed.

A few months later, the UN advised us they had launched a voluntary repatriation program and Liberians, who were comfortable doing so, could have transportation to Monrovia by ship, returning home at their own risk. Most of those who were not Krahns or Mandingos, and had never worked in the Doe administration, accepted the UN offer to return to Liberia.

Abel and I were now a committed couple, and neither of us felt safe returning to Monrovia, for rebel forces were still in control of much of our country. My cousin Alfred, however, decided to accept the UN's offer. Within a week, he and Gmaa sailed to Monrovia and we heard Gmaa and her mother were happily reunited.

Our own plans were to leave the country and head to Guinea. Abel earned a little money each week from soaps he made at the camp and sold in Freetown; I received a quarterly stipend from the UN to help pay for school supplies. However, it was several months before we could save enough to pay for transportation.

One day, in early 1995, I returned to the Waterloo refugee camp from the Fourah Bay College campus just in time to see a Sierra Leonean military officer with one boot missing and a rifle in his hand run screaming through the camp. In his Creole tongue he shouted, "Me fambo! Me fambo! Oh! Me mama, Ae don lef na wata!" He had said, "My family! My family! My mother was drowned!"

"What's happening?" panicked refugees pleaded. With terror in his eyes he screamed, "Rebels de come, them de come, them de come!" We were horrified to learn he had just escaped an onslaught in which rebels had massacred his family and comrades.

Abel was away in Freetown selling his homemade soap, but I expected him back shortly. I immediately ran inside our makeshift palm-branch hut to grab whatever I could lay my hands on. As I tossed our belongings together I could hear Abel desperately yelling, "Louise! Louise!" In a moment, his terrified face appeared in the doorway. "Louise, I was afraid I had lost you!" he panted. With a bearlike hug, he practically squeezed the air out me. I picked up the bag I had just packed and shoved it toward him. Without wasting another second we ran out of the camp as fast as we could, joining thousands of other fleeing refugees. Families despairingly abandoned the old, sick, and physically handicapped who were no longer able to move on their own, leaving them behind to receive the merciless rebels.

A tidal wave of RUF forces was making its way toward Freetown, Sierra Leone's capital, and we knew that wave would first slam into the town of Waterloo. Anyone who did not evacuate the camp soon would end up caught in the crossfire between rebels and the Sierra Leonean forces.

We ran with a multitude of refugees and headed south as fast as we could. In a few hundred yards, the sound of gunfire coming from the direction we were heading stopped us in our tracks. I truly thought we would all perish, and implored, "Lord, Jesus, please help us!" We quickly turned around and headed north; running for the cover a nearby palm plantation might afford us.

After an hour of non-stop running, scraping ourselves on thorny palm branches and poisonous ivies in the process, we reached the main road. We bent over in pain from severe cramping and sheer exhaustion. There was no sound except that of our heavy breathing; hundreds of lungs filled and emptied, plying the air as one massive bellows. The muscles in our legs and thighs began contracting uncontrollably, and some of us collapsed on the pavement, suffering from the spasms.

As soon as we could, we ran down the road coming upon a band of Sierra Leonean soldiers who were getting ready to launch a counter-attack on the invading rebels. Since rebel soldiers often changed into their victims' clothing, they made us all strip so they could search us for rebel markings. They forcefully removed from the group anyone who appeared the least bit suspicious. The soldiers shoved them to the side of the road and shot them. Even though we had seen this scenario played out time and time again, we were horrified. After assuring themselves the rest of us were a band of refugees, the soldiers directed us to Devil Hole, which was about four miles up the road toward Freetown. Although there was no camp there, and we would have to do the best we could, they felt Devil Hole was the best place for us to be until a new camp could be set up closer to Freetown.

While most of the refugees followed their orders, Abel and I, along with a number of others, felt Devil Hole was far too close to Waterloo to be safe. We felt we would be better off heading toward the more heavily guarded capital. After walking for four hours in the direction of Freetown, we encountered a group of ECOMOG soldiers. ECOMOG stands for the Economic Community of West African States Monitoring Group, a West African, multilateral, armed force established by the Economic Community of West African States in 1990. Their initial purpose was to intervene in the civil war in Liberia, but they had been deployed into Sierra Leone to help stop the RUF rebellion.

The ECOMOG soldiers, just as the Sierra Leonean soldiers had, commanded us to head to Devil Hole. They told us it would not be safe to go to Freetown just yet. In a few more hours, we reached Devil Hole, an area infested with mosquitoes, scorpions, and many other biting bugs. We threw together a makeshift camp. There were no provisions other than water from near-by streams and the bit of food local villagers might be able and willing to share with us. Once again, there was nowhere to sleep but out on the open ground.

Situated in a very deep valley surrounded by craggy and treacherous mountains, Devil Hole had received a very appropriate name. Mountains hemmed us in on three sides—and to make matters worse, we were only a few miles from Waterloo, the town we had just evacuated. At any moment, we fully expected rebels would overrun and kill us. Freetown may not have been safe just yet; however, we wondered how safe we were in Devil Hole. Being located on a peninsula, there were only two ways for us to go—either toward the invading rebels, or toward Freetown and the ocean.

The UNHCR did what it could to help us. Established by the United Nations in 1950, it was an agency mandated to lead and coordinate international action to protect refugees, and to resolve refugee problems worldwide. Although its primary purpose is to safeguard the rights and well-being of refugees, they were often hampered, even forced into total ineffectiveness by the bureaucracy and obscure policies put in place by the host countries in which they operated. As refugees, we were completely at the mercy of these policies. We had no choice but to accept whatever treatment the host country decided to mete out—even if that treatment was inhumane.

If we did not die at the hands of the rebels, we still faced the risk of dying at the hands of a soldier who, in the name of national security, may decide we were a risk. Those who didn't suffer this fate still faced the risk of starvation when corrupt officials decided, in their own interest, to intercept food items and other critical supplies (and often, in turn, sell them at the local markets) that had been earmarked for refugees.

Corruption even crept into some weak-minded representatives of the UNHCR. Food distribution was inconsistent, but refugees could earn food through various methods, including sexual favors. We had no choice but to complacently accept the uncivilized living conditions.

Two weeks after arriving at Devil Hole, fearing for our safety, the UNHCR decided to relocate us to a new camp in Jui about seven miles up the road and only a 45-minute walk from Freetown. We packed the little we had and headed out on the three-and-a-half-hour walk to Jui. The Jui camp was as devoid of critical supplies as any other was. Children died of treatable diseases, such as cholera, due to the lack of clean drinking water, adequate food, and essential medication.

I watched as a beautiful, five-year-old boy died of cholera while lying in his mother's arms. Cholera is a form of infectious gastroenteritis caused by toxin-producing strains of bacteria. It is transmitted by eating contaminated food, or by drinking contaminated water. It is one of the most rapidly fatal illnesses known, and a healthy person can die within three hours if he or she receives no medical treatment.

Earlier that day, he was a happy-go-lucky little boy. He ran around and explored the far ends of the camp with his friends in search of food. Being extremely hungry, they ended up scavenging for food at a nearby garbage site. A few hours after returning home the boy doubled over in pain and began vomiting and having diarrhea. Unfortunately, the main clinic had been locked up for the day. His poor mother ran up and down the camp trying to find medication to control her son's condition. Hearing her wailing and pleading, many of us ran to her aid. We gave the child warm salt water and natural herbs in the hopes of saving his life. His body expelled everything we gave him.

He experienced a rapid loss of body fluids; the dehydration and rapid drop in blood pressure eventually led to shock. His little legs pulled up tightly to his chest from the severe muscle cramping. His heart raced, his body grew cold and clammy, and he shivered and twitched as if he had been out in a cold rainstorm. Lying in his mother's arms, he drew his last, labored breath and left us. Once she realized he had stopped breathing, his mother let out a woeful wail heard in every corner of the camp.

In anguish, she attempted to prepare her son's body for burial. Tenderly washing the perspiration from his face, she ended up sobbing so uncontrollably that another woman had to take over. The mother collapsed onto his little chest and kissed him, crying out his name. She reluctantly allowed others to wrap her beloved, lifeless child in a white sheet and place his body gently inside the wheelbarrow waiting outside her hut. As they wheeled her precious son away to the gravesite, she followed.

The boy was the only child and the only family this woman had left. Sierra Leonean soldiers had killed her husband when we were in Seminary on suspicion of being a member of the invading rebel forces. She was in such pain that we feared she might throw herself into the grave with her son. Even though she did not, we all knew she buried her heart with him.

As strange as it sounds, it was during this time, and in this dreadful place, that Abel and I chose to refer to ourselves as common law husband and wife. He made me feel complete, and was very attentive to my needs, doing everything he could to take care of me. He was my protector and I learned I could depend on him for this; I knew he felt the same way about me. Even though life did not change in its provisions, we had drawn together and our relationship gave us a sense of home and family, something we could count on during these dark times.

CHAPTER 14

Against All Odds

A calming breeze and the warmth of early morning sun soothed me as I leaned against a fallen tree at the edge of the expansive river, gazing at the muddy embankment riddled with footprints. My attention was drawn to the river's edge, where strong men were dexterously yanking on nets they had set the night before. Shouts of elation came from a father and son team who had just pulled their nets full of shrimp, crabs, and catfish from the estuary. The noise of the catch brought the young refugee children hurrying, adding their tiny footprints to the mottled depressions already in the mud. Seeing the pleading eyes of the hungry gathering, good-hearted fisherman threw shrimp to each of the children. They scurried after their prizes, grabbing the hard shells in tight fists. Scampering up the slippery riverbank with their treasures in hand, they headed straight to their mothers in the camp. I smiled at the charity of the Jui village fishermen who were willing to share their catch with refugee children.

Closing my eyes, I listened to the laughter of the children, and daydreamed of the joys of village life when I was five years old, before my mother returned to the Ivory Coast and left me with my father. I fondly recalled my mother grabbing the handcrafted, hoop-shaped fishnet that hung neatly inside our hut door. I remembered how she would flip it over her head and let the rim rest on her forehead while the net draped down her back for easy carrying. I smiled as I thought of a time when she had donned the net, and led me out into the cool morning air, just as someone sang out, "Let's go!" I gleefully joined the dozens of village children as we raced ahead of our mothers in a mad dash for the river.

As we neared the water, we leapt in great strides, hoping to be the first one in. Many ran, sloshing along the shallow edge, while others swam toward the designated spot upstream. Once there, we splashed, laughed, stomped, shouted, and splashed some more; it was our job to make as much noise and commotion as we could, driving the startled fish downstream toward our mothers' nets. The melded joy and pride of accomplishment for our antics filled us as our mothers' nets filled with their catch.

The fishermen's shouts jolted me back to the present as the last nets were hoisted from the river, and children again ran up and down the bank in the hope of securing a kind handout.

Sierra Leone, not unlike Liberia, had been reduced to an endless expanse of bloody battlefields, where rebels and government troops fought for the control of the country. The rebels forced any civilians or refugees whom they captured, and did not instantly kill, into joining their ranks. If the civilians or refugees refused, the rebels tortured them to death. Whenever rebels captured women refugees, they did not only use them as domestic servants, but sexually exploited them as well. In addition, they forced the women into labor, transporting heavy arms and ammunition.

Language barriers, the local citizens' mixed political sentiments concerning refugees, ethnicity, and religious differences all contributed to the refugees' feelings of hopelessness. No matter how despondent and destitute we were Abel and I tried to keep our spirits up by maintaining positive attitudes and praying to God to rescue us from our condition.

It appeared we would be stuck in Jui for some time. Realizing that my educational pursuits continued to be critical to my independence, I sought and received a new UNHCR scholarship, allowing me to cross-train in a technical field as an auto mechanic technician. Although I had wanted to pursue a four-year-degree in Library Science at Fourah Bay College, trade school scholarships were the only first-year scholarships available—and I wanted to learn something new to keep myself busy. Making the best of it, I considered my new choice to be an adventure into a new frontier, and I had great hopes of soon being able to earn a living.

Because it was a three-hour walk to Freetown from the Jui refugee camp, students on UN scholarships obtained an allowance to pay for living quarters in Freetown. The torturous memory of my flogging and near-lynching in Freetown made me think twice about making the move, but I could not afford to take the bus into town, so I decided it would be better to deal with my memories than to walk six hours a day to school and back. Giving up my scholarship and remaining a refugee at the camp was not an option in my mind.

As Abel and I made the move to Freetown, we hoped the upcoming 1996 elections would end the conflict. When the ballots were all counted, a celebration broke out amongst the people. Alhaji Ahmad Tejan Kabbah of the Sierra Leone People's Party, a party promising to end the conflict and usher in lasting peace, had been elected the third president of Sierra Leone. On March 29, 1996, he was sworn in.

President Kabbah said his primary focus was on ending the rebel war, and in November 1996, in Abidjan in the Ivory Coast, he signed a peace agreement with Corporal Foday Sankoh of the Revolutionary United Front (RUF). The agreement became known as The Abidjan Agreement or the Abidjan Peace Accord, and it included a proclamation that read, "The armed conflict between the Government of Sierra Leone and the RUF is hereby ended with immediate effect. Accordingly, the two foes will ensure that a total cessation of hostilities is observed forthwith."

Under the agreement, the RUF was to disarm and transform itself into a political party. In addition, there was to be no official or judicial action taken against any member of the RUF, "in respect of anything done by them in pursuit of their objectives as members of that organization." More surprising, members of the RUF would be allowed to join the country's military.

In spite of our desire to see an end to the conflict, many civilians, and most refugees, felt the agreement had gone too far. For us, it was unfathomable that a group of rebels who had waged a heinous war on the innocent villagers of their own country, and on thousands of refugees from Liberia, could transform into a peaceful organization overnight simply by swearing allegiance to the new government leaders.

We wondered how those who had tortured and killed thousands of men, women, and children, and who had destroyed girls and boys by turning them into killing machines, could be expected to lay down their arms overnight and transform themselves into part of Sierra Leone's own armed forces.

Soon, Sankoh revealed his true intentions. In spite of his assurances to the contrary, he used the Abidjan Agreement as an opportunity to gain a tactical advantage. Instead of disarming, in March 1997 officials arrested him at a Nigerian airport with illegal weapons in his car.

Two months later, on the 25th of May, a group of Sierra Leonean soldiers, under the banner of a new Armed Forces Revolutionary Council (AFRC), overthrew the fledgling government and President Kabbah. They forced him into exile, in neighboring Conakry, Guinea.

Major Johnny Paul Koroma, who was in jail at the time of the coup, became Chairman of the AFRC. He stated that the previous government's failure to implement the Abidjan Agreement caused the coup; Koroma advocated making a peaceful settlement with Sankoh and allowing him and other RUF leaders to enter Freetown and unite with his government. He immediately announced the suspension of the constitution, banned all demonstrations, and abolished all political parties.

Chaos reigned as rebel forces entered the city and began looting local shops and homes. Shop owners quickly closed their businesses and the moral fiber of the community deteriorated as, within days, families began to starve. Whether they were looting or loitering, everywhere we turned, we saw four or five rebel soldiers. Much like what previously occurred, UN personnel and the Red Cross aid workers packed up and left town, leaving us to fend for ourselves.

I was tired of running, yet I knew staying in Freetown would be an act of suicide. Abel and I needed to leave quickly. On June 4, 1997, only ten days after the coup, we rushed to the local bank to gather the small savings we had stashed away, only to find the bank had locked their doors, telling those outside there was no more money.

On our way home, we used a back route that took us behind the State House, the official residence of the president and the seat of the Sierra Leonean government. All of our senses were on high alert, and our stomachs were in knots from fear. As we passed a group of soldiers who were guarding the president's offices, we immediately picked up the Liberian idiom they were using. I whispered to Abel, "They're Liberian RUF soldiers!"

The soldiers stopped us and said, "Your pass, your pass, we fini takin care of the terrain," meaning, "You all can pass here, we have this place under our control now." We hurried past them, nodding and keeping our eyes focused on the ground. We dared not speak because they might have killed us on the spot if they had recognized our Liberian accents.

We ran back to our apartment to throw together a few necessities. While we were packing to make a run for it, I came across my Bible, quickly opened it, and found the passage that reads, "But the Lord stood by me, and strengthened me; that through me the message might be fully proclaimed ... and I was delivered out of the mouth of the lion." I grabbed Abel's arm, looked squarely into his eyes, and said with conviction, "Abel, God's Word is alive, and I see His promise to deliver us from the mouth of the lion. You know *Sierra Leone* means "mountain lion," and He *will* deliver us out of Sierra Leone."

I could see Abel was having a difficult time believing we would find a way out, so I encouraged him with, "Don't worry Abel. I have an idea; let's go to the Freetown-Lungi International Airport. From there, we may be able to find a way to leave the country and travel to Guinea."

Abel looked stunned and incredulous. He snapped at me and said, "We don't have enough money. We don't have enough food. And we don't know anyone there!" I snapped right back with confidence, "Oh yes we do!" I took a deep breath, and with unbending faith responded, "We know somebody there. The same God who has been with us here will be there!"

Abel was surprised at the strong and determined tone of my voice. He took both of my hands in his, looked me in the eyes, and prayed, "Holy Father, you are our refuge and our strength, an ever-present help in times of trouble. We cannot find our way to safety without you. We trust you will direct our steps." We agreed to head for Lungi Airport, and knew we had to act swiftly.

A rapid knocking on our door almost made me jump out of my skin. Abel cracked the door open and found two sad and forlorn figures—Moses and Cecelia, fellow refugees—a couple from Liberia who were also living in Freetown and who had become our friends. They were terrified. We hurried them in. Moses, with his slender, youthful build, braced Cecelia against his chest. Fear deeply etched their faces. They clearly did not know what to do or where to turn.

They had brought with them one small bag of personal items, and another small bag containing the only food they had left—a little farina and eight lumps of sugar. Cecelia held up their small bag of food and said, "This is all we have, but we will share it with you." I hugged her close, and we both cried. I whispered, "Jesus multiplied two small fish and five little loaves of bread to feed thousands, and I am confident He can do the same for us."

We quickly shared our newly created plan with them, and they agreed to follow us to the Lungi Airport because they believed God was leading us; they felt better following Abel and me than anyone else they knew.

Abel and I had managed to scrounge up fifteen dollars and, trusting that God would somehow open a door for us, we grabbed our Bibles and the food we had stuffed into a small plastic bag. With that, and a lot of faith, we quietly locked the door of our house to avoid drawing attention to ourselves, and stole away in broad daylight.

We slowly strolled along, acting as if we four were on a casual afternoon walk or a trip to the local market. We only spoke to each other in hushed tones because our accents would immediately give us away as Liberian refugees. As we walked along, we could see that the rebels had destroyed most of the stores and had broken into homes out of sheer boredom. They needed to feed their deeply ingrained hunger for constant action and destruction in some way, so they had taken to destroying the town as a means of keeping themselves busy. Already, the rebels were scooping up young girls along the way for their nighttime entertainment. We could tell who they were because of the terror in their eyes as the rebels strong-armed them—and they were not yet wild and unkempt from the brutality and drugs they would be subjected to shortly.

It was mid-afternoon and, after having walked like this for a half-hour, we reached the ferry that provided passage across the eight-mile stretch of water, which separates Freetown from Lungi. As we boarded the ferry, my mind flashed back to the horrible scene of drowning men, women, and children who had boarded an overloaded barge on its final crossing of the Moa River. I could still see their terrified faces and hear their screams as the merciless current dragged them under. I had become deathly afraid of traveling over water, and clung tightly to Abel during the interminable journey; I was greatly relieved when we at last reached the dock.

Abel flagged down a mini-bus to drive us to the airport, cutting a several-hour walk down to a half-hour ride. He paid the driver and we stepped out of the beat-up old bus and onto the paved road in front of the airport.

We arrived to find the airport guarded by hundreds of heavily armed ECOMOG peacekeeping troops from the West African sub-region. We stood wondering what to do, and where to go. I prayed aloud, "God, we are standing here in Your presence. Guide our hearts, minds, and feet in the direction you would have us go."

Abel started walking and we all followed; none of us questioned his direction. God's hand moved us. We walked right on past the heavily guarded airport because we knew we did not have enough money for tickets to anywhere. It was apparent the military had partially converted the airport into a base. Darkness descended in a constricting blanket as we entered the local business district on roads unfamiliar to us. It was a moonless night, and all lighting was off at this hour. It was so dark we could barely see our hands in front of our faces. We were afraid to keep walking, but knew we could not stand idly in the street. I trusted God would continue leading us as we moved along, and with each step, I anticipated His guidance.

It could be fatal for us to speak to anyone we came across in the dark because the local people had heard that there were Liberians in the RUF and that the rebels had invaded Freetown. They also knew what Liberian rebel invaders had done to other towns not too far away. We walked on in the darkness as quietly as we could.

Abel spoke in a throaty whisper, "I can't see where I'm going. Stay close. We don't want to lose anyone." As I held onto Abel's hand and reached back for Cecelia, a voice called my husband's name out of the darkness, "Abel?" We stopped dead in our tracks. My only thought was, *Oh Lord, what's this?* The unknown voice called out again from the darkness, "Abel, that's you, isn't it?" I gave a shiver as we cautiously followed Abel toward the voice.

A dark figure stepped out in front of us and Abel instantly recognized his old friend Jeddee, whom he had met four years earlier in the Waterloo camp. Jeddee had left the camp to live with his aunt who had a home in Lungi. Jeddee said, "Abel, what are you doing here?" Abel laughed nervously, "Oh, we're out for a lovely evening stroll." Jeddee laughed, too, and grabbed Abel with a big hug. For a moment, their excitement overshadowed our plight and lightened our spirits.

Abel said, "How did you know it was me?" Jeddee responded, "I recognized your voice, Abel. No one has a voice quite like yours." He added, "For the last four years I've been living here at Lungi. What exactly are *you* doing over here?" He stopped and looked at the rest of us and queried, "And who are you traveling with?" Abel introduced us to his friend, "Jeddee, this is my wife, Louise, and our dear friends Moses and Cecelia."

Jeddee inquired, "Where are you headed, my brother?" Abel broke down and cried in a mixture of anxiety and relief, but soon he was able to explain the difficult situation we were in. "RUF rebels have taken over Freetown, and we're on the run again. We came to Lungi trusting that God would make a way for us to get out of the country, somehow."

Abel's voice quavered as he shared, "Right now we don't have any place to go. We need a place to stay until we can make our way to Guinea." With resolution in his voice, Jeddee said, "Follow me, I have a place. By the way, all passenger flights in and out of Sierra Leone have been banned due to the military coup, and as you may have noticed, ECOMOG forces have taken control of the airport to protect it."

I poked Abel in the ribs with my elbow and whispered, "Do you trust him? Where's he taking us?" Abel shrugged his shoulders and gave an "I don't know" look while nodding at the same time. He followed closely beside Jeddee. My concerns gradually melted away as Jeddee and Abel struck up a friendly conversation about the past and what had gone on since they had last seen each other; I squeezed Cecelia's hand with assurance. "It's okay, God is leading us out of the mouth of the lion."

We arrived at Jeddee's aunt's house at around 10:00 PM. Jeddee went inside, where we assumed he was advising his aunt and uncle that, during his evening walk, he had run into a friend he had known several years earlier in the Waterloo refugee camp. When they learned we were standing outside, they rushed out to greet us. They asked us to have a seat on the porch and their five children, ages six to eighteen, joined us. The family was hungry for news of what was happening in Freetown.

As Jeddee's aunt put a pot of soup on the stove for us, we told them about how Major Johnny Paul Koroma, after ousting President Kabbah, had invited RUF rebels into Freetown and given them free reign. We shared with them how rebels were everywhere in the capital, and had even taken over the State House. "They were running the streets, harassing and intimidating people, hijacking cars, looting stores, and pillaging homes while waiting for orders from their commanders." Many of the rebels were boasting, "We're in Freetown now, and no one can take it back." Jeddee and his family were horror-struck, and deeply concerned that the rebels might attack Lungi in an attempt to seize the airport.

Since it was late, and they could see we were in need of rest, they welcomed us to stay with them for as long as needed. Jeddee's family may have had little money, but they had wealth of a different kind. Their kindness to us is most assuredly recorded in Heaven. It was a blessing to be able to stay with Jeddee and his family for the next ten days.

Jeddee gave up his bed to Abel and me, but we passed the offer on to Cecelia and Moses. I kneeled before retiring, and thanked God for going before us and bringing us to this home. Abel and I lay on a bamboo mat on the concrete floor next to the bed. Abel rolled over toward me and whispered, "You were right." I smiled and asked, "Right about what?" He said, "We do know someone in Lungi. *God* is here, and He sent Jeddee to find us. As long as I live I will never forget this night."

"Nor I Abel, nor I," and I drifted off to sleep. The pain of our bony bodies pressing against the strips of bamboo on the hard floor made it difficult to sleep deeply, yet our spirits rested in the peace of knowing that God was making a way for us to escape.

The next morning we joined the family on the porch for a breakfast of bread and boiled eggs, and continued our conversation of the night before. Abel and I shared how we were living in Freetown and going to school on UNHCR scholarships when the rebels had entered the town. The news especially upset Jeddee's aunt. "If they attack us here, we have nowhere to go. The only way out is by boat, and even if we did leave, where would we go? Where could we stay? We worked so hard to build a home and a life here. If the rebels attack this town all we've worked for could be destroyed." She was also very worried about the safety of her five children.

I yearned to fill her with words of comfort. After experiencing what the rebels were capable of, all I could do was share the truth about what we had seen in Freetown, trying to assure her that I believed, with all my being, God would take care of us. For most of the day, we stayed glued to the radio as we listened to BBC broadcasters reporting live on the situation in Freetown. We learned that the United States was evacuating American citizens as expediently as possible, using Marine helicopters, as were the British.

When Sunday morning came, we followed Jeddee to church. It was a beautifully warm and sunny day, and a pleasant breeze blew off the ocean, easing our frayed spirits. Swaying coconut palms graced the peacefully flat landscape. We walked arm-in-arm along a paved road to downtown Lungi, not far from the airport. Church was in an old, unfinished, unpainted schoolhouse that had no glass in its dark window openings. I smiled at the humble surroundings, and wondered what we would find once we were inside.

We were early, and as we strolled up to the building, we passed a goat munching on bits of grass in the yard near the front entrance where a temporary door made of bamboo was precariously propped. Jeddee repositioned it, allowing us inside. As soon as we stepped into the large room, the smell of goats overwhelmed our noses. Since the building could not be secured, goats walked in and out as they pleased. A middle-aged woman who was sweeping away goat droppings and other debris looked up at us with a bright grin, nodding a greeting in our direction.

Long, gray-painted wood benches lined up on the bare concrete floor. As people streamed into the room, the hum of voices began filling the space. We followed Jeddee to a bench in the back and sat down. For the next few hours, we determinedly left behind hellish experiences and approached Heaven's gates with hearts full of gratitude.

The lead drummer put his drum between his legs and began softly palming it while the other drummer readied his instrument by strapping it under his left arm. Seated next to the drummers was a musician who played an African piano made of different sized wooden slats; he played it with mallets, much like a xylophone. A woman began playing the *sasa* and swept me back to when my mother would play hers and sing blessings to those in the village. I could not help but weep as I recalled her love.

As the music swelled, we all rose to our feet. The Spirit of God moved over us, and the joy of the Lord filled our hearts to overflowing. The worship leader, his wife, and the pastor's wife led the singing. We joined in the well-known songs, praising God for his goodness and love.

The tempo of the drumming increased and many began dancing as their spirits soared. Some began a trek around the room, twisting, turning, and twirling together as their delight rose to Heaven, and they shouted praises to God. Our drab surroundings came alive with colorful clothing and beautiful voices and happy people. We swayed, danced, clapped, and stomped to the music and filled the House of God with sounds of joy. Cries of, "Amen" and "Hallelujah" rang out until our energy was spent.

Perspiration glistened on our faces and we collapsed onto our benches as the music ended. Fortunately, a refreshing ocean breeze blew through the windows, giving us all some relief as women fanned themselves with their *lappas* and men cooled themselves with country fans made of feathers.

Before preaching, the pastor called for a time of prayer. Then he opened the service to any who might be moved to speak. I stood up and prayed, "Father God, I thank you for life. Every day is a gift from Your hand. Thank you, for Your daily provisions and protection." At that moment, I received a troubling vision and felt the need to share it with everyone. Empowered by God, I said, "I see trouble coming. In just three days, trouble is coming to Lungi. I see rebel soldiers filling the streets, and Lungi will be attacked—but God is with us and will not forsake us." A hush had come over the congregation and all eyes were on me. I looked from face to face and saw their concern. I continued, "Everyone gathering here today in this church will be safe. We all will survive!" I took a deep breath, and sat down.

Immediately after the meeting had ended, an old soldier crossed the room in long strides. He was not very tall, but his broad frame was commanding. He was heavyset and very dark—almost black, with a rugged, yet worn-looking face. He was dressed in an ECOMOG military uniform and had slung his rifle across his back. I had noticed him earlier, because he sat by himself. One young man who was sitting on the same bench had gotten up and moved across the room when the soldier sat down and placed his rifle on the seat.

As he came up to me, the old soldier's eyes looked deeply into mine. He paused, the silence only strengthening his conviction; then came his words. "Oh, little girl! When you prayed, I felt the power of God move in you, and I was touched by God." He continued, barely taking a breath, "I'm just an old ECOMOG soldier from the Nigerian Contingent who loves Jesus." He smiled and held out his hand to shake mine and asked, "Where do you live?" I felt safe in his presence, and did not question his sincerity. I said, "My husband and I are staying with our friend Jeddee." After the service, the Old Soldier, as we referred to him, followed us home so he could see where we were staying.

Jeddee invited the Old Soldier to stay for lunch. He listened to the story of our plight, and seemed deeply touched. Before he left he said, "I was meant to meet you today. God be with you." I felt a connection with this man, and wondered what part he might possibly play in securing our safe passage out of Lungi.

Shortly before dark, we heard a knock at the door. Jeddee went over and opened it. There stood the Old Soldier with four of his soldier friends. He had gone back to his base and told his friends about a woman who heard from God about a coming rebel invasion on Lungi Airport. Out of concern for their lives, as well as curiosity, they had come to meet me. It was a fulfilling evening; under a dark sky and the promising sliver of a new moon, we sat and talked about God's love and the vision I had seen that morning in church. Before we knew it the night was nearly spent, and the soldiers hurried back to their base.

At the crack of dawn someone rapped on the door. Jeddee stumbled his way over and opened it to find the Old Soldier smiling at him. "May I come in to visit with the praying people?" The first words out of his mouth when he saw me were a very enthusiastic, "Good morning, woman of God!" His face beamed brighter than the morning sun. I thought, *God is smiling on this man.* The Old Soldier wanted to tell us that he had been so concerned about my vision of an imminent attack that he had shared it with the general, who was the commander of his outfit. The rumors of a woman visionary in Lungi had begun circulating throughout the base, causing many to come to the Old Soldier to hear more.

That same day the BBC announced that RUF rebels were surrounding the Freetown-Lungi Airport, and were planning to capture the terminal. Everyone knew that my vision was about to become a reality.

Three days later, in the middle of the night, rebel soldiers invaded Lungi. The noise of gunfire and rocket-propelled grenades (RPGs) rapidly filled the air. Abel and I were in the living room, and ran to the bedroom to hide. As soon as we had scooted under the bed, Moses and Cecelia tumbled from the bed and joined us on the concrete floor. Glaring light traversed the walls and floor of the room as RPGs shot past our windows. Adrenaline pumped through my tiny frame and my heart seemed to be pounding as loudly as the bomb blasts that shook the house. I soon became sick to my stomach from the screaming I heard outside.

The battle raged about us, bringing its shattering sounds of screams, gunfire, and explosions. A pregnant woman who lived next door joined in the drama of the terrifying battle. Her screams were audible above all the other noise and tore at us as we huddled under the bed. After the battle had ceased and all seemed quiet, Jeddee's aunt slipped out the back door in hopes of helping her neighbor. The agonizing labor spasms ceased as the battle had, and the baby finally entered the world; one of grave uncertainty.

Not long after Jeddee's aunt had returned home from delivering the baby, loud thumping at the door startled us. We were too frightened to open it and everyone stayed hidden. Abel and I were still under the bed with Moses and Cecelia. The pounding grew louder and we finally heard a muffled voice yelling, "Louise, Louise, open the door! It's me, and the pastor. We're going to take you to the base, where it's safe." As he shouted for us, the Old Soldier's voice faltered with the fear that we might have all perished during the night's bloody battle. We scurried out from our hiding place, and when he saw us, indescribable relief filled the Old Soldier's face. The Old Soldier and the local church pastor had been going door-to-door to fetch people from their homes and escort them safely over to the ECOMOG base for protection. The woman who had just given birth earlier that morning came out of her house with her newborn in her arms. She leaned on her husband for support while she raised her hand, acknowledging Jeddee's aunt.

The morning sun revealed the aftermath of the night's battle. Dead rebel boys, still clenching their rifles, lay crumpled on the ground. I was afraid to step over them, thinking they might somehow awaken and shoot us. Quavering, I paused before them, and was sure even the dead could not be trusted.

As we approached the airport, I was surprised to see six .50 caliber machine guns mounted on the street, manned by soldiers with ammunition belts draped across their chests. I looked around at the makeshift base and wondered which building we would go to for protection. I was becoming very uncomfortable and did not want to stay outside any longer than necessary, knowing another rebel attack was imminent.

All the townsmen who had gathered at the base received orders at gunpoint to strip naked so the ECOMOG soldiers could look for rebel markings. These soldiers were kinder than the Sierra Leonean soldiers had been, but even they could not take any chances that a rebel might have dressed in the clothes of a dead civilian and snuck in among us. They inspected the women and children by asking us to lie flat on the asphalt so they could search our bodies for rebel markings.

After assuring themselves there were no rebels among us, an officer said, "Everyone stay where you are. We've decided that we can protect you better here on the road than inside the base because the base has been under heavy fire. From here, we can easily see the rebel forces, no matter which angle they attack from. All of you men lie down now, on the road with the women and children!" I screamed inside my head, *I don't want to stay outside!* At this moment I did not care what their reasons were, I just wanted to hide inside one of the buildings as far away from the battle as possible.

At about 10:00 AM, just as we had all settled on the blistering hot road surface, a band of rebels began shooting right over our heads at the ECOMOG soldiers. One soldier shouted, "Don't move! We're firing over your heads." Instantly, we were plunged into the middle of an intense confrontation as troops hunkered down—so close that many of the civilians held onto the soldiers' boots while the battle blazed around us. Children's terrified screams were deadened by the deafening sounds of AK-47 gunfire buffeting our eardrums. Scorching brass casings pelted us, singeing our skin and clothes as smoke filled our lungs. The ground shook violently as rebel RPGs exploded nearby. Parents shielded their children's bodies with their own, cradling their heads and covering their ears as they pleaded, "Don't move! Stay down!"

Agile young rebels climbed onto nearby rooftops and began taking sniper shots at the soldiers. In an instant, the THUMP-THUMP-
THUMP of the powerful .50 caliber machine guns reverberated
through our bodies and several roofs caught fire from the barrage of
bullets. As rebels crawled toward us on the ground, some of the soldiers
dropped down on their stomachs and fired into the tall grass along the
edge of the pavement. The soldiers were in a three-tiered configuration
with some flat on the ground, some kneeling, and others on chairs
operating the machine guns atop the ground-mount tripods. When
the machine guns fired into the grass at the advancing rebels, it looked
like an invisible tiller was violently churning up the soil. Clods of grass
and earth jumped into the air, and sand sprayed out a few feet in all
directions as the bullets struck the ground.

In an attempt to overwhelm the ECOMOG forces, a seemingly
unending flow of wild-eyed rebel children continued swarming at us
from all directions, scrambling onto roofs—snarling and screeching at
us. It was clear they believed nothing could confound them. Thankfully,
the ECOMOG soldiers maintained the upper hand with their superior
skill and firepower. Adrenalin-charged, they returned fire. "Over there!
Motherf'in' rebels! Kill 'em! Mow down those human-eaters! Blood-
thirsty bastards! They're not human! Take 'em all out!"

The entire time, I felt that I would be dead in the next moment.
I felt as if a jackhammer had been strapped to my skull and I choked
from the fumes that lay close to the ground. The unbearable heat of
the unforgiving sun intensified the foul scent of the hot asphalt and the
acrid smell of the gunfire. We were drenched in our own sweat as well
as that of the soldiers performing their duty above us. Some parents
had a difficult time holding onto their young children who tried to
jump up and run away from the madness. I too had a nearly uncontrollable urge to run.

At one point, I nearly passed out, and felt my spirit leave my body—
much like when I had been beaten and tied to the back of a motorcycle
in Freetown. I drifted into a surreal state, still present, but slightly

removed from the intensity of it all. I floated there, taking in all the sensations, but not being affected by them. I was able to contemplate whether I would live to see another normal day. As my mind wandered, I remembered the various ways God had worked in my life. I remembered my vision of Lungi being under attack by rebels. Once again, God had warned me of things to come; once again, I had nowhere else to go—but I was still alive.

The battle raged on like this for six long and punishing hours. Finally, at around 4:00 PM, the gunfire ceased. We were told to stay where we were, in case it was only a lull in the storm. I held my breath and prayed that the battle was over. It was a true miracle that not one of us who had placed our lives into the hands of the ECOMOG soldiers had been harmed. The soldiers shouted to each other, "Did we kill all the bastards?" A few troops spread out to secure the area, making sure there were no rebels lingering in the bushes or hiding on rooftops. When they gave the all-clear signal and said we could get up, we wondered where we could go and be safe.

Knowing the battle could commence again during the night, one of the officers spoke with the pastor we had met three days earlier, gaining his permission for everyone to stay in his home; they felt they could better protect us there after sundown. The smell of asphalt and gunpowder was still thick in our nostrils and adrenalin still coursed through our veins, causing some to vomit.

Parents covered the eyes of their children as we weaved our way through the death and debris. A chill went through me as I saw the blank stares of the dead who had seen their last battle. I was stunned seeing their bodies; they were little boys as young as seven lying beside AK-47 rifles nearly as tall as they were. These once innocent children had been forced into training, told the voodoo talismans they had been given would make them impervious to bullets, and had been drugged into a frenzy and placed on the front lines as fodder to test the strength of the ECOMOG troops.

Terrified farm animals and family pets scurried and dashed in all directions—barking, bleating, clucking, and flapping. Once they noticed us they headed our way, and many of them joined us in the pastor's home. Still frantic, they ran in circles, jumped over furniture, and slammed into walls.

Many of us wanted to close the doors, but the pastor said it would be best to keep them open in case we had to make a quick exit at the next attack, or if the house caught fire. No one dared leave because the ECOMOG soldiers had told us they would shoot at anything moving outside. We packed every inch of floor space in the pastor's moderately sized home like sardines in a can. Our little group remained together in a corner of the living room, and I thought, *If we're going to die, we're going to die together.*

Soon after we arrived, the ground began to shake and windows shattered as an RPG just missed the house and exploded nearby; a torrent of gunfire immediately followed. We all screamed and tucked ourselves low to the floor. The rebels attacked until they ran out of ammunition. Those who were able to escape fled into the night while the ECOMOG soldiers cut the others down.

In the morning, the military announced the battle had ceased. We ventured out, finding bullet-riddled homes and previously well-manicured yards cratered and smoldering. Buildings had sections torn out by RPG blasts. Glass from blown-out windows mixed with the blood from the bodies that littered the neighborhood.

Abel and other men were asked to aid the soldiers in collecting the dead for disposal. It was an appalling job. When Abel saw the mangled bodies of the rebel children he was incapable of moving. He went into shock trying to comprehend the tragedy strewn over the lawns of this once serene town.

After the streets and yards were cleared, everyone was advised it was safe to return to their homes—what was left of them. The destruction was so extensive we knew it would take many months, possibly years, to repair the area.

CHAPTER 15

The Old Soldier

Wars, rumors of wars, and living in constant fear had taken a toll on our emotional and physical health. Having been in Lungi for only a week, we had already suffered two days of bloody battling; we jumped at the slightest sound and panic came up in our throats at every rap on the door.

In the midst of it, our faithful Old Soldier friend came once or twice daily to visit and be encouraged as we shared God's Word with each other. He often brought many fellow soldiers along with him.

One morning the Old Soldier knocked on the door with his special knock. When I opened the door, I was surprised to see an especially large group of uniformed soldiers with him. I smiled and giggled under my breath, "Good morning, friend." He smiled back saying, "I brought you some more friends." Abel, Jeddee, Moses, and Cecelia joined me at the door, and we all walked outside so we could sit comfortably under the shade of a tree.

The Old Soldier looked at his friends and, as he rested his hand on my shoulder, he declared, "These are the 'praying people' I told you about, and they are the real deal. Their faith in God is astounding, and no one has greater faith than this woman."

All of their eyes focused on me; I stood and said, "Thank you, so much, for saving our lives. You deserve great honor. All of you were willing to expose yourselves to the enemies' bullets to protect us." I praised them for their bravery, and prayed for them to have God's protection and long life.

The Old Soldier pointed at us and spoke again. "I've only known these people for a week, and they have changed my life." He turned to me and said, "Louise, tell them how God's miracles have protected you."

I looked into the eyes of the soldiers and instantly knew what I must share with them. I opened my heart, not holding anything back, and said, "There's a beautiful promise in God's Word that says we know that all things, whether they are good or bad, work together for good; for those that love God, and are called according to His purpose."

I continued by sharing some of my struggles, and how I had been forced to flee Liberia. I told them of how Uncle Nyoun had saved my life and what a miracle it had been for our small group to run into Jeddee when we first came into Lungi. I shared again the vision I was given while praying in church of a rebel invasion of Lungi that would come in three days; a vision we all knew came to pass.

"I praise God for each of you, for you were willing to be used by God to protect the town of Lungi, and we are all enjoying the precious breath of life today because of your faithfulness." Jeddee, Abel, Moses, and Cecelia all nodded in agreement and expressed their appreciation by reaching out and touching those selfless men. We lifted up these heroic young troops with words of praise and thanksgiving, but no matter how many words we used, I knew there was no expression great enough.

One soldier asked, "What will you do now?" I told him, "As Liberian refugees it is not safe for us to stay here in Lungi. We need to find a way to travel to Guinea." The soldiers wanted to help, so it was suggested we write a letter to their commanding officer requesting his assistance. The Old Soldier said, "If you write it, I will gladly deliver it to the general."

A renewed sense of hope and energy washed over me; I jumped up and ran into the house with Jeddee at my heels. He knew exactly what I needed, and quickly located a pen and paper. After listening to everyone's suggestions, I went to work drafting a letter to the general, stating the facts of our situation. I mentioned the story of Esther from the Bible—how she prayed, fasted, and pleaded with her husband, the Persian king, for the lives of her people, the Jews. Without his help, we would perish.

When I had finished my letter, the Old Soldier reached out for it and said, "Louise, it is God's will that you survive. This letter will go before you, and we will all see God's mighty hand move the minds and hearts of those in authority."

Just like Esther, our group made a pledge to fast, not eating or drinking for the next three days. We devoted ourselves to prayer, and at the end of our three-day fast, there came a knock at the door. I opened it to find the Old Soldier smiling from ear to ear. He stepped toward me, swept me up in his strong arms, and gently put me down. He gave Abel a robust hug as he said, "The general wants to meet all of you."

Our shouts of joy filled the house. After exchanging more hugs, we prayed and sang praises to God. The Old Soldier politely interrupted us to say, "He's waiting right now to meet you." Not hesitating, and motivated by our excitement, we followed him out the door and toward the base. We practically had to run to keep up with him.

From a distance we could make out a tall, thin, but strong figure standing stiffly just outside the closed doors of the airport terminal. As we got closer, we could make out his strikingly handsome face and smooth features. He wore an officer's cap with a gold bird on the front, and his uniformed chest was covered with medals. The Old Soldier dipped his head toward us and whispered, "Wait for my introduction before you speak." He walked up to the general and saluted. Not revealing his emotions or thoughts, the general returned a trim salute. The Old Soldier said, "Sir, I have brought the people, as you requested."

The general nodded approval and turned toward us. His austere manner somewhat diminished our level of excitement. With military firmness he inquired, "Who is the spokesperson for this group?" I immediately gave a bow in his direction and said, "Me, sir. I am Louise Barton, and this is my husband, Abel; these are our friends Moses and

Cecelia. We are pleased to meet you." He cracked a smile. While holding up a piece of paper in his hand he said, "Who wrote this letter?"

Even before seeing the handwriting on the paper, I knew it was
mine, and responded, "I did!" Without taking a breath I continued,
"We are innocent people. We are Liberian refugees trapped in Sierra
Leone. We tried to get our money out of the Freetown bank so we
could leave before the war broke out, but, while we were standing in
line, someone came out of the bank to tell us the money was all gone.
At that point they locked the doors."

I kept on talking, barely pausing for breath, for fear he might brush
us off and not want to hear the entire story. I continued to share the
facts of our plight. "We had to walk out of Freetown in the midst of the
violence, in broad daylight. We took nothing except a couple of parcels
and our Bibles. We hoped the rebel troops who were keeping watch
around town wouldn't notice us."

I took a quick breath and continued. "We came to Lungi about ten
days ago, not knowing anyone here, but trusting God would provide
a way. He led us to Jeddee, an old friend of Abel's, who miraculously
showed up in the middle of the night on the dark road where we were
walking. Jeddee has kindly allowed us to stay at his home since our
arrival. At his church, week before last, I had a vision that Lungi would
be attacked in three days by rebel forces."

The general looked over at the Old Soldier who was standing to the
side, out of the way. Knowing the general was looking for confirmation, the Old Soldier spoke out in a strong voice and, without hesitation, said, "Yes sir! I was there when she had that vision, and the rebel
attack happened just like she said it would."

The general had listened attentively, and looked directly at me to
say, "Well, that's an amazing story. What do you want me to do?" I continued, allowing a pleading tone to come into my voice, "Sir, you are
our only hope. We need to be taken by one of your planes to Guinea."
That seemed like a reasonable enough request to me, since there were
many planes sitting on the tarmac.

He softened his voice to answer me, "I regret to tell you this, but I cannot transport civilians on military aircraft." He added, "It's against military policy, and I would be disobeying if I agreed to your request. Besides, it would be quite dangerous for you to travel in our aircraft because rebel forces shoot at our planes every time we fly."

I began begging him on my hands and knees, "Sir, if you don't help us we will all perish." The general maintained his stoic expression, but as he turned and walked a few paces away, we could see him battling with his emotions. Getting up from my knees, I ran in front of him and cried out in desperation, "Please, don't turn from us, sir. I wrote to you about the story of Esther in the Bible; a woman who had only one chance to enter the king's presence and win his favor if she hoped to save her people from annihilation. You are that king and we need to gain your favor or we will die."

He turned on his heels, visibly disturbed that he could not help us. I moved in front of him once more and begged for his mercy. "We are like the Israelites who left Egypt crying out for help in the wilderness. They had no food and no water, and they knew that if God didn't come through they would all perish. We are trapped as refugees in this country that can no longer protect us. Please do whatever you can to help save our lives so we may be able to live to tell the story of how we survived this war, and how God used you as his instrument."

The general wiped his hand across his brow and down the side of his face. Slipping his hand into his pocket, he took out his well-worn wallet and flipped it open. His gaze traveled across our faces and then he looked directly at me. With his thumb and forefinger, he managed to wriggle two photographs from their protective sleeves and silently presented pictures of his own children. After a pause he said, "Louise, you remind me of my daughter."

I smiled at the photos and thanked God that the general was a father. I pushed further, "You have beautiful children, sir. Please consider my father and the love he has for me. Please help save another father's daughter from certain death."

The general put away the pictures, pushed the wallet back into his pocket, and apologized, "I understand your plight. I would want someone to help my children if they were in this predicament; but like I said, my hands are tied and I cannot help you. The fact is I would be violating orders to transport civilians in military aircraft, especially during time of war! It's not allowed, and wouldn't be safe for you."

I did not let up. I could not believe we came this far for him to turn us away. As I continued with my pleas, he raised one eyebrow and said, "Like you, my daughter never takes 'No' for an answer." He looked toward the sky and his face began softening. The corners of his mouth began to lift in a smile as he reminisced about how his daughter managed to get almost anything she wanted from him. When he looked back at me he said, "She is as persistent and persuasive as you are; so much so that I can never resist her requests." He brought out his wallet again, but this time he slowly counted out one hundred dollars in US currency.

Handing me the money he said, "Louise, you should be proud of yourself. You have saved not only your life, but the lives of your friends, your husband, and your future children." I was ecstatic, and grabbed him tightly around his neck. We all blessed him profusely and thanked him for his kindness.

We continued pouring out our gratitude on the general as he walked away and went inside the building. As we huddled together in our excitement, our friend, the Old Soldier, came over and wrapped his arms around our group. We cried and laughed together, knowing we had just seen God move on the general's heart.

We immediately began preparing for the next leg of our miraculous journey. We were happy, yet filled with sorrow because we would be leaving Jeddee and the Old Soldier behind. We had come to Lungi with practically nothing and were leaving with newly made friendships and one hundred US dollars.

Two hours after our meeting with the general the rebels launched a minor offensive to let the ECOMOG soldiers know they were still there and still strong. The skirmish did not last long, but we knew it would not be the last.

At 10:00 PM, the Old Soldier arrived with four of his soldier friends, joining neighbors who had come to bid us farewell. We prayed and sang for the next two hours, outside in the moonlight, thanking God for saving our lives and asking for his continued protection.

The hundred dollars was more than enough to buy Abel, Moses, Cecelia, and me passage aboard a large canoe-like boat called a *pam-pam* that would take us to Conakry, Guinea. It would be over seventy-miles through part of the Atlantic Ocean.

We realized we would be heading out on another trip that could cost us our lives because, less than a year before, a report had spread through town that a similar canoe, filled with merchants and other passengers, had capsized on its way from Conakry to Freetown. The canoe, filled with more than eighty people, struck a rock during the night; thirty were reported drowned and another thirty missing. Traveling in the Atlantic without life preservers and not knowing how to swim would be a frightful experience; however, leaving Sierra Leone by boat was our only option. Aware of the danger we would be facing, our newfound friends hugged us and cried. They were very afraid for us, and promised to pray for our safe arrival to Guinea.

We got to sleep around midnight, but were up at 4:00 AM to prepare for our walk over to the small wharf where the weekly boat launched. As we ate a breakfast of fish and rice, about thirty neighbors and church members who knew we were leaving showed up to pray with us. It was wonderful to be loved like this.

The Old Soldier arrived just a few minutes before 6:00 AM. His eyes were red from crying on the way over. He said, "You guys are good, strong people who are called by God. He has brought you this far and He will take you the rest of the way. I am trusting in His goodness." He walked the whole twenty-five minutes to the wharf with us, as our unauthorized escort, to make sure we made it safely to the launch. He was not about to allow a chance rebel attack to take our lives on his watch. He said to Moses, Cecelia, and Abel, "Louise is a woman of God who has been an inspiration to me, and whenever she tells you anything, be sure you listen to her. God will be with you wherever you go." His words of encouragement were filled with emotion and his voice trembled.

The boat launch was a small wharf with a palm-frond-roofed shack where they sold peanuts, and other tantalizing foods. The aromas filled the air along with the smell of the ocean. I closely examined the narrow, open *pam-pam* tied to the wharf, noticing the thick, hand-hewn wooden sides and counting the boards mounted in place as seats for its passengers. It seemed sturdy enough to my uneducated eye and I attempted to settle my fearful thoughts and memories of my past watery escape. I allowed myself a brief pause and began enjoying the reflection of the vessel's brightly painted sides as they played on the calm surface of the water. Pure white puffs of clouds marched across the brilliant sky and the sounds of the shore drew my attention. I took a deep and reassuring breath while gazing out at the horizon that divided the two blue expanses—sky and water. A sense of gratitude for life overwhelmed me.

The *pam-pam* to Guinea traveled once a week, that is, once a sufficient number of passengers had arrived to fill the boat. Unfortunately, not nearly enough people showed up that morning, so we were all told we would have to wait indefinitely, until the right number of customers presented themselves.

Our faithful Old Soldier friend reluctantly said goodbye, and continued to look over his shoulder, waving to us as he walked out of sight. As he disappeared, I thought about how friendships like these are rare and precious gifts.

The boat captain told us he hoped to leave by evening, but needed at least twenty more paying passengers. By sundown, however, there still were not enough for the voyage. We would have headed back to

Jeddee's home for the night except it was not safe to walk back in the dark with rebels still casing the town, so the captain kindly invited us to stay in his home for the night.

His home was a storehouse for the local merchants and he had filled it with onions, garlic, ginger, peppers, and an array of spices. The fumes from the spices permeated the air so strongly that we all suffered from endless sneezing and watering eyes. Trying to sleep, the four of us dozed in and out of consciousness while sitting up on a little couch. By morning, everyone's eyes, except the captain's, were red and blood-shot. He looked just fine, having grown accustomed to the fumes over the years.

It was not until 7:00 PM the next day that a sufficient number of passengers arrived to make the journey a worthwhile one. As I boarded the *pam-pam*, I again recalled the tragedy at the Moa River, where everyone onboard an overloaded barge had drowned. As over eighty passengers squeezed in with me, I could see that this boat was also being overloaded, and I had to fight back the panic as everyone crowded into their seats. I silently prayed, *Lord God, please give me peace so I can endure this two-day journey.*

CHAPTER 16

Thrown into Jail

Eighty-seven souls, and their belongings, crammed as tightly as possible into an oversized canoe with one small outboard motor. A captain and two crewmembers manned it. I looked at the boat and wondered how it could possibly be seaworthy with the load it was to carry.

The boat had eight narrow benches that each sat five to six passengers, if they hunched their shoulders sideways. Five or six others sat on the floor between each bench. We four were fortunate enough to secure bench seating. Abel sat on my right, Moses and Cecelia on my left.

After everyone was onboard the captain hospitably announced, "Welcome aboard the Atlantic shuttle from Lungi to Guinea. This trip will take us the good part of two days. I have made hundreds of trips traveling these waters over the past eighteen years. I have never lost a single soul, and I don't plan to change that any time soon."

Before we pulled away he added, "We are expecting good weather for the entire trip, and if we are lucky you will be able to see some ocean life up close and personal." I cringed at that thought. The captain added, "Please do not stand up while we are underway, and keep your hands and other body parts inside the boat at all times."

The wooden boat creaked as it rocked gently back and forth on the waves that were washing up with slaps against its sides. The captain untied the dock lines and stepped into the boat. A couple of swift yanks on the pull rope, and the motor sputtered and started up. We edged away from the wharf and were under way.

We headed out for deep water as we watched the Lungi International Airport disappear from sight. The loud pulse of the motor, the wind blowing in our faces, and the occasionally drenching ocean spray kept me awake and alert. In silence, I prayed for God's protection and braced myself for the long and highly anticipated journey.

Three hours into the trip, after we had left the protection of the shore, a storm began forming. The wind began to blow in gusts. The waves rose, and broke over the bow of the *pam-pam*. It was rapidly taking on water. The once clear sky continued darkening, the clouds became heavy, the wind blew more steadily, and the waves grew much higher. Their tops blew off into spray that whipped at our faces. Most of us could not swim, and none of us had life preservers. Fearing the boat would capsize and sink, the majority of the passengers cried out to the captain that they wanted him to turn back. I cried out to God, "Please save us. Have mercy Lord—stop the storm, calm the waves. We can't turn back. We must find refuge in Guinea."

The captain steered the boat into the oncoming waves to keep us from rolling over. He screamed out over the wind, "I am the master of the sea! I know all the secrets of the ocean! We will be fine—trust me!"

Without mercy, our small, overloaded vessel was battered. Most of the passengers were panic-stricken and seasick, and each lurch and roll of the boat caused them to empty the contents of their stomachs and their bowels alternately all over themselves and the boat. The waves crashing down on us blended and splashed the vile mixture, causing those who were not sick from the motion to join in the misery. We might have lost a few passengers in the tumult if we had not packed ourselves into the boat so tightly. Parents held onto their children and merchants tried to keep their baskets and bags from washing overboard.

The captain once again yelled over the storm, "The Spirit of the Ocean is angry, and is demanding an offering." He held tightly to the motor's tiller and the wind whipped away his bellow, "This area of the

ocean is always unpredictable, and I tell my passengers they must give
up offerings." When we nearly tipped over from the next wave, he
screamed louder, "The spirit requires an offering of gold and silver, and
any other valuable items you might have."

I supposed that was what he had meant by his earlier words, "I
know the secrets of the ocean." The captain asked one of his two crewmembers to pass a hat and take up the offerings. As it passed along each
row, the crewmembers would enjoin, "The Ocean requires a gift from
each of you."

I saw husbands and wives removing their wedding rings and neck-
laces, and placing them in the hat. Each person gave what he or she
could in hopes that the Ocean would accept the gift and calm the waves.
When the hat came to me, I simply passed it on. I did not contribute
anything because I knew God would save me from the onslaught. I was
not about to put my faith in anything other than Jesus Christ, the Son
of God.

As soon as the hat passed through eighty-seven pairs of hands, the
crewmembers emptied the contents of the basket, swiftly and unceremoniously, into an oncoming wave. The valuables fell to the depths
of the ocean floor. The storm subsided and the mountainous waves
shrunk down; the boat rocked gently from side to side. The passengers
were astonished to see a rough ocean suddenly made calm. I knew it
was prayers, not the jewelry, that had calmed the storm.

During the storm, our canoe had drifted off course and our captain,
the master of the sea, had become lost. We motored along for several
more hours in the wrong direction, causing us to lose valuable time.
Although we were escaping a war that might have killed us, we found
ourselves battling the sea instead. Our hope of making it to safety was
dwindling with every passing hour. We traveled all that night, all the
next day, and into the next night.

A cry of, "Thank God," escaped the lips of the passengers as a
Guinean Coast Guard boat headed our way. They came along side and
gruffly ordered the captain to follow them to a Coast Guard base. Our

captain spoke up, "We ran into a terrible storm, and I lost my bearings. My passengers have been sick, and we have run out of drinking water and food. Some of them are violently ill and need medical attention, and I need to take them directly to Conakry." The Coast Guard ignored him and ordered, "You will follow us." Our captain did not have any choice but to follow the Coast Guard. *It's a miracle they found us,* I thought; and the anticipation of their sending us on our way to Conakry filled my heart.

A low rumble of weakened cheers arose from the passengers when land appeared on the horizon. The moment we pulled into the dock a small band of soldiers rushed over and demanded that we get out of the boat. We were relieved to step onto something that did not move, even though almost three days in a small boat made many of us sway from side-to-side as we walked, causing us to look as if we were drunk.

For some reason, the soldiers singled out and brutally beat some of the passengers. The rest of us could only huddle together in shock and confusion, hoping we would not receive the same treatment.

The commanding officer ordered, "Have all these people stripped and searched!" Guinean soldiers stood by with their rifles in their hands to enforce his command. Men, women, and children all stripped in one large group. Their methods of search and interrogation were cruel and unusual. The soldiers manhandled men as well as women during the process, irreverently poking, prodding, and even fondling us, under the pretense of looking for rebel markings.

Ongoing bouts of sickness still came in waves over those who were ill. Abel was one of them, and he was suffering terribly; I was afraid for him. Finally, at the end of the long, drawn-out strip search, the Coast Guard Captain felt satisfied that we were all innocent passengers. Since it was getting dark, he announced he would escort us to Conakry in the morning.

The local people had heard that the Coast Guard had captured and arrested a band of rebels, but once they realized we were not rebels, they took pity on us and offered assistance. A kindly woman waved at our little group of four and said in French, "*Venez ici*," meaning, "Come here." She guided us to her small cinder-block home, where she boiled water in a large pot so we could scour off the filth that covered us after our difficult voyage. She made a large pot of fish soup and while we were eating, she compounded an herbal remedy to help Abel, who had apparently contracted cholera from one of the passengers.

In the morning, our captain and crew tried to remove the drying efflu-ence that clung to the benches and insides of the boat, but they did not have sufficient time to do a thorough job. Worn-out, haggard, and sickly passengers formed a disorderly line at the dock. Their pallid countenances revealed their persisting illness. I supported Abel as much as I could. He had become so weak that he had great difficulty making it out onto the dock and could barely stand while waiting to board the *pam-pam*.

Those in front of us began inching their way forward ever so slowly. The crewmembers gave a hand to the weak and infirm as they boarded. We scrunched as closely to each other as we could and exchanged queasy looks, pinched smiles, and tight but hopeful nods.

For the next three hours, the Guinean Coast Guard escorted us toward Conakry. Each minute seemed like an eternity. The boat began to fill again with sea spray and more uncontrolled eliminations by the passengers. The captain finally announced that we had entered the waters off Conakry. We were elated and rejoiced at knowing we would soon disembark and be free to contact the UN for assistance. The Coast Guard motioned for us to continue on our way without escort, and our captain was again in charge of our voyage.

After five more difficult hours, we entered a small, shallow harbor at Boussoura Port in Conakry. As we neared a low, concrete wharf, designed to accommodate the many *pam-pams* that surrounded it, a *pam-pam* filled with immigrations officers made its way toward us. The officer in charge shouted, "Who's the captain?" Our captain waved his hand and replied, "I am." Fearing he might be carrying rebels, the officer said, "You are overloaded. There are too many males onboard. You must return to Lungi."

Our captain knew the immigrations officer as well as most of the *pam-pam* captains in the harbor. It seemed to frustrate him that the immigrations officer apparently did not trust him. Our captain tried to stay calm, but, in his exasperation, he answered tersely, "We've already been stopped by the Guinean Coast Guard, and my passengers were subjected to a humiliating strip search. They determined that my passengers are not rebels and they escorted us here. Many of my passengers have become critically ill and require medical attention." The officer waved us away, ignoring our captain's pleas, again ordering us to leave the harbor and return to Lungi. At this point, other passengers joined me in begging the officer to reconsider. Our voices rose together as we implored him for our very lives.

Our captain entreated, "We will all die at sea, we do not have enough food, water, or fuel for the journey." He added, "Even if I did have enough fuel, as you can see my passengers are very sick, and I might lose some of them."

At this point, a young man, one of the many who plied the shallow water bare-backed and in cutoff shorts offering themselves for hire to run errands or to load cargo, came near our boat. The tide was out and the water was shallow enough for him to be only waist deep. Our captain called to him, asking him to take a fuel can and some money to buy fuel for us.

The immigrations officer did not interfere and gave the order for his small vessel to return to the wharf. Our captain had dropped an anchor by this time and he got out of the boat in order to follow the immigrations boat so he could continue trying to make sense to the officer.

During all this confusion of negotiations for fuel, wailings of the passengers, and yelling back and forth between our captain and the immigrations officer, another storm had begun to brew. As we waited, the pleasant weather rapidly deteriorated into a violent storm with hurricane-force gusts and driving rain. Even in the shallow water, the wind churned up enormous waves that tossed the boat violently. Screams of terror from the passengers blended with the howling of the wind and our boat began to fill with water so fast that there was no doubt it would sink.

The roof of the small, harbor-side guard post ripped off and those on the wharf and on shore ran for cover as flying objects tumbled past them. Someone in authority yelled out. "Get those people out of the water. Bring them in!" Our *pam-pam* had filled so much with water, though, that it could not make way on its own, and another boat hurried out to rescue us.

By the time the rescue boat arrived, our boat was nearly submerged. We were completely awash and our belongings were being carried out of the boat with each new wave. There was no way to wade ashore; the waves would have knocked us under. The wind and waves were so strong that as passengers stood up to transfer to the other boat they tumbled backward into ours. Somehow, we all managed to scramble aboard the rescue boat and made for the wharf.

The moment we got off the boat, the men received orders to form one line and the women another and we hurried into the Security/Customs facility. The officer in charge scowled and looked our way. He pointed at the line of men, said something gruffly in French, which he translated, "The women and children can stay. All the men must return at once to Sierra Leone."

Although a few of the men were merchants and had not brought their wives on the trip, the major portion of our group was couples having the sole intent of escaping the civil war and finding refuge in Guinea. The women protested and begged the officer to allow the men to stay. Everyone pointed out how ill they were, too ill to survive a return voyage.

We were relieved when, after a long debate, the officials finally reconsidered and the officer in charge said, "Okay, the men may stay as long as they have their papers. Please proceed."

I watched as they trudged forward; Moses had to hold Abel up. When they reached the customs counter Moses said, "We are from Sierra Leone, and are running from the conflict." Moses' Liberian accent gave away his nationality, and the customs officer immediately retorted, "Oh, no you're not! You're a Liberian. You are the ones who brought the war to Sierra Leone, and now you've come to Guinea to do the same thing." His voice carried through the entire room and the hatred in his eyes pierced us to the core as he blasted out, "We don't want you here! And we don't want your war here either!" With finality he ended, "You're going back, and that's that!" All attention focused on Moses and Abel.

I thought, *Oh Lord, please no!* Cecelia and I broke out of line, ran up to the officer, and loudly protested, "No! If you send them back, it will mean certain death. We had to flee Liberia because our lives were in danger from rebel forces, and we are seeking refuge in Guinea." The official said, "The two of you may stay, but these men must return to Sierra Leone!" I responded with firm and unbending conviction, "If they go, we go. It would be far better for us to die together than for us to be separated from the men we love!"

My resolute stand apparently startled the officer and he paused to think for a moment. He took a deep breath, stared me in the eyes, and in complete exasperation said. "Are you serious, madam?"

"I am very serious!" I cried out. The officer pointed to Abel and said, "Look. This man is already dying. He's not likely to live even if he stays here in Guinea. Unless you really wish to die with him, you and your friend need to go with the other women. These men are returning to Lungi."

Our refusals to separate from Abel and Moses made the officials even more suspicious of Cecelia's and my intentions, so they summoned security guards to intervene; they shuffled us to the side. I hoped our plea had actually struck a few heartstrings, and that they would reconsider how best to help us.

The next thing we knew, a military truck with its cargo section covered in a green tarpaulin, roared up and skidded to a stop in the gravel outside the guard post. A Guinean soldier was pointed in our direction; he marched over to the four of us and gesturing stiffly, stated in French, "That's your transport. Get in!" Other soldiers carrying rifles began prodding us from behind and herded us into the back of the truck.

We had no idea where they were taking us. As the truck sped along, the driver seemed to hit every bump and dip in the road and whipped sharply around every corner, so, by the time we stopped we were quite bruised and banged up from being thrown around during the ten-minute ride. The truck had stopped in front of the Bonfi Police Station where, to our horror, we were all officially declared and documented as rebels.

Here we were in a French-speaking country, unable to understand fully what was being said about us, and we were being declared as Liberian rebels infiltrating Guinea from Sierra Leone. I wondered dispiritedly, *God, what's happening? How can this be?*

The police station's holding cells were evidently full, so we were forced back into the truck. After another few minutes of rough ride, the truck pulled to a stop. The driver jumped out, ran to the back, and in broken English shouted, "Get out of truck" followed by, "Move it!" Moses and I helped Abel out and onto his feet, bracing his limp and frail body between us. We were terrified.

The officers had delivered us to the Matam Police Station, known in French as the *Commissariat de Matam*. I cried aloud to God. "Please save us!" No one else could utter a word and I watched the already dim light in their eyes extinguish as their hopes fluttered away.

The driver handed us over to a police officer who took the papers drawn up at the Bonfi Police Station; papers we could not even read because they were written in French. He scowled at the papers and looked at us with a sickening smile. My deepest desire was for them to question us and, after telling our story, for them to declare our innocence. Instead, we were roughly handcuffed and escorted down a dark, grimy corridor as roaches and other vermin scurried from our path. I pleaded, "Where are you taking us? We're innocent!" The officer apparently spoke no English. He led us to a steel door, unlocked it, and yanked two prisoners out of the cell. They could barely walk, and looked like cadavers. Their eyes were sunken in, their bones protruded at the joints, and they reeked of human excrement.

The officer shoved us inside the cramped cell, and then bent down to place heavy leg irons over our ankles. After taking off our handcuffs, he gave Moses a swift, hard kick in the back that shoved him into me, causing us to both fall on our elbows and knees and skid across the concrete floor. Cecelia stumbled over to her boyfriend's side crying, "Moses, oh God!" She looked up plaintively at the officer who smiled down at her smugly.

Abel, who could hardly stand, staggered over to where I had landed and, bending down, tried to lift me up. The cold steel jail door slammed shut, leaving us in darkness. We could see nothing and I shuddered, thinking that this could become our tomb.

In less than an hour after setting foot on Guinean soil we were locked in a dark and gruesome cell in the Matam Police Station's jail at the mercy of a system well known for its practice of holding the accused indefinitely; a system in which the incarcerated would often languish for years before being tried or released. What crime had we committed? We were Liberian refugees who had endured both the Liberian and Sierra Leonean civil wars while being chased halfway across Liberia, and all the way across Sierra Leone. The fact we were Liberians was deemed sufficient evidence for us to be held as rebels. We had no means of pleading our case, and had no hope of release.

When our eyes became accustomed to the darkness, we noticed that there were no beds, no toilet; we were in an empty room. The only sources of light were two small holes. One hole, no wider than the length of two thumbs, led to the outside, and provided us limited ventilation. The other was a small hole in the steel door that police officers used to observe us with their flashlights.

As our senses returned to us, we began smelling the awfulness of our surroundings. We were sickened to see maggots, roaches, and other crawling things making their way through urine soaked feces left piled in the corners. The smell of the fetid excrement gagged us and we all choked back the urge to vomit.

As soon as the roaches realized there was fresh flesh to feast on they flew, swarming around us. They bit us and entangled themselves in our hair. The noise of their wings as they landed on our faces tormented us.

I pushed myself up off the filthy floor and took a step toward the middle of the tiny room. As I stood there I cried, "Jesus, Jesus, Jesus, hear us and come to our rescue. Save us and deliver us from this torment."

Man's inhumanity was clearly exposed in this dark and filthy place. After two days with no food and water, Abel's condition worsened. I cradled his limp body on my lap and cried out to God, begging Him to do something. Abel suffered with tremors, rapid pulse, shortness of breath, and muscle cramps. His limbs tingled as nerve endings protested. Reduced to skin and bones, his skin draped loosely over his immobile frame. I will never forget his heart-wrenching whimpers as he lay dying. Every thought became a prayer; I knew it would take a miracle for him to survive.

On the third day of this nightmare, a police officer opened the door and threw in a bag of something that thudded onto the floor. At first, we did not know what it was because the light streaming in blinded us. After he slammed the door shut, Moses hobbled over to see what it was. He reached into a plastic bag and found five smaller bags; each contained life-giving water. Each bag came tightly tied at the top, yet they were thin enough to tear a small hole in with your teeth. Moses took two of the bags of water and gave them to me. I bit into the side of one and poured the water into Abel's open mouth. He had such an intolerable thirst that he gasped and bit at the air as he tried to gulp the water down. I bit open the second bag and started to give him mine, but he noticed and refused it. I could not argue and rapidly consumed it myself.

A little while later, an officer squeezed a chunk of stale bread through the tiny vent hole in the door. As it fell onto the contaminated floor, we rushed to it; dividing it amongst ourselves, we devoured it. Our frantic hunger was enough to conquer any hesitancy we might have felt over eating from the putrid slab of concrete.

To lift our spirits I shared Bible stories I had memorized, such as the story of Paul and Silas, who were chained in a jail like ours. "Do you know what they did? They decided to rejoice, and sang praises to God. Do you know what happened while they were singing?" I rose to my feet and said, "The chains fell off their hands and feet, and the doors to their cell flew open." With that, we sang gospel songs and praised God for our coming deliverance. We were convinced the chains would fall from our ankles, and the jail door would open. A revival broke out in our cell, and we kept on singing, and kept on praying. The fear of death lost its hold on our lives.

Frustrated officers banged on the steel door, yelling, "*Fermez vos bouches!*" (Close your mouths!) and "*Tais-toi!*" (Shut up!). First, we did lower our voices and sang in whispers. However, the more we sang the more emboldened we became, and we began singing our hearts out to God with as much passion as we could muster. The harder they banged on the door, the louder we sang. After all, we had turned our fate over to God and we knew there was nothing to lose. A renewed spirit of hope and gladness gave us strength and peace in the midst of our torment; no matter how threatening the situation, we remained unrelenting in our conviction that God would hear our prayers.

We persisted into the next day—much to the consternation of the officers who had never encountered anything like it; they continued to bang their disapproval on the metal door. We could hear one of them grumbling to someone. Our small group was in the middle of singing "Jesus Loves Me This I Know," when we heard them outside our door. We caught our breath for a moment, listening, and when nothing happened, we sang even louder. We soon heard keys rattling and the door banged open. As we squinted to see who was there, I cried out in English, "Who's there? Who are you?" The brightness in the hall was blinding, but we could make out a slim and rather tall man dressed in civilian clothing standing with a group of officers. This shook us up a bit, and I wondered if they would separate us. The thoughts came to me that they might throw us into solitary confinement or take us out back and shoot us in order to put an end to our singing.

The man in civilian clothes put his hand over his nose and mouth, turned to the officers, and spoke in French. He was saying something about, " … not rebels! Hear what they sing?" The officers shrugged and looked at each other in doubt. They seemed surprised when their friend, who understood the words, began translating and singing our simple song. I cried out again, "Please help us! We are innocent refugees!"

We were in a wretched condition and I am sure it was difficult for this man to look at us, but I managed to make eye contact with him and I was not about to let go of his attention, so I shouted, "God, come to our rescue. Tell this man we are innocent!" The man appeared to understand what I was saying and he signaled with his hand for me to remain calm. This gave me faint hope and the thrill choked in my throat as a sob.

We were all astounded when he began to speak to us in broken English, asking our names, backgrounds, and reason for being in Guinea. I looked down at my feet at that moment, fully expecting the shackles to fall away. Communicating with him in English and with the little French we knew, we informed him we were Liberian refugees who had recently come from neighboring Sierra Leone, where we had earlier sought refuge. "Look at our condition," I cried to him. "My husband is at death's door. He needs medical assistance now. We came seeking refuge from the Sierra Leonean civil war. Instead, we're being treated with suspicion."

At the end of our conversation I beseeched our visitor to help impress our innocence upon the Guinean authorities and to ask them to set us free. We were nothing but innocent victims and I suggested to him that he contact the office of the United Nations High Commissioner for Refugees for further verification of our status, since we were under their protection and Abel and I had been on academic scholarships.

Touched, the visitor turned to the officers and said, "These people are not rebels, but victims of poor speculation. From what you described, I expected to see half-crazed, blood-thirsty rebels, not innocent Liberian refugees struggling to stay alive." After translating this to English for us, our newfound advocate assured us that he would contact the authorities on our behalf and ask them to contact the UNHCR to verify our story. I pleaded, "Please don't forget us!" He was visibly moved by our plight and promised that he would do all he could to help.

The officers closed the door; with the sound of the key in the lock and once again in darkness, I wondered if the stranger would follow through on his promise. Asking for divine intervention and for a prompt release, we all prayed and thanked God, and with more gospel songs, glorified Him in the midst of our adversity.

Later that same day, our door was unlocked again and a police officer, waving his hand, beckoned us to get up and come out. As we clasped hands and supported each other, he bent over and unlocked our shackles. He was setting us free. Notified of our plight, the UNHCR had verified that we had been refugees under their jurisdiction while in Sierra Leone. On that glorious day, June 20, 1997, we boarded a police van, which delivered us to the offices of the UNHCR to be handed over to their care.

God had heard our prayers, and had sent an ex-police officer our way. When he had decided to change his plans that day and drop in on his old friends at the jail for a visit, he had no idea God would use him as an instrument to change the course of our lives.

CHAPTER 17

Blue Skies

Four police officers escorted us by police van to the UNHCR offices to be placed under their care. We arrived at the gate of the UNHCR compound, and our driver leaned out of his window to show the guard the official papers concerning our release from the dreadful jail at the Matam Police Station. The guard gave a quick nod and an aloof wave of the hand as the gate opened.

The UNHCR flag flew in the center of the compound—the flag was white and displayed the UNHCR logo of a person in silhouette standing between two hands forming a protective roof; an olive branch wreath encircled these. What a welcoming site this was after the past four hellacious days.

I took a deep breath and thanked God for, once again, sparing our lives. We were finally safe in the hands of an agency whose primary purpose is to safeguard the rights and well-being of refugees. Food, water, medicine, and a comfortable place to sleep were foremost in my mind.

The driver parked the vehicle and went inside the building. He returned shortly with signed papers in hand and opened the van door, telling us to get out. He got back into the driver's seat, speaking under his breath to the other three officers, and with sneering laughs and guffaws, all four officers said, *"Au revoir,"* as they drove off, leaving us standing in the parking lot all by ourselves.

I was stunned! All our mouths hung open and our eyes grew wide as we looked at each other and then around the parking lot. We guided

Abel over to the UNHCR flagpole so he could sit down. As he rested against Moses' legs, I headed inside, approached the receptionist, and stated, "We are Liberian refugees who are under the care of the UNHCR; we were just dropped off by the Guinea police." Before I had a chance to say anything else she jerked her head and signaled with her eyes toward the stairs where the UNHCR chief officer happened to be.

I bolted toward him as he headed out of the building and reached him before he could open his car door. "Excuse me, sir." Startled by my having run up behind him, he backed away as he turned to see what I wanted. He was even more shocked to see a woman who looked and smelled the way I did. The filth from the Matam Police Station jail cell still clung to me. His eyebrows shot up and before he could speak, I blurted out, "I am a refugee from Liberia. I was unjustly accused of being a rebel and just spent four days in jail." I whipped my hand toward the flagpole, and pointing, I said, "My husband is over there under the flag." I was nearly in hysterics. "He's dying and needs immediate medical attention. Something needs to be done for us right now!"

Swiftly, and without pause, he headed back to the building and shouted as he entered, "John, JOHN!" In a moment, a short, stocky man with a questioning look on his face came running out of the building. The chief pointed to the flagpole and commanded loudly, "We need to help these people. They need to be taken care of right away." I joined Abel and the others as the two men hurried over to evaluate our condition. The chief officer addressed John, saying, "John, I need you to take care of this deplorable situation and get these people registered; they need medical attention quickly." John agreed he would take care of everything. Satisfied, the chief returned to his car, leaving us in John's custody.

As soon as his boss was out of sight, John straightened up and backed away from us, saying contemptuously, "Why come here? You're all a mess. You guys need to go to the camp." "Camp!? My husband's dying! He needs to get to a hospital. When we arrived in Guinea four

days ago we were accused of being Liberian rebels, and we just got out
of jail. Please. Abel and I are students on UNHCR scholarships, and
I know you can verify that from your records. Please—sir—we need
you to register us and get Abel to a hospital." Shooing at me with his
hands, John repeated condescendingly, "Go on. Get out of here. Go to
the camp."

Every refugee under the jurisdiction of the UNHCR needs to be
registered when they enter a new country, and refugees are entitled
to emergent medical care. If we attempted to navigate the city on our
own without a UNHCR registration paper for each of us to identify
ourselves as refugees, we would, especially in our unkempt condition,
risk being mistaken for rebels again. John, however, was attempting
to walk away, refusing to register us, refusing to provide us with the
documentation required to secure emergency medical care for Abel. He
obviously wanted us out of his hair.

The refugee camp John was referring to was in Forécariah, Guinea,
which was nearly sixty miles away. The UNHCR had a bus for such
purposes; however, we found that John was not willing to put it into
service for a group as small as ours. It would have taken us at least three
days to travel that far on foot, and in our weakened condition, we
would die making the attempt; Abel more than likely would have died
before he could even walk out of Conakry.

As John backed away from us with his face screwed up in disgust, he
continued making gestures with his hands for us to leave the UNHCR
compound. Unbelievably, when we did not comply, he stalked over to
Abel and shoved his debilitated body to the ground. I cried out and
reached for Abel as Moses leaned forward in an attempt to prevent him
from falling over. We both helped to readjust Abel, once again leaning
him against Moses' legs.

I was infuriated, and shouted, "John, can't you see my husband is
gravely ill? You can't just throw us out. You have to do what your boss
told you to do, and if you don't we'll stay here under this UNHCR flag
until we die—and the whole world will know what you've done! We

would prefer to die here under the protection of this flag than to die on the streets of Guinea."

John was withdrawing hastily, but I ran in front of him and continued demanding his help. He ran in spurts and I kept intercepting him. "You have to register us—you have to do something!" By this time, many other refugees and UNHCR workers had gathered to see what all the commotion was. Realizing a small crowd was watching him; he glowered at me from beneath a heavily furrowed brow and snarled under his breath, "Get away from me. Immediately!"

He turned to run, but realized I fully intended following him right into his office if he headed into the building. He spun back around, looked straight at me and gruffly repeated, "You– go– to– camp!" A rage filled me, and I bellowed, "I don't know where the camp is, and we are not leaving here without being registered!"

At that very moment, a woman, who appeared very calm and composed, walked over to see first-hand what was going on in the UNHCR parking lot. She was dressed immaculately, wore beautiful long dreadlocks neatly tied at the nape of her neck and carried a sleeping baby on her chest in a bright, colorful sling. Moved by the scene, she wanted to see if there was any way she could assist.

As she approached us, she let out a screech that caused the baby, whose hair naturally stood straight out from its head, to come awake with wide eyes and open mouth, and John nearly to jump out of his skin. "Oh my God, Louise! Is that you? Where did you come from?" Still in the middle of running and ranting, I came to a halt, recognizing Lydia Cole, a fellow refugee who had been with us in Sierra Leone. I stumbled, almost falling, and cried, "Oh, thank God! Lydia, we need help." I knew Lydia as a take-charge person and felt she could somehow fix our situation. She walked right over to me and, in spite of the horrid smell and filthy clothing, she and her baby gave me a big hug. I found myself clinging to her and I began crying uncontrollably.

John's face and body had stiffened when he heard Lydia call my name. Gathering what was transpiring, she shifted her gaze to John, fixing him with an icy glare. I proceeded to fill her in on our story. "Oh Lydia, we were just released from the disgusting jail at the Matam Police Station, and we were stuck in that horrible place for four days! The police just now brought us to the UNHCR for help—and this man ... " I pointed sharply at him for emphasis, "John, refuses to help us!" I held both hands out toward Abel and said, "And my husband is near death and needs medical attention."

That is all Lydia needed to hear. Her muscles tensed and the arteries in her neck stood out. She was fully acquainted with the insensitive and unethical ways John treated every refugee who crossed his path, and this time he had gone too far. Her nostrils flared as she leaned forward and squinted at him, yelling, "What do you think you are doing? You wouldn't have a job if there were no refugees." Tilting her head toward us while she continued to glare at him, she said adamantly, "These people need to be registered so they can get food and emergency medical attention." She looked down at Abel, shook her head, turned back to John and chided, "Can't you see how sick he is?"

The wrath of God seemed to well up from within her as she admonished, "You say you work for the UNHCR. What in the world do they pay you for?" Pointing up at the flag she shouted, "Do you know what it means to work for the refugees and the honor of this flag? Apparently not! We are going to stand here until you do your job!" Lydia took a quick breath, pointed a stern finger in his face, and said, "You need to register these people. Sign the registration papers!"

John hunched his shoulders in defiance. He did not seem pleased at Lydia's taking him down a notch in front of an audience that was growing larger by the minute. "It is not your concern, mind your own business," he responded.

It turned out he had vastly underestimated Lydia's resolve and willingness to stand up for what was right. Like a skilled defense attorney advocating for her clients, she fired back, "What? Mind my own business! I know this woman and, for your information, every refugee *is* my business, and my concern; and should be *your business and concern*, because that's what you're being paid for!"

I thought a riot might break out because Lydia was not alone in her thinking; other refugees in the compound agreed loudly. Unfortunately, John's resolve to ignore our pleas equaled Lydia's insistence that he step up to his duties. She was ready and willing to continue the fight until she noticed Abel's eyes roll back in his head.

Exasperated, she said, "I can't wait here while this man dies under this flag. These people are my refugee family; they are my brothers and sisters—and since you are obviously bound and determined to do nothing, I'm going to take care of them myself. I'll deal with you tomorrow." She looked at me and said, "I'm sorry Louise; arguing with John is getting us nowhere. Follow me." She turned and headed toward the street. Moses and I helped Abel to his feet, and held him between us as he attempted to support his own weight.

Lydia flagged down a taxi and motioned for us to get in. I eased into the seat, pulling Abel's limp frame while Moses pushed until he was safely inside. Moses and Cecelia came around to the other side and got in next to me. Lydia sat in the front with the driver, giving directions. Before pulling away, the driver glanced back at us to see whom he had picked up. I fully expected him to be disgusted at his new fare; instead, I recognized compassion, especially when his eyes came to Abel.

As we traveled, Lydia shared some of why John had such distaste for her. He did not care for Lydia because she had recently taken on the unauthorized role of refugee advocate. She knew well the UNHCR's policies concerning refugees and how they should be treated.

Lydia directed the taxi driver to a street corner where vendors sold used clothing. She stepped out and purchased a change of clothes for each of us. When she returned to the taxi, she asked the driver to take us to the beach. Lydia turned to look back at us and said, "This is the only place I know where you can clean up." As we arrived, we could hear the squawking of seagulls and the roar of the incoming waves; the air smelled so clean.

She stepped out, opened the back door, and helped us get Abel to his feet. Moses and I again braced Abel between us for the slow walk down to the water. Lydia followed us with the bag of clothing she had bought for us earlier. At the water's edge, we removed our wretched rags and dipped our worn and filthy bodies in the water.

The healing salt water washed away much more than the encrusted filth. It cleansed our wounds and raised our spirits. The panic eased away and, even though they were too rough to relax in, I found the sound of the waves lulling me into a pleasantly euphoric state. Abel needed my help, though, and I knew I must stay determined and focused. He rested at the water's edge, waiting for help. After I had bathed myself and dressed, I knelt down next to Abel and scooped water over his frail body. I could feel every bone. He looked up at me with his once beautiful brown eyes; how they used to sparkle! All I could see was the darkness that was trying to overtake him. I thought he would die right there in my arms.

Once I had bathed him, Moses helped me get him dressed. Lydia gathered our old rags and placed them in the plastic bag that previously held our new clothes, and said, "Follow me, I have a plan. I'm sorry we have to walk to get there, but it won't be too far." Moses, even in his weakened state, cradled Abel's body and carried him as best he could. Abel's feet dragged along the ground with each step. It was an excruciatingly painful one-mile trek.

As we walked, Lydia told us that we had to watch out for men like John. She warned, "Many refugees get taken advantage of because they don't know their rights under the protection of the UNHCR." She looked at me and said, "Louise, you are a smart woman. You did right to speak up and take charge. Don't ever be ashamed. Hold your head high and speak what's true, and what's in your heart."

Before long, we saw a large, dilapidated building whose foundation was being undermined by incoming tides. She said, "This building used to be the residence of the Liberian ambassador and his family. It's a pretty big place isn't it?" She added, "As soon as Samuel Doe was murdered, the ambassador left with his family. Now it has been home to hundreds of Liberian refugees who have waited to be taken to Forécariah and other refugee camps."

When we entered the building, she directed us to what used to be the banquet hall, where heads of state and other ambassadors would come to dine. This great hall had become a dormitory for many refugees. They used stones they had scavenged from the beach to partition off small sleeping areas. Every square inch of the building was spoken for. I noticed all the glass in the windows had been broken out, and the ocean air blew freely through the building.

Lydia met with the staff of the compound and made all the necessary arrangements for our temporary stay. She ran to a nearby pharmacy to pick up medication for Abel's continual vomiting and diarrhea and an electrolyte drink to help replace essential minerals he had lost over the past week. I thought, *What would have happened to us if we had not run into dear Lydia? We would probably have found our demise on the streets of Conakry.*

After spending four days in jail with only a stick of bread between us, we desperately needed solid nourishment. John's refusal to register us as new refugees in Guinea had left us with no food allotment, and Abel was entirely too weak to make the trip back to the UNHCR office so we could complete the registration process.

A man named Derek, a fellow refugee whom the Liberian Embassy appointed as chairperson of the facility, recognized our plight. He worked with the other refugees who willingly shared their meager stores to provide us with an adequate supply of food until we could secure our own rations. For five days, we subsisted on handouts from others while we waited for Abel to gain enough strength for the trip back to the UNHCR compound where we would be officially registered. The kindness of equally unfortunate brothers and sisters who placed others' needs above their own touched me. Often, those who have the least to give, give the most—much like the impoverished widow in the Bible, who gave everything she had.

There were many other deficits to overcome or live with, though. The clean, life-giving ocean breeze that blew through the open window frames by day became a difficulty for our emaciated bodies at night. We could not maintain our body heat and the wind kept us awake as we shivered and wrapped ourselves in each other's arms.

This slowed the return of Abel's strength, but once he could manage it, the four of us went with Lydia, our empowered advocate, to the UNHCR compound. Lydia took us directly to John's office. He was not pleased to see us; however, this time he was compliant and completed our registrations immediately. Although we were registered, the UNHCR only provided rations for refugees once their office processed all the paperwork, following a protocol that could take weeks.

When we returned to the old ambassador's residence, I overheard a couple of refugees mention a man named John Quia who worked in the control tower at the Guinea International Airport. They said he was a kind and charitable man who often helped refugees, and they were going to visit him the next morning. I was thrilled to hear his name, because when we were in Lungi, Jeddee and his friends from church had told me of this man, a man well known for his generosity. He used to work at the Lungi Airport, and while we were trying to flee Lungi, others who knew Mr. Quia had confided, "Oh Louise, if the ECOMOG forces had not shut down the airport, and if Mr. Quia were still here, he would have put you on a plane to Guinea."

I felt sure he was the one they had spoken so fondly of because the airline he worked for had moved to Guinea before the military took over the Lungi Airport. I joined the refugees in the morning and, when we arrived at the control tower, a receptionist picked up the phone and told Mr. Quia he had visitors. She must have told him we were refugees because he immediately came down to see us and handed a couple of dollars to each person.

When he looked my way I said, "Mr. Quia, I heard about you from Jeddee and other friends of ours in Lungi." He allowed me to continue, so I explained our journey and difficulties, ending with, "We were finally able to register with the UNHCR yesterday, but still face a long wait before receiving supplies. Up to now we have been subsisting on the kindness of other refugees who have been sharing their rations with us."

He reached into his pocket and handed me twenty-five US dollars. You could see the sympathy on his face as he said, "Take this, and buy medication and food for you and your husband. Please feel free to come again to visit me, and please bring your husband when he feels better."

I thanked him profusely for everything, saying, "Mr. Quia, I will never forget your kindness, and everywhere I go I will tell people how you blessed us." Mr. John Quia's light shown resplendently in the darkness of war and injustice and brought hope to many who were lost and forgotten.

I was finally able to pay for medical assistance for Abel and buy food to sustain us until we received the long awaited UN rations. Abel soon began to thrive and the spark of life grew brighter and stronger. I was thrilled to see his vitality return.

Upon our arrival, there had been less than one hundred refugees at the former ambassador's residence. The conflict in Sierra Leone raged on and, in a month's time, our number had swollen to nearly one thousand due to a heavy influx of Liberian and Sierra Leonean refugees— who were reported to have grown to at least five percent of Guinea's population. Every evening, a Guinean military officer made rounds and conducted a roll call to ensure no rebels had snuck in, masquerading as refugees. The space was divided and re-divided, as some left, others came; everyone shared, generously admitting newcomers to the fold. Even still, lack contrived to have its way, causing depression and stirring up arguments, tempting frazzled tempers to flare. Abel and I spent long hours listening to, comforting, and praying with other refugees. They would share their drama and we, in turn, would share ancient words of wisdom from the Bible, words that have encouraged and comforted people over the millennia.

On August 2, 1997, just over a month after our release from the atrocious jail at the Matam Police Station, Charles G. Taylor was elected president of Liberia. Prior to the election, thousands of his youthful supporters were heard chanting, "He killed my ma, he killed my pa, I'll vote for him!" Taylor was the leader of the National Patriotic Front of Liberia (NPFL) whose rebels had reportedly killed over one hundred thousand innocent Liberian civilians; he had also helped fund the Revolutionary United Front (RUF) that killed tens of thousands of Sierra Leonean citizens and fleeing refugees.

A new Liberian ambassador to Guinea, assigned by President Taylor, replaced the one who had fled as Samuel Doe, the former president, was murdered. Derek, who had been serving as the chairperson of our holding camp, met the new ambassador, who informed him he was on a departure list and would soon be leaving for another country. Derek suggested that Abel and I would be ideal replacements as chairpersons. There had not been a dual directorship before, but we worked well together and were able to help men and women on a much more personal basis than he had been able to. Derek believed this would be a positive move in many ways.

A few days later, the new Liberian ambassador called at the old residence. He brushed aside the small crowd of refugees who had gathered in the doorway to see who had just driven into the compound, and asked for me and Abel. We were summoned, and soon found ourselves standing before a heavyset man of medium height who had a round face and a broad nose. With his freshly pressed clothing, stern countenance, and curt mode of speech, he maintained a commanding disposition. Upon being introduced to us he announced, "I heard from Derek, as well as others, that you are a humble and honest couple, and that you are always praying. I will soon be asking the residents to vote for Derek's replacement, and I want you to be on the ballot, because I've heard everyone loves you and wants to vote for you."

The next day, Derek called an impromptu meeting and asked everyone to vote. Abel and I immediately became the new chief mediators between the UNHCR, the Liberian Embassy, and the refugees living at the residence. They affectionately called us "Chairlady," and "Chairman." In our new positions we were responsible for keeping written records of issues, disputes, critical needs, and illnesses; as needed, we reported them to the embassy or the UNHCR.

With the growing number of newly arriving refugees awaiting rations, theft of food was a mounting problem. In addition to their nagging hunger, many were on edge from sleepless nights spent on cold floors. Whenever a conflict came to me, I insisted the persons having the problem join me in prayer before we began any discussion. Miraculously, answers would come to me as we prayed, causing word to spread. "The chairlady hears from God." I was busy around-the-clock trying to cool tempers and lift spirits as people sought my assistance.

One day, Guinean authorities found a partially blind, eighty-year-old man, whom they thought was lost, eating out of dumpsters. He was only semi-coherent, but when they heard his accent, they knew he was a Liberian, and since they did not want to have any Liberian refugees dying in the streets, they took him to the Liberian Embassy, where they were told to bring him to our compound.

When the old man came to us, he looked like a wild man with hair that stood out like a lion's mane. Well-established filth completely covered him. Abel and I led him to the beach where he soaked in the salt water. After giving him a thorough scrubbing, I secured a pair of scissors and a razor and gave him a haircut and shave.

Having catered to his bodily needs, I wanted to know what more we could do to assist him. "Where is your family?" I asked. He dropped his chin on his chest and forlornly said, "My wife and my five children were killed in the war." When I asked him why, he said, "We were Krahns."

He rubbed his forehead with the palm of his hand, breathed in deeply, and looked up; abruptly changing the subject, he asked, "Where am I?" I put my arm around his bony shoulders. "You're staying with us now, at the former Liberian ambassador's residence—and if you ever need anything, just ask me, I'm Louise, the chairlady."

This endearing, eighty-year-old man, who introduced himself as "Old Man Moses," suffered bouts of dementia and would often forget who and where he was, yet, everyone loved his charmingly colorful, innocent, and funny demeanor. He would often wander around aimlessly, not knowing where his place was. Realizing he had special needs, Abel and I made it our business to watch over him as if he were our own family. Every night, after I directed him to the old piece of cardboard on which he slept, and before he drifted off to sleep, he would say, "God bless you, Chairlady. God bless you, my daughter."

Old Man Moses cried whenever I went to the market. When I returned he hurried over to me, dried his tears with the back of his hand, and rummaged through my bag like a child, asking, "Do you have a donut for me, my daughter?" At each meal, he would refuse to eat until I had properly prayed over his food, and would ask, "Can I eat it now?"

After spending a year with us, the UNHCR transferred Old Man Moses to the Forécariah refugee camp. Less than a month later, he left the compound to take a walk. When he found his way back to camp, everyone could see from the lacerations on his face and his bloodstained clothing that someone had badly beaten him. When a few refugees ran over to him he sobbed, "Four boys bothered me, and made me angry. When I told them to leave me alone, they beat me up."

He was taken to a nearby clinic where his wounds were dressed, but the equipment required to do a thorough assessment of his condition was not available. After a friend told me what had happened, I immediately arranged UNHCR transportation to the hospital in Conakry for him. The staff ascertained that he did not have any broken bones, and sent him back to the camp.

Three days later, news of Old Man Moses' death came to us. He had been complaining that his chest, back, and head hurt; I suspected he had suffered undetected internal injuries. As happened with any refugees who died in the camp, Old Man Moses was taken in the back of a car to a nearby refugee gravesite and buried with no coffin. He had died hundreds of miles from his homeland, lost, and with no family. Hundreds of refugees wept for the death of this simple old man who had lived among us.

The crowded conditions at the compound made it especially difficult for the disabled and, as we had for Old Man Moses, Abel and I kept a watchful eye on anyone who needed extra attention. One terribly stormy day a man, crippled since youth by polio, arrived with his son. In his weakened condition, and with his twisted feet, he had to resort to scooting around on the floor in a sitting position.

When I first saw him, he was sitting on the floor, leaning against a wall. I went over to introduce myself, and asked, "How are you?" He had a large, broad smile and his loud booming voice echoed from the walls. "I am well, thank you. My son and I have just arrived and we have no food." He chuckled and added, "Other than that, we are doing fine." His mellow laughter rolled like far-off thunder, and I could not help but laugh with him. He continued, "My name is Jerome Quaye, and this is my son." In that brief exchange, Jerome had touched my heart and I resolved to do all I could to help him.

As newcomers to our facility, their rations had not yet caught up with them and Abel and I decided to share our standard rations with Jerome and his son. It was not long before we learned that, much like us, they had escaped from Liberia into Sierra Leone, and relocated to Guinea. Jerome had recently been declared a political refugee, and was waiting to receive a stipend and relocation.

After hearing the story of my flight from Liberia, and noticing the fact that I was related to the Doe family, Jerome said, "Louise, if you document your situation, I am confident you will also be granted political refugee status by the UNHCR." The thought that I might be afforded this status had never crossed my mind. I was excited by the possibility; if I were classified as a political refugee, I would also receive a monthly stipend to pay for room and board outside the refugee compound. I prodded Jerome, "Do you really think I have a chance?" He looked at me, "Yes, I am *certain!*" Encouraged by his confidence, I immediately began to document my case.

Almost daily, people who had family members in Liberia or Sierra Leone would drop by the residence to see if any of them had arrived in Guinea. One afternoon, a young Liberian man looking for family came in, and he happened to mention that his mother-in-law, who was one of the first Liberian refugees to escape to Guinea, worked as a cook at the American Embassy. Moses immediately recognized that the young man's dialect was the same as the residents of his home town, so he asked the young man what his mother-in-law's name was, and where she was from.

When the young man said, her name is "Mary Kamara," and told Moses what town she was from, Moses said, "Your mother-in-law is from my home town. I don't recognize her married name, what was her maiden name?" When he heard the name he immediately said, I believe I'm related to her! Can you ask her if she knows me? The young man said he would be happy to ask his mother-in-law if she knew Moses, and then asked Moses for some personal information he could share with her.

The next day, Mary Kamara dropped by the residence on her way home from work. After sharing a few stories, and the names of family members, Mary and Moses soon realized they were cousins—and they both cried out with joy at the good fortune of having found each other. Mary insisted that Moses and his girlfriend Cecelia pack up their belongings and immediately come with her to live in her two-story home, which was about thirty minutes away by car.

When people share the same adversity and hardships, their lives become intrinsically interwoven. I mourned their move as if it was a permanent loss. I cried tears of joy for their good fortune, and tears of sadness at the thought of losing daily contact with my closest friends. Moses and Cecelia left the old ambassador's residence, but made it a point to drop in on Abel and me as often as they could.

Soon after I had submitted all the required paperwork in application for political refugee status, I scheduled an appointment with Mr. Gregory Moose, the UNHCR protection officer who reviews and approves such cases. Arriving for my appointment, I knocked on the door of his office and heard a light-hearted, "Come in." His blond hair and blue eyes startled me. "Hello, Mr. Moose." He motioned for me to sit down.

He picked up my file, momentarily glanced at it, and in a relaxed manner said, "Louise, I've looked over your file thoroughly and decided to reclassify you." He paused and smiled. "You are now officially a political refugee." I wondered briefly if I had heard him properly, but I knew I had when he said, "That will provide you with a monthly stipend that will pay for room and board for you outside the refugee compound." I was overjoyed. Mr. Moose signed the official documents saying, "I will process this right away." He added, "Also, I believe you would qualify for political asylum and resettlement in another country. I highly recommend you apply for that as well." He gave me a form to take home and fill out.

Within a week, Abel and I moved to a modest neighborhood in Conakry, where we lived while waiting for word regarding our asylum application. I was overjoyed to learn that Mary Kamara's house, where Moses and Cecelia lived, was only a five-minute walk away. Living so close to each other allowed us to enjoy each other's company often.

I was beginning to believe that I might actually be nearing the end of my very long and arduous journey. Although I could not know what God had in store for me, I knew I was under His care wherever I went—had it not been for His blessings and grace, I would not have made it so far.

CHAPTER 18

Liberty Lady

Before long, Abel and I learned from a friend that there was a little church nearby. The pastor was a fellow Liberian refugee. He had secured a part-time job, which allowed him to rent an unfinished house that he used for church meetings.

It was a few months after we moved into our rented room in Conakry, and on a fine and balmy Friday evening, that we had an urge to visit our new pastor and his wife. We walked down the narrow road under the light of a magnificent full moon and were happy to find them sitting with a friend on benches in front of their home, enjoying the fresh night air. As soon as the pastor saw us approaching he called, "Louise, Abel, what a pleasant surprise! Please, come, sit with us." Ruth, his wife, stood to give me a hug, and said, "Louise, it's so good to see you." Turning to their friend who had been sitting next to her, she said, "Let me introduce you to my good friend, Rachel. Rachel, this is Abel and Louise. Rachel's a merchant from the Ivory Coast. She's dropped by to see us on her way through town." I smiled and said, "It's so nice to meet you."

Ruth said to Rachel, "Louise is a Krahn girl, too." Rachel's eyes lit up as she looked my way and asked, "Ah. Where are you from?" I responded, "Zwedru. I'm of the Naio Community. Most Naio Krahn live in Janzon or Polar, but I'm from Bawaydee."

Divine appointments often occur when they are least expected. Rachel practically knocked me over as she jumped up. "What? The Naio Community? That's where I'm from. I was born and raised there!"

"Really?"

"Yes! Who's your father?" she asked emphatically.

"My father is Charles Barton, but all his friends call him Kohoun Charley."

She gasped, "What?! I knew your father. My family lived right across from him. We were neighbors. I can't believe it! A long time ago I remember meeting one of Kohoun Charley's little girls." She paused, held her palm out a few feet above the ground, and said, "When she was about this high. If I remember correctly, her name was Géesedeh."

"That's me, I'm Géesedeh!" Rachel reached out to me and we embraced in an ardent hug. She leaned back, holding me at arm's length for a good look, and said, "I can't believe it. All grown up." Shaking her head she added, "What a small world!"

Rachel told me she had moved to the town of Nzérékoré in Guinea, learned to speak French, and had become a traveling merchant. A hopeful thought began to form and I said, "When I was a little girl, my mother, Josephiné Barton, moved from Liberia back to the Ivory Coast to the town of Blaidee-Jojason. Most folks know her as Boahn Sophené. Do you happen to know her?"

Rachel said, "No, I'm sorry, I don't." Disappointedly I said, "I've been through so much. I'd really like to see her again. It's been over twenty years since I last saw her." I did not hide the sorrow that flooded through me.

"I will see what I can do. Maybe I can hire someone to look for her." Rachel seemed moved by my story and I could tell by her face that the offer was genuine.

I could no longer speak and began crying. I knew God had led me to this place, on this evening, so I could meet Rachel. As she put her arm around my shoulders, she spoke with great conviction, "Sweetheart, don't worry. I will make it my job to find your mother. I will not stop until I find her. I promise you."

I told her between sobs, "I want to give you some money to take to my mother ... in case you do find her ... so she can travel to Guinea to see me ... if she is able." She responded, "I will be visiting here at Ruth's until next Friday when I will be leaving for the Ivory Coast."

The following Thursday I headed back to Ruth's home, and was very happy to see Rachel again. When I gave her the money she said, "God must have led you to me. I am so happy to be able to help you find your mother. If I don't find her in Blaidee-Jojason, I'll keep looking for her wherever I travel." I was grateful for God's blessings in my life.

One early morning, three months after meeting Rachel, a dream about my mother woke me up. In the dream, I had taken a taxi to the market and picked her up. I woke up and was so excited about the dream that I shook Abel awake and told him about it. After a big yawn and in a groggy mumble he said, "Um hmm," and promptly fell back to sleep. With a smile and a nod, I quietly whispered, "Ma, I will see you one day soon, face to face."

I lay in bed wondering if the dream was a word from God, or just the longing of a child who missed her mother deeply. When I looked at the clock, I realized I did not have time for contemplation because I needed to hurry to the UNHCR office for my weekly visit to check on the status of my political asylum application. Since I usually had to stand in line for eight or nine hours with other refugees taking care of various types of business, I always left early in the morning so I could make it home before dark.

There was still no word on my asylum application, so after standing in line all day, I headed for home. As I was heading down the road, a few minutes after having left the UNHCR building, I heard someone calling my name. I turned in the direction of the voice and saw Lamine, a boy who rented a room where we did, running toward me.

In a teasing voice, Lamine said, "Hey Louise! Guess who's at your house?" I was too tired for a game, but I smiled and asked back playfully, "I don't know. Who?" He answered, "Louise! Your Ma! She's at your house."

For a moment, I stood totally stunned, the smile still hanging on my lips. As it dawned on me what his words meant, I gasped, "What? My mother?" I couldn't move; my feet were firmly planted in place and all I could do was blink. His head was bobbing up and down. "Yes, she came with two other people."

Before he could continue, I interrupted in total disbelief, "My mother is at my house right *now?*" He laughed and giggled in great hilarity. "Yes, they went to the pastor's house first. Ruth said when she answered the door she knew instantly the woman was your mother, because she looked so much like you. She brought your mother and the others to your house, and they have been waiting there all day for you. You better hurry."

When I neared the house, I could see a tall, thin woman pacing back and forth on the porch. As I came closer, she looked my way and I could see the years had worn the youthfulness from her face. The moment she saw me, my mother cried out to the others, "I see Géesedeh coming!"

I ran down the last bit of road and into the yard. Flying up the steps of the porch, I fell into my mother's arms. We cried and held onto each other; we were not aware of anything or anyone else. Our world was complete, and enveloped us in its loving warmth. She held me so tightly that I could feel her heart beating against my chest.

I yearned for this closeness and was totally caught up in the moment. I basked in the emotion and love that radiated from her. As my mother rocked me back and forth, she sang praises to God. Her heart beat against mine and I was finally at peace.

As I still clung to my mother, my face buried in her neck, I noticed a man with his hand on the shoulder of a young girl who stood next to him. I soon realized it was my cousin Alfred Dorlu who had worked at the Robert International Airport in Monrovia before the war broke out. The young girl, now age twelve, had been adopted by my mother when she was just an infant.

My mother was beside herself with the excitement of having found a daughter whom she thought had died long ago. She began to speak to me and bless me in rapid French. My cousin Alfred, who knew both English and French, introduced himself, and young Veronica, who was very shy and quiet. He then offered to translate what my mother was saying.

My mother held my face and asked, "Is it really you?" I laughed and nodded as tears continued down my cheeks. "Yes, Ma, it's me." She cried bitterly, showering me with kisses, and said, "When the war came I thought you died." Her grief came spilling out with her tears. My mother said, "Whenever a Liberian escaped to the Ivory Coast I asked them, 'Do you know my daughter, Géesedeh?' My heart broke every time I heard, 'No.' I asked everyone who came from Liberia. I never forgot, and never stopped asking." She repeatedly shook her head in disbelief. I wanted to comfort her. I said, "I also prayed that I would be able to see you again, Ma, and here you are!"

She closed her eyes for a moment, then continued, "I petitioned God and told Him, 'I have served You since I was a little girl. Please let my daughter be alive, and please let me lay my eyes on her one more time.'" She smiled at me. "I told God I would be happy beyond words if I could see my daughter once again." Alfred's voice mingled with ours as he translated back and forth, and he, too, shed a few tears as he became caught up in our emotion.

I told my mother of the dream I had of her coming. She smiled and said, "Géesedeh, you are God's woman! You not only have Charles Barton's beautiful eyes, you also have your Heavenly Father's eyes, ears, and mouth; and you speak what He tells you."

Then my mother shared the amazing story of how she first met Rachel, the woman who promised me she would find her. She said, "When Rachel came to my village, I was out in the fields, singing to those who were planting. The village chief, who knew that I prayed daily for your safety, even though I feared you were dead, was afraid the shock of someone telling me you were actually alive might be too great a strain on my heart. He told Rachel it would be best for her to set up her table in the village as she normally did while traveling; he would make sure I came by. When I eventually got around to Rachel's table, we had a polite conversation. Rachel told me she had lived in Zwedru. So, I asked, as I always do, 'Do you know my daughter, Géesedeh? She's from Zwedru.' She told me she had met you in Guinea, and when she said you were alive, I passed out right there on the ground. My friends who were standing beside me thought I had died.

"When I came to, my friends picked me up and brushed me off. I asked Rachel, 'Did you really meet my daughter, Géesedeh?' She said, 'Yes, as surely as I am standing in front of you now—she is alive!' I nearly fainted again and collapsed into my friends' arms. She said you told her your father was Charles Barton and your mother was Boahn Sophené. When she handed me one hundred dollars and said it was from you, I immediately knew she was telling the truth because in Africa no one just gives away money."

My mother stopped talking and allowed her love to pour out over me. Looking at me with tender eyes she continued, "Oh, Géesedeh, you've been raised from the dead. That day I began to breathe again. I couldn't wait to see for myself that my precious daughter was alive and well. I told Rachel I was ready right then and so hoped she might be able to bring me to you. She said she was sorry she would not be able to take me, because she wasn't going back to Guinea for several months. It took me three months to find someone who could travel with me. We had just started the planting season and I wasn't able to travel until your cousin Alfred, who agreed to come with me, had finished."

There were many obstacles keeping us apart for those twenty-two years. The primary reasons were that my mother lived in a primitive village with no telephones and had no money to travel, and I, being a servant girl and a refugee, had not had the freedom to search for her.

After staying on for about four months to help as a translator, Alfred headed back to the Ivory Coast by bus. My mother, however, was not ready to return, wanting to spend as much time with me as she could, so she and Veronica stayed behind.

It had been nearly two years since I had applied for political asylum, and my application was taking much longer than I expected. Considering the amount of time Abel and I had been together, the UNHCR allowed me to apply for asylum with Abel classified as my common law husband. The delay was partially due to the fact that a new protection officer, Mr. Gregory Sinai, had replaced Gregory Moose, the UNHCR protection officer who initiated our application for political asylum and relocation. When Mr. Sinai was appointed, all pending resettlement cases had to be re-evaluated using an updated process.

During the re-evaluation period, Abel and I decided to fast and pray. At the end of our three-week fast, I met with Mr. Sinai, the new protection officer. He asked if I wanted to resettle in a particular country. I told him my primary concern was for our safety, not in what country we would resettle. I advised him, "I will accept any country the UNHCR deems fit." Mr. Sinai assured me that his office was making every effort to ensure wherever we resettled we would be free from political persecution.

Nearly a month later he told me he had forwarded my case to a country for consideration; yet, he did not disclose what country they had selected. I did not want to know anyway, just in case it did not go through, but with Mr. Sinai's assurance, I again turned to the Lord to request His intervention by fasting and praying.

One night, during a church prayer meeting, I had a remarkable vision about my application. In the vision, I saw a list on which my application for asylum ranked third for resettlement in the country the UNHCR had chosen. I still did not know which country had been selected. When I shared my vision with the others at the meeting, many of them, who were not aware of my gift, said they thought I must have been hallucinating, however, I remained confident we would be approved and hoped we would soon hear where we would be going.

Eight months after my mother's arrival I heard that we had been approved to relocate to the United States; just as I had foreseen, we were third on the list. My mother was elated to learn I would be resettling in America. There was little time for excitement, however, and time flew by because news of my prophetic gift had quickly spread. People came in droves to my home for spiritual guidance.

Four months later, my mother developed a fever, and began to feel weak. Although I was concerned, she brushed it off, saying she had experienced the same symptoms while living in the Ivory Coast, and they had always subsided. She assured me she would be fine.

A few days later, while we were sitting and talking, she slowly fainted and fell out of her chair, dropping to the floor. I ran to her side and asked, "Ma, are you okay?" When she failed to respond, anxiety began to build in my chest. I grabbed a glass of water and splashed a little on her face. "Ma, wake up. Ma, are you okay?" In about thirty seconds, she looked up and, with a confused expression, queried, "Why am I on the floor?" When I told her she had just fainted she responded, "Wow, I don't know what happened."

Later in the day a few friends dropped by, and I told them of my mother's condition. The next day, Meme Yekeh, a good friend and fellow refugee from Liberia who was fluent in French and had heard the news, came over to see how my mother was doing. After questioning my mother about her condition, she strongly suggested we take her to the hospital for further evaluation.

Although my mother was able to walk with Meme and me to the corner, and she seemed okay during the fifteen-minute bus ride, soon after our arrival at the hospital she began vomiting. The examining physician said he wanted to admit her so he could run some thorough diagnostic tests. As documented refugees, the UNHCR would cover the cost of any critical care Abel or I might need, but my mother was not classified as a refugee. The hospital staff said they would go ahead and admit my mother, but asked that I head over to the Red Cross office and get her registered as a member of my family.

When Meme and I arrived at the Red Cross office, she advocated for me, in French. Barsee Harris, a fellow Liberian refugee who had become a Red Cross representative, patiently listened to the details of my mother's situation. Meme later told me she had pleaded with Barsee, "We can't let her die here in Guinea just because she isn't registered as a refugee."

Sensitive to our plight, Barsee shared our situation with the Red Cross coordinator, who immediately and generously approved the Red Cross' paying for my mother's diagnostic tests, and any subsequent medical care. In less than an hour, Meme and I returned to the hospital with all of the paperwork required to document the Red Cross' agreement, fully funding my mother's stay at the hospital.

After two days of testing, the doctors told me that my mother urgently required abdominal surgery. After the surgery, the chief surgeon, Dr. Barry, and Dr. Mohammed Soumah told me that it was good I had brought my mother in, because the surgery had corrected a life-threatening condition.

I stayed at the hospital with my mother day and night. During the day, I was there to attend to her every need; each night I slept on the floor next to her. My friend Meme kindly prepared our meals and brought them to the hospital every day so we could eat food we were accustomed to, instead of the standard hospital meals. One week after my mother's admission, the doctors told us she was well enough to go home. When we returned home, Elizabeth Deah, another dear friend who was more like a sister to me, shopped for us at the market so I could stay by my mother's side during her recovery. I marveled at how God had brought my mother and me together again, and how He had provided access to a life-saving operation that would not have been available in her little village in the Ivory Coast.

I have never seen a woman express love for a daughter as my mother did for me. More than once each day, she would stare at me and say, "Is it really you?" It was as if she just could not believe we were actually together again. She would often touch me on my back and say, "You were dead and are now alive. I have seen the glory of God."

My mother spent fifteen wonderfully fulfilling months with me before deciding it was time to go home to her village in the Ivory Coast. She finally felt she could live in peace. I was very sad to see her go, yet I was thrilled at the miraculous reunion God had helped arrange with the mother I had not seen for over two decades.

My mother's visit had been timed perfectly, during a period when Sierra Leonean and Liberian refugees were allowed to live in Conakry and other Guinean towns in relative peace. The international community praised Guinea for its generous policies regarding the sheltering of refugees. The country had offered refuge to over 100,000 Liberians and over 300,000 Sierra Leoneans who had fled harsh civil wars and gross human rights violations in their homelands.

Unfortunately, there were other forces at work in Liberia and Sierra Leone, led by Charles Taylor, who had become president of Liberia. It was their aim to upset relations between the refugees and local Guinean citizens and to force the refugees to return so they could capture and eliminate any "dissidents."

On September 1, 2000, just two weeks after my mother ended her visit, Liberian rebel forces attacked the Guinean border town of Massadou; over forty Guinean civilians were said to have been killed. Less than a week later, Sierra Leonean RUF rebel forces attacked the border town of Pamelap. Dozens of Guinean civilians were killed and the town was devastated. These, and other rebel incursions, led to a rapid disintegration of formerly good relations between the citizens of Guinea and hundreds of thousands of innocent refugees—refugees who they came to suspect of being rebels and treated them as such.

A xenophobic panic erupted. Some Guineans became overwhelmed with fear and hatred for foreigners and this resulted in refugees being attacked, raped, robbed, and rounded up for detention. The international outcry was enormous and, within days, the Guinean president issued orders that the round-ups and harassment cease and that any detained refugees be released. The die had been cast, though, and refugees were once again running for their lives during another period of destabilization.

It had become open season on Liberian and Sierra Leonean refugees; Abel and I were so terrified that we spent nearly two weeks hiding under the bed in our apartment. To be living in a complex owned by a Catholic Guinean soldier, a soldier who had grown to respect us and who would let us know when it was safe to venture outside, was yet another blessing from God. I thank God for this man's integrity and his willingness to watch out for our safety.

The morning of October 18, 2000, began like any other day; it was a beautiful, sunny morning, and the delightful, carefree sounds of birds filled the air. Abel and I prattled along making mental lists and discussing how excited we were to have recently learned that we would be flying to the United States in just two weeks. Our landlord assured us we could safely venture out, and Abel decided he would drop in on Jacqueline Glenn, a close friend of ours. I told him I was heading over to see Edith, the sister of Mary Kamara whom Moses and Cecelia had moved in with, because Edith had agreed to braid my hair in preparation for our upcoming trip to America.

I arrived in about thirty minutes, having enjoyed the pleasant mile-and-a-half walk. Edith and I sat on the front porch so she could braid my hair and I began telling her how thrilled I was that, in a couple of weeks, I would be traveling to a completely new world. We chattered intently for so long that, by late afternoon, Edith had only completed braiding the back half of my head.

In the early afternoon, the UNHCR and the International Organization for Migration (IOM)—the leading inter-governmental organization that aids in the orderly management of migration—received an urgent request from our sponsors in the United States to get us on the next flight to America. Two representatives from the UNHCR and IOM hired a taxi and drove straight to our apartment, only to find we were not home. They knew they had to find us and get us packed and to the airport no later than 5:00 PM because the next flight out was at 8:00. Hoping to find us at the marketplace or out for a walk on the street, they scoured the city. When they did not find us, they decided to head back to our apartment.

Fortunately, they arrived at the apartment complex just as Abel returned by bus. It was 4:00 PM. When they told Abel the news, he jumped into the taxi and directed them to Edith and Mary's house.

When I saw a taxi pull up to the curb and Abel jump out and run toward the porch, followed by two men, I thought something terrible had happened. I immediately jumped up from the chair, with my hair combed and fluffed out in the front like cotton candy and braided in the back, as all three men started talking simultaneously. Finally, one of them said forcefully, "Louise, you have to stop everything and come with us, right now! We have under an hour to get you to the airport so we can get you on the 8:00 PM flight to America!"

"You must be kidding," I said, "we're not supposed to leave for two weeks." The man replied, "Please, just get in the taxi with us so we can get you packed. We'll explain on the way." I gave Edith a big hug and asked her to please tell all our friends about the sudden change in plans, and tell them all goodbye for us.

The men filled us in on the details in the few minutes it took us to get back to our apartment. When we reached our apartment complex, the man in charge said, "Please pack only a few clothes. Quickly! Leave everything else. We'll wait here in the cab for you and get you to the airport." We only had minutes to grab a few belongings and bid farewell to our neighbors. We did not have time to shower or even change our clothes; we threw what we could into a big, square, plastic zippered bag we had previously been given for the trip, and ran out the door.

Thirty minutes later, we arrived at the Conakry airport looking like we had never flown before. It was true, yet, with a bit more notice, we could have been much better prepared for our journey. We tried not to let the suddenness of our departure dampen our excitement. However, as the UNHCR/IOM representatives paid the taxi driver and escorted us to the airline counter to get us checked in, we looked around the terminal and realized we were surrounded by other refugees making the same trip. They were well dressed and had obviously had more time to plan for the journey, while we looked rather wild and frazzled. I did not even have access to a comb to try to fix my hair, and with all the last-minute paperwork and other preparations, I realized I would have to fly to America looking this way.

Still, we were thrilled that we were finally heading to our new home. We thanked God that the time of suffering was finally ending for us, and that we were leaving behind all the bloodshed and pain. This time we knew where we were going and we would be safe when we got there.

Edith and our neighbors had gotten the word around that we were leaving on an 8:00 PM flight, and by the time we were to board the aircraft a small group had gathered to see us off. We hugged, cried, and hugged some more before we climbed the steps to the plane.

I stepped on board wearing a simple dress, a pair of worn out flip-flops, and with my hair half-braided. My hands trembled; I took one last look at the city of Conakry and waved goodbye to my loving friends. The noise of the engines drowned out the flight attendant's words as she motioned for me to follow her to my seat.

Once we were airborne I chanced a look out the window; I was deathly afraid, and held tightly to the seat in front of me. I saw the beautiful city of Conakry, the capital of Guinea, below—and with mixed emotions of relief and sadness, I realized I was leaving Africa for the first time in my life, and I was finally free from over a decade of relentless persecution as a Liberian refugee.

As I sat stiffly in my seat, I reflected on what I had endured from the time I was a child. At twenty-seven, I was leaving all my suffering behind on the war-torn shores of Africa. I closed my eyes and tried to imagine what America would be like. What kind of life would I have there? Would there be palm trees, palm nuts, and palm oil? Would I learn to drive a car or possibly own a home of my own? I ached inside and silently whispered, *Africa, oh Africa, what have you done to your people? Why must we flee from the land that once embraced us?*

As the engines droned and we flew into the night, deep feelings of peace washed over me—and I leaned back to drift off to sleep. Dreams, dreams, peaceful, beautiful dreams circled in my mind like a gentle breeze on a warm, lazy, summer day. Once again, the touch of my mother's hand guided me under the safety of the cocoa tree where she had first given me her blessings. Her tender voice gently lulled me deeper into sleep, "May your life be full. May success follow you. May you live very long to see every strand of hair on your head be as white as these grains of rice, and may many years lie before you. Blessings will flow from above, and you will be strong and great."

I was jolted awake by other passengers excitedly exclaiming, "There she is!" My husband, who had held my hand while I was sleeping, had dropped it suddenly and was craning his head to look out the window.

I turned just in time to see her, standing in the harbor, strong and tall, dressed in a long, green, flowing gown, embracing a tablet and extending a torch of welcome. My breath escaped in a long, "Ohhhhh," as I gazed at the majesty of the Statue of Liberty. Her noble countenance extended to us and welcomed us to her shores. Unrestrained tears spilled from deep within my war-torn heart as I realized that after running so far, and for so long, I was no longer a tired servant or a poor refugee huddled in hiding—I was, at long last, free!

ABOUT THE AUTHOR

Louise G. Barton and her family currently reside in Atlanta. In addition to being an avid advocate and supporter of those who remain refugees unable to return to their homes, Louise often appears publicly to promote awareness of their plight.

To Contact Louise
Visit Louise's website:
sofartorun.com